# How to Make a Living from Music

**Second Edition**

**By David Stopps**

Creative industries – No. 4

D1592306

**WIPO**

WORLD
INTELLECTUAL PROPERTY
ORGANIZATION

How to Make a Living from Music

*Music*
INDUSTRIES

# TABLE OF CONTENTS

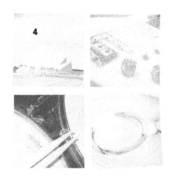

6

# PREFACE

The World Intellectual Property Organization (WIPO) is pleased to present this second edition of the Creative Industries book *How to Make a Living from Music*. The book is designed for musicians and music professionals who wish to hone their knowledge of the music business. It offers practical information to help authors and performers appreciate the importance of proper management of their intellectual property rights, in addition to providing instructive advice on how to build a successful career in music by generating income from musical talent.

The book provides useful definitions of grassroots concepts and identifies the basic income streams for authors and performers. Special attention is given to copyright and related rights, and their particular application in the music context. The book underscores the importance of artist development and management, and provides guidelines on establishing fair arrangements for benefit sharing resulting from songwriting and performances.

*How to Make a Living from Music* is written, first and foremost, as a practical tool for creators in the world of music who are still in the process of establishing themselves in the market. Hence it offers a style that is designed to reach out to a broad audience. Secondly, the publication explores the interface between the creative process and all the necessary management arrangements which need to be in place from the moment of creating the music material until the moment it reaches the audience, thus providing valuable insights on synergies between creative and entrepreneurial approaches. Thirdly, it looks into the importance of using the enabling infrastructure such as collective management organizations, registration systems and available compensation schemes. The value of the presented material is reinforced by the detailed annexes which can guide music professionals through the practical complexities of the music business.

8

This book is intended as a tool for musical authors and performers both in developed and developing countries. Many international examples have been included, making it a useful instrument for creators worldwide. The content is not meant to be used as a substitute for professional advice on specific legal issues.

*How to Make a Living from Music* was commissioned by WIPO and written by David Stopps,1 a seasoned music manager with vast international experience. The author is not an academic or a lawyer. Rather, he is a working music business artist manager, event promoter and entrepreneur with over 40 years' experience in dealing with copyright and music monetization issues at the music industry's coalface. This book is therefore written from the point of view of a practitioner and tends to take a pragmatic, practical approach, rather than a theoretical or academic one. The views expressed in the book are those of the author and do not necessarily reflect those of the Organization.

# INTRODUCTION

This is a very exciting time for music artists. A music artist is always a performer (someone who sings and/or plays a musical instrument) and is often also a music author (a composer, songwriter, lyricist or arranger). Never before in the history of the world music business have there been so many opportunities for authors and performers to get their music heard and sold on a global level.

So much has happened since the first edition of this book. We have seen the emergence of Twitter as a major marketing tool for music, and continued expansion and innovation from Google, Apple, Facebook and Amazon (often collectively referred to as GAFA). We have also seen Myspace falling into decline after it was purchased by News Corp and then seemingly revived in 2013 under the stewardship of Justin Timberlake. Cloud computing and storage are emerging as the next major phase in the development of digital music services, as we move from a copy economy (CDs and downloads) to an access economy (streaming). Artists are discovering that 'data is the new oil' as they constantly find ways to grow a database of fans which will be key to their success in the new digital ecosystem, an ecosystem increasingly being driven by artists and artist managers. More and more music is becoming social, with sharing and recommendations being at the heart of music discovery and digital music marketing. Whereas in previous times fans were regarded as consumers, they are now a vital and active part of every business model.

Google's YouTube has become the world's biggest music discovery website, which has increasingly resulted in music moving from audio-only to an audio-visual format. Korean artist PSY's 'Gangnam Style' video received over one billion views on YouTube in 2012, making it the most viewed video in YouTube history. The audio version of the track was successful, but not as successful as the video, which shows that fans want the full multimedia experience. Meanwhile Lady Gaga has created her own social network, 'Little Monsters', created by Backplane, which uses Facebook as a feeder. More and more artists and managers are taking the DIY (Do It Yourself) route, but that cannot function in a vacuum. Fans expect artists to nurture their digital presence by constantly updating their website and their social media artist pages, and by providing regular and interesting tweets and Facebook posts. Real-time analytics are proving invaluable, as they can reveal exactly what type of fans an artist has and, more importantly, where they live, which greatly assists successful tour planning. In the digital services landscape we are increasingly seeing 'freemium' offerings such as SoundCloud, Dropbox and Reverbnation, which provide the basic version free to download and use, whereas more advanced features or increased capacity have to be paid for. We are seeing traditional financial advances from third-party phonogram producers (record companies) becoming more scarce, and financial crowd-sourcing directly from fans providing an alternative source of finance for artist projects. Where recording agreements are on offer, phonogram producers are increasingly demanding a 360 degree contract wherein they will receive income from live work, merchandising, branding and sometimes publishing in addition to recording income. When it comes to recording, recording hardware is becoming ever more sophisticated and less and less expensive.

Telecoms are also getting involved with music content and are developing their own music stores and services in some countries. New innovative digital services are constantly being launched, but innovation in the coming years will be driven by the competition between Apple's iOS system and Google's Android in the mobile ecosystem. Anyone doubting the true value of music should consider that Apple became the world's largest corporation in 2011, with music being one of the main drivers of that achievement. When Steve Jobs launched iTunes and the iTunes music store, he was not focused on selling music but rather on using music to sell iPods and computers. iTunes enabled Apple to take a massive market share in the portable digital music player market and by association the personal computer market. Apple later expanded the same music storage ability from the iPod to the iPhone and the iPad.

As the Internet is geographically neutral, where an artist is based has become far less important. In previous times, it was often advisable for an author or performer to move to one of the world's major music business centers, such as Los Angeles, Paris, Hamburg, London, New York or Nashville. With the advent of the Internet, that

is far less important. If an artist can create and record great music, all that is needed is a table, a chair, a computer and a broadband connection and he/she is in business on a global level. Provided an artist can create a good website and have an active presence on the key social networking sites, all the world's markets are at their fingertips, no matter where they live.

Philosopher and composer Friedrich Nietzsche famously said 'Without music life would be a mistake'. How right he was. The whole world is mad on music. Even in the very poorest countries, singing, dancing and making music are an important part of daily life. In the developed world, interest in music is increasing all the time mainly due to the ease of access that the Internet and the digital ecosystem are providing. Music is deeply embedded in the culture of every country. In the past, the only music that could easily be purchased was that stocked by record stores. Due to the limitations of the size of any particular record store, the stock carried represented only a small fraction of the music that had been recorded worldwide. The Internet has changed all that. The diversity of music now available means that anyone with an Internet connection has access to a record shop measuring ten kilometers by ten kilometers, and it's always expanding.

Age is also becoming a significant factor. In the developed world, older people are regarded as digital immigrants whereas younger people are digital natives. Developed countries are seeing a significant reduction in youth crime as computers, smartphones, social networking and video games take away the youth boredom factor.

This book is designed to identify and explain the basic income streams that exist in the worldwide music industry for musical authors and performers (and also for phonogram producers, publishers and anyone involved in the music industry). It is intended primarily to reveal to authors and performers the most effective way to generate income from their talent and endeavors, and the best way to achieve fair arrangements for the exploitation of their songwriting and performances without being ripped off. It also explains the importance of good management and provides guidelines on finding a manager and reaching a fair agreement regarding the conditions of an artist/management contract. A comprehensive example of a long-form artist management agreement can be found in Annex C on page 223. Artists and managers have found this to be particularly useful. It also fulfils the function of pulling together all that is contained within this book in a practical way. Basic guidelines on starting a record label, publishing agreements, recording agreements, band agreements, music in film, TV, advertising and video games, collective management, live work, building a fan base and the basics of digital marketing are all to be found here. There are also recommendations for further reading or online information if the reader wishes to learn more about a particular topic.

In all of the above areas we are seeing spectacular changes as music fans' preferences move from desktop and portable computers to mobile smartphones and tablets. We are seeing a revolution in advertising. Instead of blanket advertising such as a TV or newspaper ad where 95% of those viewing have absolutely no interest in the product, it is now possible, by using Facebook Ads and Google Ads, to target only those consumers who are likely to have an interest in a particular type of music. The statement 'There is no innovation without disruption' manifests itself almost every week as new and exciting digital services are launched.

The live music industry is also seeing sweeping changes, with companies such as Intellitix revolutionizing the music festival experience. By issuing ticket holders with a wristband containing an intelligent microchip and transmitter, it is possible to reduce the time ticket-holders stand in line. It is also possible to load the chip with cash or credit so that food, drink and merchandise can be purchased without cash transactions, which has been found to boost sales. In addition, it allows festival organizers to know where every ticket holder is, manage festival staff and integrate with social networks. However, even this is being leap-frogged by new finger vein recognition technology which scans a person's finger and creates a unique biometric identifier. Vein recognition technology is already being used to replace credit cards and could even replace passports in the future. In smaller venues fans now expect direct contact with the artist, so rather than relaxing in the dressing room after a show, artists are expected to come out and not only do a meet-and-greet with fans but also actually sell and sign merchandise.

Whilst it is hoped that this book will be useful to anyone wishing to be part, or who is already part, of the music industry in the developed world, it is also intended to address the opportunities for authors and performers in developing countries. There has never

been more interest in the developed world for music originating from developing countries. The world music sections of record stores and online stores based in North America, Europe, Japan, Australasia and other developed countries are constantly expanding, as music fans discover the richness of the wonderful music emerging from the world's developing countries. Whilst legitimate sales of the bestselling 5000 albums in the world are declining, sales of the next bestselling albums from 5001 to 10000 are increasing, showing that diversity is becoming a reality. With the introduction of low-cost computers and low-cost broadband connections, we live in a time of revolutionary change, and music is in the front line. Never before has music been so accessible. However, the Internet has also created a situation where copyright, particularly in recordings, is under attack, and it will probably be some time before new structures emerge to properly pay authors, performers, phonogram producers and publishers and protect them from or compensate them for the unauthorized use of their works and performances. With up to 70% of the world's music being acquired without authorization, the industry has temporarily been in a state of market failure. Tackling this problem will require a backdrop of greater global harmonization of copyright law, combining associated reasonable enforcement measures with simpler, easier and faster licensing structures at price points that consumers find acceptable. Whilst it is essential to have a legal backdrop, the emphasis needs to remain on innovation and new attractive, convenient and legal digital services that music fans like using. The music industry, technology companies, consumer organizations and governments will need to work together to find ways to monetize the anarchy. Education will be a key element. There is also a tension between a completely open internet where it's difficult to sell anything digital and a closed internet which restricts access to knowledge. Neither of these extremes are desirable, with a part-open, part-closed internet giving us the best of both worlds. The development of apps for smartphones and tablets is moving information away from the open internet and on to closed or semi-closed platforms.

In the interim, those artists who are both authors and performers are finding that the majority of their income is coming from publishing, live performances, merchandising and branding rather than from the exploitation of their recordings.

In developing countries, some of the institutions and basic structures such as Collective Management Organizations (CMOs), access to the Internet and the ability to open a bank account may only now be in the process of being established, or may not yet exist at all. It is hoped that this book will be of use to such authors and performers to give them an insight as to how things work in the developed world and what may be just around the corner in their own countries. It may be that where a country has no national Collective Management Organizations, authors and performers can join foreign CMOs. However, unless artists and artist managers can get access to a broadband connection easily, development will be slow, not only in a country's music industry but in most other economic sectors too. Research has shown that if a country facilitates an increase in broadband penetration of 10%, this results in an increase in GDP of around 1 to 1.5%. Similarly, the rollout of 3G and eventually 4G mobile networks will be crucial for economic growth. It is hoped, therefore, that governments can prioritize the rollout of broadband and 3G/4G so that not only their music industries can grow, but also their economies in general. The movement from audio-only to audio-visual requires greater broadband capacity, making broadband infrastructure ever more critical. If Internet access and access to bank accounts are problematic, it may be possible for authors and performers to get together and form a collective with a broadband connection and a joint bank account, so that they can receive income from sales of their music online. In other cases it may be that governments are able to provide these facilities to authors and performers, with network access being provided by a local satellite dish at community centers.

As we move into the digital age, the role of collective management organizations will become more important, and efficient licensing mechanisms, operation, regulation and governance of CMOs will be increasingly highlighted. As the music industry becomes more and more global, ease of licensing will be key, although provisions need to be in place to ensure that the value of music does not become forever lower. As in the developing world collective management is still in its formative stages, the concept of mechanical rights, for example, is sometimes non-existent. This book will explain the importance of the establishment of CMOs and the importance of registration and data management with CMOs to ensure proper compensation for authors, performers, publishers and phonogram producers. It will also stress the need for the world to come together around a global repertoire database containing accurate identification of authors, performers, copyright owners/licensees, studio producers, country of recording, international identification codes etc. for every recording ever made. WIPO has launched the IMR (International Music Registry)

initiative (http://www.internationalmusicregistry.org/portal/en/index.html), proposing a broad stakeholder dialogue as a first step towards this concept.

Where money has been mentioned in this book it is expressed in US dollars, as this is the most widely-used currency worldwide. Digital marketing and digital services are changing so rapidly that some of the services and digital tools mentioned in this book will become less relevant and other more innovative and disruptive services will take over. The reader is therefore encouraged to keep abreast of the new changes and services that will inevitably emerge in the digital arena.

It is hoped that this book will provide a useful overview of the various income streams available, and that it may open doors so that music authors and performers can reap the benefits that they so richly deserve.

**David Stopps**

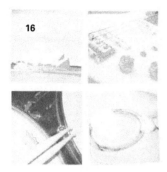

# DEFINITIONS

When using this book it is useful to refer to the definitions section (Annex A on page 195) to fully understand all the terms used. The term 'author' will be used to describe songwriters, composers and arrangers. This includes those who write lyrics for songs and those who write both the music and the lyrics, as well as those who write, compose or arrange instrumental music. The output from a songwriter, lyricist, composer or arranger will be defined as a 'work'. The term 'performer' will be used to describe those who sing or play musical instruments or make any audible sound on a recording such as hand-clapping. This could be in front of an audience on stage or in the recording studio. If a performer makes a recording, their performance would be 'fixed' and becomes a 'fixed performance', otherwise known as a 'recording'. Some performers are pure performers and do not write the songs or music which they perform, whilst others are both authors and performers. The result of a performer's work will be defined as a 'performance' and a recording will be referred to as a 'recording' or in the legal context 'a phonogram'. The broad term 'artist' will be used to describe performers and performers who are also authors. In this book, the name 'artist' will be used to refer to a single performer or a band or group of performers. So both Beyoncé and her former band Destiny's Child would be referred to as an 'artist'.

There are some definitions that can be a little confusing. For example, the term 'producer' is commonly used to describe the person who supervises the recording process in a recording studio. Quincy Jones, for example, who supervised the recording of Michael Jackson's 'Thriller', is often referred to as a 'producer' or as a 'record producer', whereas the record label Sony Music Entertainment, which owns the copyright in this Michael Jackson album, is referred to as the 'record company'. In the world of copyright law and intellectual property, however, Sony, in this example, would be referred to as the 'phonogram producer'. For the purposes of this book we will call the Quincy Jones role a 'studio producer' and the Sony role a

'phonogram producer'. We will also refer to collective management organizations (which in the past have been referred to as collection societies) as CMOs.

The following diagram shows how the rights for authors and performers are defined. In the examples given, Lady Gaga and Bob Marley are both authors and performers, as they wrote most of the works on their recordings. Elton John also qualifies as both an author and a performer, as he writes most of the music for his recordings (but not the lyrics) and is also a performer. Bernie Taupin is a pure author, as he only writes lyrics for Elton John and does not perform in the recording studio or on stage. Elvis Presley was a pure performer, as he relied on others to write works for him. It is important to always remember these two sets of rights in anything to do with music. Thinking of rail tracks with one rail as authors' rights and the other as performers' rights is a good way to think about it.

## Artist

| Author | Performer |
|---|---|
| **Songwriters/Composers Lyricists/Arrangers** | **Singers/Musical instrument players** |
| Create 'Works' | Create 'Fixed Performances' also known as 'Recordings' |
| Rights are Copyright (or Droit d' auteur) | Rights are 'Related Rights' (or 'Neighbouring Rights') |
| Copyright protection Usually life of author plus 50 - 70 years | Copyright protection Mostly 50 - 70 years from first release to public. (Except US see page 38) |
| Exploited by Music Publishers | |
| *Examples* Bernie Taupin Lady Gaga   Elton John Bob Marley | *Examples* Elvis Presley Lady Gaga   Elton John Bob Marley |

The World Intellectual Property Organization (WIPO) is an agency of the United Nations, based in Geneva, Switzerland. It seeks to create and harmonize rules and practices to protect intellectual property rights and to promote cultural diversity, economic growth and to ensure a fair balance of rights in the field of intellectual property. The vast majority of the world's countries are members of WIPO and they are referred to as Member States: in 2012 there were 185 Member States participating in WIPO processes. By providing a stable environment for the marketing of intellectual property products such as music, WIPO and the WIPO treaties enable Member States to trade with each other with legal certainty, for the economic benefit of all participants. (www.wipo.int)

# CHAPTER 1
# WHERE THE MONEY COMES FROM

In the modern music industry there are many different income streams available to authors and performers. Here is a summary of the main income streams:

## 1.i  Authors

(a) Income from public performances on radio, television, downloads and streaming online, live performances, concerts, bars, shops, hairdressing salons and any location where a work is played or heard in public;

(b) Income from mechanical licenses when recordings are distributed on physical sound carriers such as CDs, cassettes, vinyl and DVDs and are sold to the public. Mechanical licenses are licenses issued by authors and publishers to phonogram producers, allowing them to legally exploit recordings and audio-visual productions containing a work;

(c) Income from mechanical licenses when works are the subject of audio or audio-visual downloads, streaming via the Internet or as ring tones, ring-back tones or real tones;

(d) Income from synchronization licenses when the work is synchronized to visual images, video or film;

(e) Income from the sale of printed sheet music and scores or from online digital sheet music downloads;

(f) Income from home copying levies;

(g) Income from public lending of sound carriers containing the work.

## 1.ii  Performers

(a) Income from fees for live performances in front of audiences at festivals, concert venues, clubs, public places and private events;

(b) Income from royalties when a phonogram producer (record company or label) sells a fixed performance (recording) to the public on a physical sound carrier such as vinyl, cassettes or CDs;

(c) Income from royalties when a phonogram producer sells a digital recording via the Internet as a download, by streaming or as a mobile phone ring tone, real tone or ring-back tone;

(d) Income from public performances when a recording is played on the radio, on television, or in public (such as in an arena, a discothèque, club, juke box, factory, shop, hairdressing salon etc.);

(e) Income from 'master re-use' when a recording is synchronized to visual images, video or film;

(f) Income from home copying levies;

(g) Income from sponsorship and branding;

(h) Income from public lending of sound carriers.

It is important for authors, performers and artist managers to make sure that they are on the receiving end of all the above income streams. Different countries have different rights, laws and regulations, so the entitlement for some of the above income streams may vary (e.g., in the UK performers are entitled to remuneration when their audio-only recordings are broadcast or played in public, whereas as soon as the recording is included in a music video their entitlement to broadcast and public performance income ceases. It is hoped that when the BTAP [Beijing Treaty on Audiovisual Performances] is brought into a member state's national law, it will provide equitable remuneration to performers when their recordings are used in music video in the future).

With the problems associated with unauthorized online file sharing, we are seeing the importance of some of the income streams changing. Performers are finding that recording income has become lower compared to the other income streams. This directly effects mechanical income on the author's side, which has therefore also become lower. As stated above, mechanical income refers to license fees that phonogram producers are obliged to pay the publisher/author of the work in a recording for each record/download/stream sold or accessed. On the other hand, we are seeing growth in public performance income from CMOs for both authors and performers. For performers, branding and sponsorship as well as fees for live work are growing and becoming more important. Merchandising sales can also be a

strong income stream if their sales are organized properly. We will discuss these income streams in more detail throughout this book.

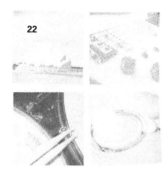

# CHAPTER 2
# BUILDING A TEAM

At the beginning of an author or performer's career, they will need to focus first and foremost on their art and making great music that an audience will like and want to listen to. In the early stages, the artist, with perhaps the help of a friend or family member, will have to do everything themselves. A pure author will need to persuade artists to perform and hopefully record their works. A performer will need to form a band or ask other musicians to perform with him/her, organize rehearsals and try and get some live work in small venues. It will be necessary for an author or performer to join the appropriate CMO as soon as any works or recordings are available to the public or are performed in public. Correct registration with CMOs is fundamental to an author or performer's career. It will also be important for an author or performer to engage a lawyer who is familiar with music business agreements. If a manager is being engaged, it is essential that the author or performer engage a separate lawyer to the one being used by the manager when negotiating the management agreement. It is essential that the author or performer receives independent advice. When some moderate success is achieved, it will become appropriate for an author or performer to start to put a bigger team in place to maximize opportunities. Only some of the roles described below will be necessary in the early stages. Most artists are both authors and performers, so they will need a combination of the following roles in each group. The roles shown below are for an author and a performer who have become a big success story.

## 2.i    Authors

For a pure author who does not perform in the recording studio or at live shows, the team could be as follows:

Some pure authors may decide not to have a manager and will just rely on their music publisher. A music publisher is a person or organization which seeks to exploit and administer an author's works so as to achieve the highest possible income. If the author is seriously interested in composing film scores, they would be advised to engage one of the big film-score agents such as Gorfaine/Schwartz in Burbank, California or Air Edel, who have offices in London and Los Angeles. They may also wish to engage an audio-visual placement agent, shown here as 'Music-in-Film Agent', who can try to place recorded versions of the author's works in film, TV productions, advertising and video games. The author will need a website as a shop window for their achievements so far and for new works created, which should be regularly updated. They may feel confident to be the webmaster themselves or else they may engage a webmaster who is competent in website management. The position of digital marketing director could also be the webmaster. This person ensures that the author has a regularly updated presence on the important social networking sites and services, thus providing a global profile. Pure authors should be prepared to personally attend meetings and networking events in harmony with their manager and/or publisher, as this can be very effective in getting results. In practice, pure authors are usually also performers to some extent, as they often write whilst accompanying themselves on piano or guitar even if they have no intention of performing in the recording studio or live on stage. It is very important that the

author organizes a professional-sounding recording of each of their works. Artists looking for songs expect to be presented with a good well-mixed recording for them to consider. In the past, these have sometimes been referred to as 'demos' which were basic, quickly put together recordings of works. In the modern music business, with the sweeping advances of low-cost home digital recording hardware, artists expect to be presented with a more sophisticated recording.

## 2.ii    Performers

For the performer who records in the studio and performs live, the team can be considerably larger than for a pure author, especially as success starts to become a reality. The performing artist's team could include all or some of the following:
To begin with, the performer themselves will probably have to fulfil all of the above functions that are relevant. The first person to engage is usually the manager who,

as we will see in the artist management chapter, will manage and administer all of the business side of the artist's career. If the artist signs to a third-party phonogram producer, they will usually provide many of the services shown above. These could include publicist, photographer, graphic designer, digital marketing director, and the 'plugger' (someone who tries to get the artist's music on radio and television). An artist should try to get as much artistic control as possible in a third-party phonogram

producer agreement, so that they can approve photographs, artwork, studio producers and digital campaigns etc. The next most important people to add to the team are usually the booking agent and the webmaster, who may also fulfil the function of digital marketing director. It may be that the manager acts as booking agent in the early stages and they may also provide webmaster services as well if they have the skills. Sometimes the artist or a member of the band has the skills to be the webmaster, which can also work very well in the early stages. The artist should always remember that even if they have a separate webmaster they must make regular Facebook posts and tweets etc. themselves. In the digital world, the artist and the fans are the two most important elements of the new music business model. The fans must be allowed to participate and the artist must also directly engage with the fans via 'meet and greets' at live shows, the artist's website, email and the social networks.

When the artist starts to draw larger audiences, it will be necessary to engage a tour manager who will, in conjunction with the manager and the artist, manage all aspects of live work. Sometimes a manager and an artist will take on a tour manager on a tour-by-tour basis or for specific dates, or it may be that the tour manager is employed full-time or held on a retainer between tours. (A retainer is a guaranteed minimum amount that is paid every month regardless of whether the artist is working that month or not). The tour manager role is an important one, as they have to deal with situations effectively but diplomatically so that the tour functions as well as possible. If the artist and manager have their own record label, then the aggregator will be very important (see page 165). They may also need to outsource graphic design, pluggers, digital marketing, CD and DVD manufacturers etc. A choreographer might be needed if the artist incorporates dance routines as part of their live performances. A roadie is someone who manages the on-stage equipment before, during and after a live show, including loading, unloading, tuning instruments etc.

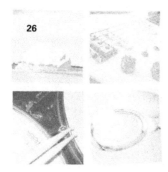

# CHAPTER 3
# COPYRIGHT AND RELATED RIGHTS

'Copyright' is one of the better words in the English language, in that it means exactly what it says. It is the 'right to copy'. If an author writes a work or a performer makes a recording, no one else has the right to make copies of it without the author or performer's permission. With the parallel evolution of technology and law, copyright has evolved to cover control by the author or performer of other uses of a work, such as communication to the public (public performance, broadcasting and making available) and distribution. Traditionally the term 'copyright' refers to an author's works, whereas the rights of performers, phonogram producers and broadcasting organizations are usually referred to as 'related rights' or 'neighboring rights', but they are all forms of intellectual property rights. In some countries such as the UK and the US, related rights are regarded as another form of copyright, but for the purposes of this book we will define the rights of performers, phonogram producers and broadcasting organizations as 'related rights'.

One has to go back to the invention and evolution of the printing press in the sixteenth century to find the first regulations concerning copyright. The right to copy books was limited to certain copyright holders. The first real copyright legislation came along in 1710 in England, but it was not until the mid-nineteenth century in France that modern copyright law began to take shape.

One of the main factors to be understood is that there are two systems in law. The system applied in continental Europe and which originated in France is referred to as 'civil law', whereas the English legal system is referred to as 'common law'. Civil law systems place far greater emphasis on the rights of the author, often referred to as *droit d'auteur*, whereas common law systems put more emphasis on the concept of copyright ownership. The civil law, *droit d'auteur*, treats the rights of authors almost

in the same way as human rights, whereas the common law system is more focused on the economic issues and regards copyright and related rights as property rights.

As England 'spawned' the legal systems in the US, Australia, Singapore etc. as former colonies, the English common law system is also to be found in those territories. In the UK, Scotland, with its historic connections to France, operates under the civil law system whereas England, Wales and Northern Ireland all operate under the common law system. Similarly, in Canada the French-speaking region of Quebec operates under civil law, whereas the rest of Canada, with British roots, operates under the common law system.

In both cases one thing is true: the legislation of rights for authors had a head start of over 100 years on those for performers. As a result, the rights of authors tend to be stronger and are of greater duration than those for performers. For example, one of the most important income streams for performers at the beginning of the 21st century is the income from public performance on radio. This right means that every time a radio station plays a record, it must pay the phonogram producer and the performers who performed on the recording, in addition to the publisher and the author of the work. Most countries have incorporated this right as harmonized, first by the 1961 Rome Convention and later by the WIPO Performances and Phonograms Treaty 1996 (WPPT). However, under Article 15 of the WPPT, Member States have the right to opt out of this provision. The largest music market in the world, the US, decided to register this opt-out and at the time of publication, the US still has no public performance right for performers or phonogram producers when records are played on terrestrial (free-to-air) radio. The US does, however, have a digital public performance right if a recording is played on satellite radio or webcast or simulcast online. For free-to-air radio broadcasts in the US, by far the biggest sector, the author and the author's publisher receive payment (via CMOs ASCAP, BMI or SESAC), but the performers who performed on the recording and the phonogram producers who own the recording do not. Performers and phonogram producers worldwide are hoping that the proposed Performance Rights Act (PRA) will become law in the US as soon as possible, which will correct this imbalance.

The duration of copy protection tends to be considerably shorter for performers and recordings than for authors' works. In the European Union (EU), for example, the duration of rights protection for performers and recordings is harmonized from 2013 onwards at 70 years after the first release of the phonogram, whereas the duration of rights for authors is 70 years after the *death* of the author. In reality, this could mean that author's rights could have copyright protection for as much as 150 years if the author wrote a work at age 15 and died at the age of 95. In other words, author's rights can be effective for over twice as long as those of a performer. The reason for this is mainly historical, in that authors rights have been around for hundreds of years as works could be fixed in written or printed musical notation form, whereas the first recording device was only invented in 1877, thus allowing performances to be fixed for the first time. The rights for performers and phonogram producers clearly have a considerable amount of catching up to do. The first international treaty for authors' rights came into being in 1886, with the agreement of the Berne Convention for the Protection of Literary and Artistic Works, whereas performers, phonogram producers and broadcasters had to wait 75 years for their first international treaty, the 1961 Rome Convention.

The Berne Convention has been updated seven times since 1886, most recently in 1971. As of 2013, 166 countries had signed the Berne Convention. The World Trade Organization's (WTO) Agreement on Trade-Related Aspects of Intellectual Property Rights 1995 (the TRIPS Agreement) has also had an effect on authors' global rights, inasmuch as it includes nearly all the conditions of the Berne Convention. As most countries in the world are members of the WTO, this effectively brought the laws of those countries that had not signed the Berne Convention into harmony with those that had. The WIPO Copyright Treaty (WCT) further extended the rights of authors, particularly in the context of the Internet.

The Rome Convention for the Protection of Performers, Producers of Phonograms and Broadcasting Organizations was the first international treaty to harmonize related rights. Related rights were also included in the TRIPS Agreement and in the 1996 WIPO Performances and Phonograms Treaty (WPPT). As of 2013, 91 countries were signatories to the Rome Convention, 151 countries were signatories of the TRIPS agreement and 90 countries were signatories to the WPPT and the WCT.

As outlined in the definitions chapter, there are fundamentally two sets of rights to consider when making commercial music:

1) The copyright in the work (songwriting, composition, musical arrangement and/or lyrics);

2) The related rights in performances and recordings (phonograms).

However music is used, everyone involved needs to keep these two separate rights in mind at all times. The importance of understanding these two distinct and separate rights cannot be over-emphasized, and anyone involved with music needs to be very clear on how they are dealt with in all transactions.

For example, if an artist wanted to 'borrow' a small section of someone else's recording and incorporate it into one of his/her recordings, as is often done in modern recording (referred to as a 'sample' or 'sampling'), the artist would need to obtain permission from not one, but two different rights holders. Permission would be necessary from whoever owns the rights in the recording (usually a phonogram producer), but also from whoever owns the rights in the work (usually a publisher). Not until an artist has received both of these permissions can he/she legally go ahead and use the sample.

WIPO and the international treaties play an important role in how the rules of copyright and related rights are formulated so as to provide certain minimum rights which each Member State is obliged to incorporate in its national laws. In this way reciprocal arrangements are more easily possible between collective management organizations in different countries, giving music greater value in terms of international trade. For example, if an author is resident in Singapore and his/her work is broadcast on Hungarian radio, the author will still get paid via the Singapore collective management organization COMPASS, which will receive the income from the Hungarian collective management organization ARTISJUS. ARTISJUS and COMPASS have reciprocal agreements with most of the other authors' collection societies all over the world. With appropriate reciprocal international agreements and laws, it is possible to earn money from far beyond the borders of an author's or performer's country. The 1996 WIPO Internet treaties (WPPT and WCT) and the 2012 BTAP (Beijing Treaty on Audiovisual Performances) have been and will be particularly valuable in bringing copyright law up to date. With the rapid advancement of technology, the role of WIPO will become increasingly important in the future, particularly in reference to global harmonization of copyright law and copyright structures.

We will now look at the main rights these and previous treaties and agreements provide. Some may find the following information too legalistic and may wish to proceed to the next chapters, but for others it may provide an understanding of the different rights that exist.

### 3.i    Rights for Authors

According to the Berne Convention and the WCT, authors have the following exclusive rights, described in general terms:

1.  The right of reproduction (the right to copy the work).
2.  The right of distribution (the right to issue and distribute copies of the work to the public).
3.  The right of rental (the right to authorize commercial rental to the public of copies of the work). (In exceptional cases a different system may apply.)
4.  The right of communication to the public (the right to authorize any communication to the public, by wire or wireless means, including 'the making available to the public of works in a way that the members of the public may access the work from a place and at a time individually chosen by them.') The quoted expression 'making available' refers to on-demand, interactive communication through the Internet, such as downloads and interactive streaming.
5.  The right of broadcasting (broadcasting is generally considered to be a subset of 'communication to the public').
6.  The right to translate.
7.  The right to make adaptations and arrangements of the work.
8.  The right to perform the work in public (public performance right – another subset of 'communication to the public').
9.  The moral rights (the rights of integrity and the right of paternity).

### 3.ii    Rights for Performers

Performers have the following exclusive rights (with the exception of point 5, which refers to equitable remuneration) in their recordings if their country of residence has signed the WPPT. Here we will use the treaty term 'phonogram' to mean 'recording' or 'fixed performance'.

1.  The right of reproduction (the right to make copies of the phonogram).
2.  The right of distribution (the right to issue and distribute copies of the phonogram to the public).
3.  The right of rental (the right to authorize the commercial rental to the public of the original and copies of the phonogram as determined in the national law of the Contracting Parties (in exceptional cases, a different system may apply).
4.  The right of making available (the right to authorize the making available to the public, by wire or wireless means, of any performance fixed in a phonogram, in such a way that members of the public may access the fixed performance from a place and at a time individually chosen by them.
    This right refers to on-demand, interactive communication to the public via the Internet).
5.  The right to equitable remuneration for broadcasting and communication to the public. (This is the public performance right for sound recordings. Under WPPT, countries can opt out of this right if they wish.)
6.  The moral rights (the right of integrity and the right of paternity. Again, countries can opt out).

### 3.iii   Rights for Phonogram Producers

Phonogram producers have the following exclusive rights (with the exception of point 5 below, which is a right of equitable remuneration) in their recordings if the country of residence has signed the WPPT:

1.  The right of reproduction (the right to authorize direct or indirect reproduction of the phonogram in any manner or form).
2.  The right of distribution (the right to authorize the distribution to the public of the original and copies of the phonogram through sale or other transfer of ownership).
3.  The right of rental (the right to authorize the commercial rental to the public of the original and copies of the phonogram as determined in the national law of the Contracting Parties (in exceptional cases, a different system may apply).

4.  The right of making available (the right to authorize making available the phonogram, by wire or wireless means, in such a way that members of the public may access the phonogram from a place and at a time individually chosen by them. This right refers to on-demand, interactive making available via the Internet, such as downloads and interactive streaming).

5.  The right to equitable remuneration for broadcasting and communication to the public. (This is the public performance right for sound recordings. The WPPT allows member states to opt out of this right if they wish.)

## 3.iv    Licensing and Assignment

It is important to understand the difference between Licensing and Assignment. If an author or performer licenses their rights, they retain ownership of the Copyright or Related Rights and allow third parties, like publishers or phonogram producers, to exploit those rights under certain contractual conditions. If an author or performer assigns their rights, they are passing on ownership of those rights to the contracting party. A useful analogy would be that assigning is like selling a car to someone else. The original owner would no longer have any interest in the car, as it now belongs to the person they sold it to. If, on the other hand, they had rented the car to someone else, that would be like licensing. They still have ownership of the car, but allow someone else to have the right to use the car under certain conditions. It is always preferable from the author or performer's point of view to license their rights rather than to assign rights. Even if the license is for life of copyright or life of the related rights, the author or performer retains ownership of the rights. In such a case, if the publisher or phonogram producer went out of business or was in material breach of the agreement, the rights would revert to the author or performer. If, on the other hand, the rights had been assigned, a liquidator would usually sell the rights of the bankrupt publisher or phonogram producer to the highest bidder.

## 3.v    Exclusive Rights and Rights of Remuneration

Exclusive rights are the right to authorize or prohibit a particular action, such as making copies of a work or a recording, and they provide complete control for the right holder, except for certain limitations and exceptions as described below. In

most countries, exclusive rights are transferable by assignment or by license, the exception being author's rights in Germany, which can only be transferred by license. If an author signs a publishing agreement with a publisher, or a performer signs a recording agreement with a phonogram producer, the publisher or phonogram producer will require the author or performer to assign or license most of the exclusive rights held by the author or performer for the term of the agreement. An exception to this would be if the agreement were an administration only agreement, in which case the exclusive rights would remain with the author or performer, and the publisher or phonogram producer would only administer the rights on behalf of the author or performer.

A right to remuneration provides less control over a work or recording, as the use can take place without the authorization of the right owner. However, remuneration rights provide for payment at a specified rate to be made to the author, performer, publisher or phonogram producer each time the work or recording is used in public. The most widely-used right of remuneration is that applied to the public performance in sound recordings. This is often referred to as an equitable remuneration right. This right of remuneration is often non-transferable in contract, which is of great benefit to performers.

In other words, if the right of remuneration is not transferable in contract, an author or performer who has signed an exclusive publishing or recording agreement will still continue to receive his/her share of the income from the remuneration right for the public performance of their recordings, no matter what is stated in the contract.

### 3.vi    Making Available

As has been stated above, the 'making available' right is an interactive right for authors, performers and phonogram producers. If an author, performer or phonogram producer makes content available so that a consumer can download or access a specific recording and work at a time and a place of their own choosing, then the making available right takes effect. If a consumer listens to the radio or an online simulcast or webcast where they have no control as to the specific piece of music they will be listening to, then the making available right does not take effect. The radio station may play a specific genre of music, but the consumer will have no control as to which specific tracks will be broadcast. The making available right is of considerable significance for authors, performers and collective management organizations.

Because the making available right is an exclusive right, it is usually transferrable by assignment or license, whereas that is not usually the case with a right to equitable remuneration. A phonogram producer will insist that a performer assigns or licenses their exclusive making available right, as without it the phonogram producer will not be able to sell downloads or license on-demand streaming, which is increasingly becoming a major part of recording income. Because the making available right is an exclusive right, phonogram producers usually license digital services such as iTunes (downloads) and Spotify (on-demand streaming) directly, whereas equitable remuneration rights are almost always administered by a CMO. Tastemaker personal radio streaming music services such as Pandora in the US and lastFM (international) are usually considered to fall under equitable remuneration rather than making available, although this is a grey area. Whilst the consumer cannot listen to a specific track, they can 'skip' tracks if they don't like them, and the tracks that are sent to them are specifically chosen around that particular listener's taste in music. If a member of the public has no control over which track is being streamed, it is sometimes called 'linear streaming' (where the making available right would generally not apply), whereas if a member of the public has the control to choose a specific recording/work, this would be referred to as 'interactive streaming' (where the making available right would apply).

### 3.vii   Limitations and Exceptions and the Three-step Test

All the treaties mentioned above contain provisions on exceptions and limitations to the rights specified. It may be the case, for example, that if a work is used for reporting news, for critical review, for education or research purposes, then no copyright permission is required by the user.

One of the basic guiding rules applied to justify such limitations and exceptions was first included in the Berne Convention for reproduction and generalized to cover all rights by TRIPS, the WCT and WPPT treaties, and more recently by the BTAP (Beijing Treaty on Audiovisual Performances). It is known as the Three-step Test and allows limitations:

1. in certain special cases;
2. that do not conflict with the normal exploitation of the work;
3. that do not unreasonably prejudice the legitimate interests of the author/right-holder.

In the digital age, some governments are looking to introduce new exceptions and limitations. For instance, it is common practice for users to transfer the music on a CD to a computer, or to transfer music on their computer to their mp3 player or mobile phone (often referred to as 'format shifting'). This transfer process is illegal in some member states but is usually ignored by the enforcement authorities as being too difficult to police.

Some member states have introduced an exception for such copying, thus making format shifting legal for users who do this for non-commercial purposes at home. To comply with the Three-step Test, it is important that governments provide some form of compensation for the right-holders when such an exception is introduced. One such compensation scheme is to introduce 'home copying levies' on recordable media and/or recording and digital storage devices. The money collected by such home copying levies is then distributed to authors, performers, publishers and phonogram producers by CMOs.

## 3.viii  Fair Use and Fair Dealing

Fair Use is a term developed in US Copyright Law to describe a limitation and exception to copyright wherein the user would not need to seek permission from the copyright owner for certain uses. The US doctrine of Fair Use is broader and more flexible than Fair Dealing, which is the equivalent term found in the copyright law of other common law countries such as Australia, Canada, New Zealand, Singapore, South Africa and the UK. Whether or not a use qualifies as Fair Use in the US can be complicated and quite subjective. In deciding whether the Fair Use was valid, a court will look at factors such as the purpose and character of the use, the type of copyright protected material used, the amount and substantiality of the portion used and any detrimental economic effect on the copyright owner. Because the interpretation of Fair Use in the USA is so complex, disputes often end up being decided in court. Fair Dealing in other common law countries tends to be more clearly defined, which results in less litigation.

By way of example, the producers of the film 'Expelled' used 15 seconds of audio of John Lennon's 'Imagine' in 2008, using both the work and the original recording, and claimed it was Fair Use. Yoko Ono, the owner of John Lennon's estate, took the film company to court to challenge that assumption. The US Court ruled that this use did indeed qualify as Fair Use.

In the UK several commercial companies found a loophole in the laws on Fair Dealing. They ripped existing audio-visual copyright protected material from bands such as Pink Floyd and Genesis and put them together on DVDs. They interspersed each clip with interviews with music journalists who would give a critique of each clip. Although they released them commercially, these companies claimed that the DVDs were works of 'review and criticism' and therefore qualified under the UK regulations on Fair Dealing, and that subsequently no permissions were required. This resulted in record stores selling a range of such DVDs by famous artists. On one occasion the author of this book counted eight such Fair Dealing DVDs by the band Genesis in a London record store and only one DVD which had been legitimately released by the band's phonogram producer.

As we move in to the digital revolution, it is becoming increasingly important that some international norms on exceptions and limitations be agreed across member states. The problem is that each member state has its own exceptions and limitations which are territorial and often different to some other member states. This is even the case within the European Union. This makes such concepts as legal cross-border distance learning very complex. Whilst the creator of such a learning course may have complied with the exceptions and limitations in their own country, the course may well become illegal in another member state, as the exceptions and limitations regulations will be different. It will be necessary for governments to work towards international norms across the whole field of copyright law if there is to be any certainty in our global Internet-based future.

## 3.ix   Moral Rights

Moral rights fall essentially into two categories:
1.   The right of integrity. This provides that no one can change a work or a recording without the author's or performer's permission.

2. The right of paternity. This provides the author or performer with the right to be named or credited if their work or recording is used or played in public.

Moral rights are exclusive rights and are not transferable in contract. They stay with the right owner even after any transfer of economic rights. In many countries, however, they can be waived in contract, which means that the author or performer may agree in the publishing or recording agreement that he/she will not assert his/her moral rights. Whilst nearly every publisher and phonogram producer will insist on the inclusion of this waiver if the law allows, it may be possible to insert other wording in the contract which goes some way towards obliging the publisher or phonogram producer to provide some of the aspects of moral rights, such as being credited where possible.

In the digital era there is some tension between moral rights and rights of remuneration. The creative process of mash-ups, wherein an artist puts together several existing recordings and manipulates and blends them with perhaps some new parts, is becoming an art-form in itself. Sometimes these mash-ups and remixes are created 'live', either for a performance in front of an audience or for a live broadcast. In such circumstances it is therefore impossible to obtain the appropriate permissions in advance. Some authors and performers are quite relaxed about this, whereas others feel very strongly that their moral rights are being violated. As new remuneration structures develop this tension is bound to become more of an issue. In the end it will be a decision for the author or performer as to whether they want control over their works and recordings or whether they would rather relinquish their moral rights (at least the right of integrity) and just settle for being paid. One approach to this problem is to establish a system where the switches are always on unless an author or performer dislikes something, in which case they have the right to turn the switch off – i.e., third parties can incorporate the works and recordings of other authors and performers in to a mash-up, but if one of the original authors or performers takes exception to such use they have the right to issue a take-down notice. This is how services such as YouTube function. Any audio-visual content can be uploaded to YouTube, but if YouTube is notified that that content is illegal they will take it down and prevent any further uploads of that particular content. This take-down procedure is defined in the US Digital Millennium

Copyright Act, which provides a 'safe harbor' for digital intermediaries and ISPs, provided that they operate a take-down procedure if they are notified of illegality.

## 3.x    National Treatment, Term of Protection and the Public Domain

The term of copyright or related right protection is governed by what is known as 'national treatment'. This means that although the country of residence of the author or performer may have reciprocal agreements with other countries via international treaties, the term of protection in the foreign country is usually limited to the term of protection in that foreign country. A more accurate definition would be that Member States are obliged to grant exactly the same protection (the same rights, with the same exceptions and under the same conditions) to the nationals of other Member States who are party to a treaty as they do to their own nationals. For example, the term of protection for sound recordings is 70 years from first release in France (effective from 1st November 2013) whereas in South Africa it is 50 years. If a French artist with French residency has recordings released in South Africa, he/she will enjoy only 50 years of protection in South Africa but 70 years of protection in his/her own country. If a South African performer who is resident in South Africa releases a recording in France, he/she will enjoy copyright protection for 70 years in France, even though he/she will enjoy only 50 years' protection in his/her own country for the same recording.

A specific example is the earliest recordings by American singer Elvis Presley, recorded and released in 1957. In 2007, 50 years later, those recordings went into the public domain in countries where the term of protection for sound recordings was/is 50 years. 'In the public domain' means that the work or recording is no longer protected by copyright or related rights and anyone in that territory can use it without needing to obtain permission or authorization. In this example, from 2007 onwards, anyone was able to release the early Elvis Presley recordings in those countries where the term of protection for sound recordings was/is 50 years, without needing authorization and without having to pay the owners of the original recording any royalties. In the US, however, the term of protection would be 95 years (if the recording was deemed to be a 'Work made for Hire' under US law), or lifetime of the last surviving performer on the recording plus 70 years if it was not a 'Work made for Hire'. The same recordings will still be protected until 2052, which is 95 years from first

release in that territory, or even longer if they were not regarded as 'Works Made for Hire'. In this example, a company called Memphis Recording Service (MRS) managed to get one of the early Elvis Presley recordings, 'My Baby Left Me', into the UK national top forty singles chart quite legally in 2007, without any permissions or authorizations in regard to the recording being required. It should always be remembered that even though the recording may be in the public domain, the work and the artwork may well not be. If the work was written in the previous 100 years, the chances are it is still protected by copyright, so royalties will still be payable to the author or the author's publisher even if the recording no longer has protection. The same will be true of any photographs and/or artwork used on the packaging of the original recording. In the Elvis Presley example above, whilst the recording was in the public domain in the UK, the work and the original artwork still have copyright protection. The company issuing the public domain recording will still have to obtain a mechanical license from, and pay mechanical royalties to, the author or the author's publisher. They will also have to obtain permission from whoever owns the original artwork/photographs on the original packaging if they wish to use those. The alternative would be to create new artwork which would enjoy its own copyright protection and which would be quite separate and unrelated to the original artwork. The creation of the new artwork would trigger its own new period of copyright protection.

### 3.xi    Copyright Registration

It is important to understand that it is unnecessary to formally register works with a government or a government institution or with a private entity of a particular country, in order to benefit from copyright protection. Copyright exists automatically as soon as the work is created. Most countries require the original work of creativity to be fixed in a tangible form, such as by writing down the musical notation with the associated lyrics, if any, or by making a recording which contains the work.

Similarly, when a performance has been fixed as a recording, the right in the recording exists and does not need to be formally registered with a government or deposited with a government institution for it to be protected by the related rights that exist. Some countries, such as the US, have a voluntary registration system intended to make a public record of a particular copyright. Copyrighted works may be registered with the U.S. Copyright Office, and although it is not necessary to register a work or a sound recording to enjoy copyright protection, there are certain advantages in doing so, particularly in a case of copyright infringement. (See www.copyright.gov.) That said, it is important to join the appropriate collective management organizations as soon as possible and to register the works or recordings with them. (See the chapter on collective management organizations on page 49.)

### 3.xii    Trademarks

Another aspect of copy protection is that of trademarks. This is particularly important in the context of a band or artist's name. As will be discussed later on page 72, it is advisable to choose an unusual name that is unlikely to have been used by anyone else previously. Once the band name has been chosen and some moderate success achieved, it is important to register it along with any logo or artwork designed around the name, with the artist's local or regional trademark office. There are always fees associated with this registration, but the expenditure is well worthwhile as soon as finances allow. The next step is to obtain international trademark registration. This is a service offered by WIPO to all countries that have signed the Madrid Agreement Concerning the International Registration of Marks and the Madrid Protocol. A person who has a link with a country that is a party to one or both of these treaties may, on the basis of a registration or application with the trademark office of that country, obtain an international registration having effect in some or all of the other countries of the Madrid Union. At present, more than 60 countries are party to one or both of these Agreements.

For more information on copyright and related rights as well as trademarks, consult the WIPO website at www.wipo.int.

### 3.xiii    Two Copyright Laws that support Authors and Performers

There are two distinct copyright laws that really support and help musical authors and performers. One is enshrined in the law of Germany and the other in the law of the United States. They are as follows:

1.  In German law, copyright in author's works cannot be assigned but can only be licensed. This provides fundamental protection for German authors. The copyright in their works will always be owned by them and any transfer, other than license, is illegal. See the above section on Licensing and Assignment to see why it is always better for an author or performer to license their rights rather than to assign them.

2.  In US law, all transfer of Copyright and Related Rights is limited to 35 years, provided the author or performer follows certain procedures. This provision was designed to protect authors and performers who assigned or licensed their rights before the true commercial value of the rights was known. This first became effective in the 1976 Copyright Act Section 203 and is referred to as the 'Termination Right'. It applies to all copyright and related rights transfers which occurred after 1st January 1978, so the first terminations can take place from 2013 onwards. The exception to this is if works or performances are deemed to be 'Works Made for Hire', i.e. if the publisher or phonogram producer acted like an employer of the author or performer. It remains to be seen if particular works or recordings are deemed by a court to fall under the doctrine of 'Work Made for Hire', but a test case took place in May 2012 concerning author Victor Willis who was a co-writer for the Village People on hits such as 'YMCA', 'Go West' and 'In the Navy'. Willis won the case, which is good news for authors. On the recording side there are different factors at play and it remains to be seen whether the 'Work Made for Hire' doctrine will apply. In the US, authors and performers should be able to enjoy reversion of their rights after 35 years, which will give them an opportunity to renegotiate better terms and advances with their existing publishers or phonogram producers, to make a new agreement with new businesses, or to manage the rights themselves. Assuming an average life expectancy, most authors and performers could look forward to getting reversion at least once in their lifetime. Go to http://www.wipo.int/wipo_magazine/en/2012/04/article_0005.html for an in-depth article by Brian Caplan on this issue.

Both of the above laws are designed to protect creators' rights and they both perform that function very elegantly.

### 3.xiv  Creative Commons

Creative Commons is a not-for-profit organization founded in 2001 by Lawrence Lessig, Hal Abelson and Eric Aldred, and provides creators with licenses which permit others to use and share their works and recordings legally for certain uses at no cost. Creative Commons licenses are based on copyright law but provide authors and performers with a legal document that provides users with effectively a free license for specific uses or, if they wish, all uses. This provides users with legal certainty, provided they do not use the content for commercial uses if they are reserved in the license. For the author and performer it allows users to use their works and recordings, which may help the author or performer become well-known and build their career. The user may be obligated to uphold the author's or performer's moral right of paternity, but may waive the moral right of integrity, which would allow the user to modify the work or recording if they chose to (subject always to moral rights being unwaivable in some countries). The right of paternity obligates the user to give the author or performer a credit when their work or recording is used. By 2008 there were an estimated 130 million plus works licensed using Creative Commons licenses, and as of 2011 the photo sharing service Flickr was hosting over 200 million photos using Creative Commons licenses. Wikipedia also uses a Creative Commons license. Creative Commons licenses can be useful for getting exposure, but authors and performers are advised to reserve commercial uses. If a piece of music is picked up by a major brand and used in a worldwide advertisement, the author or performer would get nothing if they had issued an 'all uses' Creative Commons license. (www.creativecommons.org)

### 3.xv  Copyright Infringement and How to Stop It

Whilst nearly every country in the world has copyright laws enshrined in its national law, there is still a major problem with copyright infringement, sometimes referred to as 'piracy'. In many countries this is magnified because inadequate enforcement provisions have been provided. It is pointless creating any law if the accompanying enforcement is inadequate, or, even worse, non-existent. Member states have an obligation to comply with the international treaties they sign up to, and to introduce national laws that reflect their provisions, but national laws created from the treaties are redundant unless there are necessary enforcement procedures to make them

credible and effective. It is also advisable that member states accompany any copyright legislation with public education on copyright, particularly in schools, but also across society as a whole.

In the physical world, copyright infringement usually manifests itself in small businesses and individual traders illegally manufacturing and selling physical sound carriers such as CDs without obtaining permission from, or paying, the legitimate copyright and related right owners. Until the digital CD came along, analogue illegal copies of music on vinyl or cassette were usually of inferior quality to those available from the legitimate phonogram producers, so most consumers preferred to purchase legitimate copies. With the advent of the digital CD, however, all that changed. Counterfeit copies could be made that were 'clones' of the original, i.e. almost perfect copies could easily be manufactured by illegal traders. This has resulted in every country needing to police local street markets to enforce copyright laws. This copyright infringement involves traders making money illegally from authors, performers, publishers and phonogram producers, and undermines the commercial basis of the music industry.

In the digital online environment, the problem of copyright infringement has been greatly magnified and is much more difficult to enforce. In addition to individual traders and organizations making money illegally by selling or providing advertisement-supported 'free' music, music fans are sharing music with each other with no reference or payment to the copyright owners. There is a big difference here, as file sharers are not necessarily making money (although they are saving money), but authors, performers, publishers and phonogram producers are certainly losing money as a result of their activity.

## 3.xvi   Carrot, Stick and Education

We are in the middle of the online digital revolution, and it is inevitable, since digital files can so easily be shared and distributed via the Internet, that it may take some time to adapt copyright enforcement regulations to the modern era. Various schemes and procedures are being tried in different Member States to encourage music fans to purchase or access music from legitimate services and to discourage them from going to illegal sites and services.

As we shall see later in this book, a new system of compensation may need to be developed in the online world to properly compensate authors, performers and copyright holders. The International Federation of the Phonographic Industry (IFPI) publishes regular reports on world copyright infringement of sound carriers and files in the online environment. Go to www.ifpi.org for more information.

Many governments all over the world are introducing or trying to introduce new laws to tackle copyright infringement in the online environment. Such laws often have a difficult time going through the legislative process and there is often resistance from consumer organizations, open rights groups, ISPs (internet service providers), telecoms and digital services to any further internet restriction or regulation. The open rights groups believe that all citizens should have as much access to knowledge as possible on the internet at no cost to the consumer, and that any further restrictions or regulation would be counterproductive to that goal. The creative industries community would argue that without such new regulation from governments they are on a slippery slope to disaster, as all music will effectively be 'free' and that music will be regarded as having no real value. The music industry would argue that this will undermine the entire creative process and remove the incentive for authors and performers to create new works and recordings, which are the bedrock of a nation's culture.

Some countries have introduced, or are considering the introduction of, a 'Three Strikes and You're Out' graduated response law, wherein warning letters are sent out to consumers who engage in the downloading or streaming of unauthorized music files. If the infringer continues to engage in unauthorized activity, a further letter or e-mail would be sent warning them that if they persist in the illegal activity, their internet connection would be suspended or 'throttled'. 'Throttled' means that their bandwidth will be reduced so that the connection becomes slow and only adequate for text e-mails. The first country to introduce such a law was France in 2009, when the French government passed its Creation and Internet law, often referred to as the HADOPI law. HADOPI is actually the name of the French government agency charged with administering the Creation and Internet law (Haute Autorité pour la Diffusion des Oeuvres et la Protection des Droits sur Internet). HADOPI sent out their first letters in October 2010.

According to MusicAlly and based on HADOPI's own published statistics, up to the end of 2012 1.15 million first warning letters had been sent out and 100,000 second letters. Only 340 third warning letters had been sent, of which 14 cases were passed to local prosecutors. This has resulted in one person being convicted but not fined, and another being convicted and fined $200. In 2011 it was claimed that peer-to-peer (P2P) copyright infringement levels in France declined by 26% with around 2 million P2P users stopping unauthorized activity (according to IFPI/Nielson). The running costs of the French HADOPI operation for 2012 were US$13.5 million.

The Republic of Korea, which is one of the most technologically advanced nations in the world, also introduced a similar graduated response law, but combined it with a softer approach to illegal digital services. They went to each illegal digital service and persuaded them to become legal services. The result has been that Republic of Korea has enjoyed strong growth in its digital legal services and, with a population of 49 million, 40 million of which are internet users, only 9 people had their internet account suspended for 29 days in the first year of operation. The Republic of Korea also launched a national education initiative informing the population about the importance of intellectual property rights.

In the USA the government has encouraged the music industry and the ISPs to work together to operate a voluntary graduated response approach to illegal file-sharing. There are no penalties for persistent infringers but the ISPs have agreed to notify users by e-mail if they detect unauthorized activity. Whilst this will not change the hard-core infringers, it is having a major effect on the large percentage of citizens who feel uncomfortable about participating in unlawful activities.

Another approach that is proving to be effective is that of site-blocking via the courts. Phonogram producer trade bodies such as the BPI in the UK are having success in seeking a site blocking judgment wherein the court will require the largest ISPs to block a particular site being accessed by their subscribers. Prior to the BPI site blocking court order on The Pirate Bay, The Pirate Bay was rated as the 43rd most popular site in the UK. Eighteen months later, The Pirate Bay was rated by Alexa website analytics as being the 412th most popular site, which shows the effect of such a site-blocking order. By the end of 2013 fifteen countries had blocked The Pirate Bay.

Enforcement is by no means the only answer. Education on the importance of copyright for a nation's culture and economy is essential in schools and across society generally. There is also great pressure from legitimate rights holders for search engines such as Google to traffic-shape their services to give legal sites priority. If a music fan enters the name of a track and/or artist in a search engine, the chances are that the illegal sites will come up at the top of the list, especially if the fan also puts in 'mp3'. In the UK and in some other countries, the search engine services are responding positively to this traffic shaping initiative by placing legal services at the top of the search.

Another initiative is for legal services to simply be better and more convenient for the music fan than the illegal services. It would have been interesting to be in the boardroom when the first person suggested that they put water in plastic bottles and sell it to the public. Why would anyone want to buy water in plastic bottles when they can effectively get it free from the tap? Research has shown that in most developed countries the water is actually healthier from the tap compared to the water that is sold in bottles. Despite this, a multi-billion dollar global industry based on bottled water has developed and flourished. The music industry needs to learn from this example.

How can legal services be made more attractive than illegal ones? First of all, copyright holders and the legal services need to learn from the illegal sites, e.g. it is possible to download an artist's entire catalogue from some of the illegal sites in one click. Copyright holders and legal sites need to offer the same service at a reasonable price. Legal sites need to emphasize to music fans that legal sites are virus-free. Some music fans have had their entire hard-drive wiped by downloading from illegal sites. Most music fans would prefer to be legal rather than illegal. Copyright holders and legal digital services need to ensure that they offer a more convenient, safer and legal alternative to the pirate sites.

Another very important issue to consider is: how do the illegal music sites make money? The answer is from advertising. Many established advertising agencies place ads on the illegal sites as they have proved to get the best results for the

dollar spend for the brands they represent. Often well-respected global brands are advertised on these sites without them being fully aware of it. The most effective way of bringing an end to illegal sites is to starve them of their advertising. The music industry is increasingly putting forward a 'name and shame' public campaign to make global brands aware of how their brand is being associated with illegal sites. Whilst this advertising is effective, it associates the brand with illegal operations, which can tarnish the brand's image.

Legal streaming services such as Spotify have had a very positive effect on music fans resorting to illegal services. Spotify offer a legal, free 'all you can eat' streaming service which is supported by advertising. They also offer a premium service with no advertising and tethered downloads for a flat monthly subscription of around $9-$15, depending on the country of access. A tethered download is a TPM-protected download that is rendered inaccessible if a fan ceases to pay their subscription. Music fans have taken to these legal steaming services in their millions and are enjoying the experience, which takes them away from using illegal sites.

We need laws and enforcement as a backdrop in the digital e-commerce world as a disincentive for music fans to resort to illegal services, but more importantly, we need education and innovative, attractive, virus-free new services which put illegal services in the shade.

There are various services which, for a fee, will scan the internet and take down illegal copies of a particular track. Examples are Web Sheriff and Audiolock amongst many others.

### 3.xvii  Creative Heritage Project

WIPO is doing substantial work in providing information, including intellectual property (IP) related protocols, policies, best practices and guidelines to developing countries and indigenous groups, concerning control over their cultural heritage. For example, the artist project Deep Forest used some UNESCO field recordings made in the Solomon Islands as samples in their highly successful albums which have sold millions of copies worldwide. As far as the author of this book is aware, none of the money made from the sales found its way back to the

**48**

Solomon Islands where the original sample recordings were made. It is this type of issue that the Creative Heritage Project seeks to address. For more information, go to www.wipo.int/tk/en/folklore/culturalheritage/.

# CHAPTER 4
# COLLECTIVE MANAGEMENT AND COLLECTION
# MANAGEMENT ORGANIZATIONS (CMOS)

As we go further into the technological revolution encompassing the whole of the music industry, there is no doubt that collective management is going to become more and more important to authors and performers. It is therefore crucial that authors, performers and managers understand the importance of correct registration and membership of the appropriate CMO for a particular author or performer. Poor or incorrect registration of works and performances with CMOs, or no registration at all, have resulted in millions of dollars of income going to the wrong person (or business), or people not being paid at all. The music industry is awash with money which ends up being returned to phonogram producers or publishers because, for some reason, it cannot be paid through to the correct author or performer. A good artist manager will focus particular attention on collective management and will do everything possible to ensure that the artist is receiving all the income due.

## 4.i     Why is Collective Management Necessary and what is its History?

As we saw in the chapter on copyright above, the legislation of rights for authors was the first to be established. The first attempt at collective management was the establishment of the Bureau de Législation Dramatique in France in 1777. This organization later became the Société des Auteurs et Compositeurs Dramatiques (SACD), which still functions today. The first CMO as we now know it was established in the mid-nineteenth century, again in France. This was the Société des Auteurs Compositeurs et Editeurs de Musique (SACEM). SACEM was the first real CMO for music authors and came about as a direct result of a court decision when two composers, Paul Henrion and Victor Parizot, together with a lyricist, Ernest

Bourget, sued a café called Les Ambassadeurs in Paris for playing their works without paying them. These three author pioneers were having dinner in Les Ambassadeurs when the café's orchestra played one of their works. They refused to pay for the dinner unless the proprietor of the cafe also paid them for the use of their works. The authors won the court case that followed, and this was to change authors' rights forever. Prior to this, authors had (in theory) to give individual permission for one of their works to be performed by somebody else. By the mid-nineteenth century, this was becoming impractical as it was impossible for an author to know when and where one of their works was being performed. By the early twentieth century, similar societies, often referred to as performing rights societies, were formed in most European countries and some other countries around the world. In 1926 the delegates from 18 such societies got together and formed an umbrella organization under the name of the Confederation of Societies of Authors and Composers (CISAC), which today continues to play a major role in the collective management of authors' and publishers' rights (www.cisac.org). In 1990 another organization, GESAC, was formed to specifically represent European authors CMOs regarding European copyright issues. (www.gesac.org)

The situation for performers before the introduction of the gramophone and radio was quite straightforward. The performer would perform live if the conditions for a performance were agreeable. If the conditions were not acceptable, then the performer simply refused to perform. The performer had complete control over their rights, which was the human right to perform or not. When the first recordings or 'fixed performances' came along, the whole landscape changed. It again became impractical for a performer to give permission every time someone wished to play a recording in public, so a system had to be devised where an organization would monitor and collect such payments on behalf of the performer and whoever owned the recording. Such collective management organizations are known as 'neighboring rights collective management organizations' or more accurately 'related rights collective management organizations'.

Authors and performers can still retain the right to authorize or prohibit the use of their works or performances by not signing up to any collective management organizations and only authorizing specific uses on a one-off basis as they come along. Most authors and performers, however, want their works and performances

to be used as widely as possible so that they become well-known, thus creating the maximum income. In order to achieve this, they will sign an agreement with the appropriate CMO so that it has the right to collect income on their behalf. The CMO will deduct an administration fee from such income and pass on the remainder to the author or performer. It is sometimes possible in such collective management agreements to retain a degree of exclusivity for certain uses. In advertisements, for example, the collection society might be obliged to seek specific permission from the author and/or the performer for such use. An author or performer may have strong moral views on certain topics. For example, an author or performer (or both) may not wish their creations to be used in conjunction with a political party with which they do not agree. An author who is a vegetarian will probably object to his/her work being used in a meat or fish advertisement. It is quite common for such approvals to be excluded altogether from these agreements, such approvals being in the hands of the publisher or phonogram producer. In some publishing and recording agreements, the publisher and phonogram producer may be obliged to seek approval from the author or performer as well for specific uses. For this reason, it is in the author's or performer's interest to have as much control as possible in regard to the use of their works and performances in publishing or recording agreements, so that no inappropriate uses take place.

CMOs can operate in different ways. Some CMOs insist on a complete assignment of the right of public performance for authors' rights or performers' rights. With this type of agreement, the author or performer transfers his or her ownership of the right to the CMO. Other CMOs operate as agents for an author or performer, with the author or performer retaining the right but agreeing that the CMO can administer the right on their behalf. In the UK, for example, the Performing Right Society (PRS), the authors' society dedicated to collecting public performance income, insists on a complete assignment, whereas the Mechanical Copyright Protection Society (MCPS), which collects mechanical royalties on behalf of authors, operates under an agency agreement.

## 4.ii    The Importance of Correct Registration of Works, Performances and Recordings

It is absolutely crucial that all works (for authors) and recordings (for performers and phonogram producers) are correctly registered with the appropriate CMO. One thing is certain: if registration is not made or is incorrect, no income will flow through. In some countries, such as Italy, even if only one of the words in the title is capitalized or misspelled the CMO may not pay through income and may instead designate the payment as 'unattributable' and pay it into an unattributable 'black box' account which will eventually be paid out to local publishers or phonogram producers. For example, one of the artists represented by the author of this book has had great success with a song entitled 'What is Love?' If the song is registered as 'What is Love' without the question mark, some CMOs might refuse to pay through on 'What is Love?' with a question mark. To help get over this problem, some authors and performers register several titles of songs and guess at possible misspellings and punctuation mistakes. So in this example it would be a good idea to register 'What is Love?' and 'What is Love'. Whichever CMO the author or performer joins, it is a good idea to regularly ask them for a list of works or performances so that they can be checked for accuracy. Increasingly, CMOs are making this information available online.

## 4.iii    Functions and Governance of Collective Management Organizations

CMOs vary considerably around the world regarding their remit from governments and their members. Some are purely administrative, whilst others also have the obligation to represent and lobby on behalf of their members to uphold and protect their members' rights. CMOs seem to function well as a monopoly in a country, provided they have democratic governance. One of the most comprehensive and authoritative books written on collective management is 'Collective Management' by Dr Mihaly Ficsor, which is highly recommended for anyone interested in CMOs. In this book, Dr Ficsor states:

> 'Government supervision of the establishment and operation of joint management organizations seems desirable. Such supervision may guarantee (inter alia) that only those organizations which can provide the legal, professional and material conditions necessary for an appropriate and efficient management of rights may operate; that the joint management system be made available to all rights owners who need it; that the terms of membership of the organizations be

reasonable and, in general, that the basic principles of an adequate joint management (for example, the principle of equal treatment of rights owners), be fully respected.'

And....

'Usually, there should be only one organization for the same category of rights and for the same category of rights owners in each country. The existence of two or more organizations in the same field may diminish or even eliminate the advantages of joint management of rights.'

One of the most important issues for CMOs is that they should have democratic governance. It is highly desirable, if not essential, for CMOs to have a board structure which accurately reflects the rights they administer. So if a CMO collects income for the public performance of works and distributes this income to authors and publishers, the governing board should be made up of 50 percent authors and 50 percent publishers. Similarly, if a CMO collects income for the public performance of sound recordings and this income is split 50 percent to performers and 50 percent to phonogram producers, the governing board should be made up of 50 percent performers and 50 percent phonogram producers. This democratic board structure is particularly important if the CMO has a monopoly in a particular country. A good example of a CMO that works well with this democratic board structure is the UK authors and publishers CMO, PRS for Music. PRS for Music has a monopoly in the UK, and the board consists of six authors and six publishers. Similarly, US related rights CMO Sound Exchange, which is also a monopoly, has nine phonogram producer board members (four representing the majors, three representing independent phonogram producers and two from US phonogram producer trade body RIAA) and nine performer board members (seven representing performers, one from musicians' union the AFofM and one from the singers' union AFTRA.) These two CMOs are excellent examples of democratic, fair and balanced governance.

### 4.iv    Collective Management Organizations Databases and the Concept of a Global Repertoire Database (GRD)

The way that national CMOs have evolved means that every CMO has its own database, built up over many years and which requires constant updating. This is the most valuable asset that any CMO owns. Without it they would not be able to license the correct licensees or pay out to the correct rights holders. Inevitably, different countries have developed their databases using different systems and different software which is often incompatible with other CMOs in other countries, making accurate reciprocal payments difficult. With the technological advances in recent years of database software systems and the online environment, great efficiency could be achieved if a global repertoire database could be created that each CMO could have access to. Such a global database would contain accurate information about every recording, the copyright owners in each territory, the author(s) who wrote the underlying musical work, publisher information, performer identification, ISRC codes, country and studio where the recording was recorded, studio producer details, length of the recording, when the recording was first released in each territory etc. WIPO is working on the IMR (International Music Registry) initiative to possibly facilitate such a database. The EU is also pushing for a pan-European database for music authors. This started with the UK CMO PRS for Music and Swedish CMO STIM combining their databases and back office functionality under the title The International Copyright Enterprise (ICE).

In 2009 a 'Global Repertoire Database' (GRD) working group was established, consisting of EMI Music Publishing, Universal Music Publishing, Apple, Amazon, Nokia, PRS for Music, STIM and SACEM. Following the group's recommendations document in 2010, the group was expanded to include CISAC, ECSA (The European Composer and Songwriters Alliance), ICMP (International Confederation of Music Publishers), Google and Omniphone. In 2013 it was announced that the GRD would be managed by Deloitte Touche Tohmatsu and would have its headquarters in London and its operations center in Berlin, with a launch date of 2015.

On the performer and recording copyright owner side, PPL in the UK are investing heavily in creating their own international database for performers and recordings which may eventually evolve into a global repertoire database. The ideal scenario for some time in the future would be for a combined authors, performers, publishers and phonogram producers global database to be created with compatible and harmonized software, which would result in more efficient, economic and accurate cross-border payments.

## 4.v Collective Management Organizations for Authors

If an artist is a songwriter, composer, arranger or lyricist, it is very important for him/her or his/her manager to research into which CMOs to join. Most authors quite logically and sensibly join the appropriate CMO in their own country. In this way, they will be able to visit them easily if a meeting is required and everyone will speak the same language, which makes misunderstandings less likely. Each country's CMO will almost certainly have reciprocal agreements with similar CMOs in most other countries. So, for example, an Argentinean author will register his/her works with the Argentinean authors' public performance CMO SADAIC. If the same author's works are played on the radio in Germany, the German society, GEMA, will pay through the public performance royalty to SADAIC, who will in turn pass it on to the Argentinean author's publisher and/or the author themselves.

There are generally two CMOs that an author will need to join:
1. A public performance communication to the public CMO;
2. A mechanical copyright CMO.

## 4.vi Authors' Public Performance Collective Management Organizations

An author's public performance CMO will collect royalties whenever an author's work is played in public. This could be on the radio, on television, in a discothèque, in shops, in hairdressing salons, in doctors' surgeries, in restaurants, in bars and clubs, at live events or in any situation where music is heard in a place where members of the public can hear it. It used to be the case that most of the monies collected by such authors' CMOs came from radio, but that is shifting towards income from other public performances. Karaoke, for example, where members of the public are encouraged to sing the lead vocal to backing tracks of well-known songs in clubs and bars, is becoming increasingly important as a source of revenue for such CMOs. With radio play, authors' public performance CMOs monitor, as best they can, which works a radio station has broadcast. Large and national radio stations are often monitored comprehensively so that every work they broadcast is logged, and this information is passed on to the appropriate CMO. The CMO may occasionally carry out a separate independent audit so as to ensure that the information they are getting from the radio station is correct. Smaller radio stations may also be required to log and report all the works they broadcast, but sometimes it will be the CMO who have to do such monitoring and logging. For economic reasons, it is sometimes the case that a CMO will only be able to monitor a small radio station for perhaps one day per month. The results are then expanded as if the works they played on that day were also played on all the other days of that month. If an author were lucky enough to have had his/her work played on the one day that was monitored by the CMO, he/she will then receive income as if the work were played on every day that month. If however, the work was played on twenty days of that month but not on the particular day that the CMO monitored, the author would receive nothing. It is hoped, with advances in technology such as digital fingerprinting, that systems can be introduced in every country so that every work broadcast can be logged using electronic identifiers, and the data can then automatically be sent through to the CMO.

As we have seen above, it is crucial for an author to ensure that all his/her works are correctly registered with the appropriate CMO. It is therefore essential that if there is more than one author for a particular work, an agreement is reached as soon as possible after the work is created about the writing splits.

Traditionally it has been the case that the musical composition for a song will qualify for 50 percent of the author's rights and the lyrics will qualify for the remaining 50 percent. This is still generally the case, although sometimes the musical elements are agreed to total more than 50 percent and the lyrics less than 50 percent. In modern song writing, it can often be that many authors contributed to the final version of a particular work. In all cases where there is more than one author it is advisable to draw up a simple one-page agreement, signed by each participant, verifying the percentage of the work that is attributed to each author. Although such writing splits can sometimes be subjective and difficult to assess, it is always wise to be as accurate as possible. If not, and the work is very successful, one of the writers may decide to sue the others later, and this could be very costly. For example, the famous British band Procol Harum released a recording in 1966 of 'A Whiter Shade of Pale' which was very successful worldwide, and which still receives a considerable amount of radio play and public performance today. One of the members of the band, Matthew Fisher, brought a legal action in 2006, 40 years

after the record was released, against one of the other members of Procol Harum, Gary Brooker, claiming that he had co-written the song and had never received any income due to his not being included on the original registrations. After listening to all the evidence, the court decided that he had indeed been one of the writers and awarded him appropriate compensation and costs. This is why accurate and honest writing splits need to be agreed as soon as possible after a work has been created. It is sometimes wise for the principal writer to be inclusive and a little generous with such splits to avoid any future legal action at a later date. As mentioned above, it is a good idea for an author or the author's manager to request, perhaps annually, from the author's public performance CMO a list of all the works currently on their database which are attributed to the author. This should show the percentages and publisher's details of all the author's works.

The author of this publication cites a case of a CMO attributing the wrong percentage to one of his artists' works. The mistake took over five years to correct. Since this particular work had been a hit all over the world, it was also incorrectly registered in all the other CMOs that had reciprocal agreements with the national CMO of which the artist was a member.

In many countries, live performances by an artist also give rise to a public performance payment by the promoter or the venue owner of the concert or event. In the UK for example, every promoter is obliged to pay three percent of the total box office revenues from ticket sales (after tax) to the UK author's public performance CMO (PRS for Music) for the works performed in public at that concert or event. The promoter or venue owner is also obliged to obtain a list of the works performed by the artist or artists, together with publisher information (if known), the length of each work, and the authors' names on a special form. This form and the appropriate payment is then sent to the CMO and distributed to the publishers and authors listed on the form after the CMO has deducted its administration fee. If the performer is also the author of some or all of the works performed at a live performance, it is very important for him/her or his/her manager to ensure the forms are completed correctly and either returned to the venue on the night or directly to the CMO, or preferably to both. One easy way to do this is for the artist or manager to have all the works listed on a computer spreadsheet together with information on the authors and publishers and the approximate length of each work performed. This can then be emailed to the venue and the CMO so that the correct authors get paid. If this is not done, the artist (if he/she is also the author of some or all of the works) will lose out on a valuable income stream. The larger the audience, the greater this income stream. If, for example, an artist or band were lucky enough to perform in a supporting slot to a very popular artist or band at a large arena or stadium show, and they wrote most of the works performed, the income from just one show could be many thousands of dollars. The percentage of box office payable to the author's CMO in each country varies considerably. Generally speaking, civil law countries tend to have higher percentages of box-office than common law countries, which again emphasizes the point that in civil law the author is valued more highly.

As will be discussed in the section on publishing, many authors' public performance CMOs will pay out 50 percent of the income direct to the author and the remaining 50 percent to the author's publisher. If the author has no publisher, the CMO will pay the entire sum due to the author, after deduction of its administration fees. This payment structure is very beneficial to the author, as he/she will continue to receive income from the CMO even if he/she is unrecouped with the publisher, i.e. the royalties payable from the publisher to the author have not exceeded the advance the author received from the publisher. In many countries there is only one authors' public performance CMO (e.g. GEMA in Germany), but in some countries there are two or more. In the US, for example, there are three such CMOs: The American Association of Composers, Authors and Publishers (ASCAP), Broadcast Music Incorporated (BMI) and The Society of European Stage Authors and Composers (SESAC). The latter's name may have been appropriate in 1930 when it was set up to represent European authors, but it is now a US-based authors' CMO similar to ASCAP and BMI. If the country in which the author lives does not have an appropriate CMO, it may be possible for him/her to join a CMO in another territory.

### 4.vii  Authors' Mechanical Income and Mechanical Copyright Collective Management Organizations

In some countries there is just one CMO collecting both income from public performances and income from mechanical licenses on behalf of authors. For example, JASRAC in Japan and GEMA in Germany collect both. In other countries, such as the US, there is a separate CMO (The Harry Fox Agency) which issues

mechanical licenses and collects mechanical income. Similarly in France, SDRM is the CMO for mechanical rights and in Australia the CMO for mechanical rights is AMCOS. In the US many authors and publishers will issue mechanical licenses and collect mechanical income directly from phonogram producers, without the involvement of a CMO. Most mechanical income is generated when a phonogram producer wishes to sell a recording to the public. Before the phonogram producer can legally do so, a mechanical license must be obtained from the author's publisher or the author who wrote the underlying musical work in the recording.

The mechanical copyright CMO will issue a mechanical license to the phonogram producer, in which the phonogram producer is obliged to make a payment to the CMO for every copy it sells of the record containing the work and for every download or stream it sells. In many countries there is a fixed mechanical rate which has to be paid and is not negotiable. In the UK for example, the rate is 8.25 percent of the Published Price to Dealers (PPD). In the US and Canada, on the other hand, the mechanical rate is fixed as a 'statutory rate' or 'minimum statutory rate' per track, which in 2012 was US$0.091 (9.1c) per track for works of up to five minutes, and US$0.0175 (1.75c) per minute for tracks with a duration of more than five minutes (known as the 'long song rate'). So if a track ran for four minutes 30 seconds, the mechanical statutory rate payable by the phonogram producer would be 9.1c per record sold. If, however, it ran for six minutes, the mechanical rate would be 10.5c (6 x 1.75). Unfortunately for artists, this US rate is negotiable, and many phonogram producers negotiate a rate of 75 percent of statutory as a mechanical payment when they offer an artist a recording agreement. The author of this publication can cite one instance where he could only obtain 50 percent of statutory for one of his artist's tracks if it was to be included in a US compilation album. He was told that if he did not accept this rate the track would not be included in the album.

This US and Canadian negotiable approach leads to so-called 'controlled composition' clauses in recording and publishing agreements. In such clauses in recording agreements, the artist will often have to accept that only 75 percent of the statutory mechanical rate will be received in the US and Canada. In publishing agreements there will be a similar clause indemnifying the publisher if only a percentage lower than 100 percent of statutory is obtainable. The term 'controlled composition' means works that the performer has written, i.e. that he/she controls and on which (provided the publisher agrees) he/she can therefore agree to take a lower percentage. The author of this publication had one experience in the US where two phonogram producers were competing to sign one of his artists. One of the negotiating issues used was to ascertain if one of them would pay 100 percent of the statutory rate from the first US recording sold. In the end one did agree to this, which, because the artist wrote most of the songs, resulted in far higher publishing income over the years. Phonogram producers will also try to fix the mechanical rate in the US at the rate prevailing at the time of the release. It is in the artist's interest to try to get a 'floating' rate, i.e. an arrangement where the mechanical rate goes up as and when the national minimum statutory rate is increased. Another negotiating tactic used by US phonogram producers is to try to limit the mechanicals payable on an album to no more than 10 or 11 tracks. If an artist has this clause in the agreement with the phonogram producer, he/she should think carefully before putting more than 10 or 11 tracks on an album. The international umbrella organization for mechanical rights CMOs is BIEM (www.biem.org), which represents 52 mechanical rights CMOs in 56 countries and is based in France.

## 4.viii Related Rights Public Performance in Sound Recordings Collective Management Organizations

As we have seen, performers' rights have a great deal of ground to make up when compared to authors. This is particularly true concerning related rights and related rights public performance CMOs. The WPPT provides that users should pay a single equitable remuneration to performers and phonogram producers when a phonogram is used for broadcasting or communication to the public. This means that performers and phonogram producers do not have an exclusive right, but rather have a 'right to remuneration' when a phonogram is broadcast or played in public. The term 'single' is included to indicate that users should only have to pay once for the right to use a sound recording, rather than having to pay the performers on the record and the phonogram producer in two separate payments. Whilst most countries have interpreted 'equitable remuneration' to mean that 50 percent of the income should go to the phonogram producer and 50 percent to the performers who played on the recording, it is up to individual Member States to interpret 'equitable remuneration' as they see fit. In other words, governments are free to provide that the single

payment made by users can be shared in proportions other than 50/50 between the performers and the phonogram producer if they so wish. As we have already seen in the section on copyright and related rights, the WPPT Article 15 also contains a provision for Member States to opt out of this right altogether by 'reserving their position'. It is unfortunate for performers and phonogram producers that the governments of China, Iran, North Korea, Rwanda and the US have decided to make this reservation. This means that there are no related rights in the public performance of sound recordings for performers and phonogram producers in those countries, except that the US does have the right for digital broadcasts by satellite, simulcast or by webcast. With the US accounting for some 35 percent of the entire world music market, this represents an important loss of compensation for performers and phonogram producers worldwide who have their recordings broadcast on terrestrial radio in the United States. As the related right in the public performance of sound recordings is usually a reciprocal right between countries, and is also based on the criteria set by the Rome Convention and the WPPT, US performers are unable to receive income when their recordings are broadcast in countries that do have the appropriate related right for the public performance of sound recordings, as they are deemed to be 'non-qualifying'. As is well known, the US has produced many performers who are exceptionally successful worldwide. For some radio stations in countries outside of the US, US performers account for up to 50 percent of all records broadcast. This means that US performers are severely disadvantaged compared to their foreign counterparts. Performers based abroad who have success within the US also suffer, but US performers are the biggest losers as they receive nothing when their recordings are broadcast in their own country on terrestrial radio, and they also receive nothing when their records are played outside of the US, either terrestrially or digitally, if they are deemed to be 'non-qualifying'. As previously stated, the US did introduce a related right in the public performance of sound recordings for digital satellite broadcasts and webcasting over the internet when it passed the Digital Performance Right in Sound Recordings Act 1995, but this did not cover analogue or digital broadcasts on free-to-air terrestrial radio, which is the largest music broadcasting sector. The CMO that collects digital webcasting and satellite income on behalf of performers and phonogram producers in the US is Sound Exchange. They will also distribute this digital income to foreign performers and phonogram producers, so if a performer has any recordings released or played on a webcast or satellite radio based in the US, it

is important to join Sound Exchange (www.soundexchange.com) or to instruct their national related rights CMO to collect from Sound Exchange on their behalf. If the PRA (Performance Rights Act) ever gets enacted in the US, it will bring substantial benefit to performers and phonogram producers worldwide, and will create a level playing field in the US for competition between free-to-air radio broadcasters on the one hand, and satellite broadcasters and webcasters on the other. The PRA has so far made little progress as, not surprisingly, the powerful US broadcasting lobby is unenthusiastic. It is to be hoped that those countries that do not have a public performance right in sound recordings will establish such a right, and that effective CMOs are set up worldwide, so that income can flow freely across international borders to the appropriate right holders.

Some countries have a joint related rights CMO which collects income for both phonogram producers and performers, such as LSG in Austria, Gramex in Denmark, GVL in Germany, SOCINPRO in Brazil, PPL in the UK and SENA in The Netherlands, whilst other countries have related rights collection societies that collect exclusively for phonogram producers, such as some IFPI national organizations, and others that collect exclusively for performers, such as ADAMI and SPEDIDAM in France and GEIDANKYO in Japan. Although there should be reciprocal agreements between countries, there have been many difficulties in achieving this, due to the different ways these CMOs have developed and to the fact that, whilst authors' CMOs have had CISAC as their international body since 1926, the international body for performers' related rights CMOs, SCAPR, was only formalized in 2001.

For example, some performer-only CMOs have refused to pay out to foreign performers where there are several different related rights CMOs in the country concerned, resulting in income due to foreign performers reverting to domestic performers. In the UK, remuneration is allocated to all performers irrespective of whether they, or the recordings on which they perform, qualify for equitable remuneration. This income allocated to non-qualifying performers (mostly US performers) is then paid to the UK phonogram producer copyright owner. US and other non-qualifying performers should try and get a provision in their recording agreements whereby their share of UK equitable remuneration is paid through to them in the US by their phonogram producer (even though they are non-qualifying performers). If the US Performing Rights Act is successful, US performers and

recordings would qualify automatically for the allocated share of equitable remuneration in the UK and elsewhere, and non-US performers whose records are played on US radio would receive a share of income generated in the US – so performers everywhere should support the US PRA initiative. Should this legislation go through, it will automatically regularize PPL income collected for non-qualifying US performers in the UK.

One way that US performers can become qualifying performers is to record in a qualifying territory. For example, if a US artist were to record in Canada or Sweden, or any country that has incorporated the provisions of the Rome Convention and the WPPT (with no reservation on Article 15), they may become qualifying performers and would receive public performance income globally. By recording in a qualifying country, many US managers and artists have opened up a very substantial new income stream.

There is clearly some way to go in streamlining and harmonizing related rights CMOs and providing performers and phonogram producers with an efficient reciprocal transfer of income across borders. It is hoped that in future this flow of income can be achieved in the same way as that enjoyed by authors.

The important issues concerning related rights in the public performance of sound recordings for performers start in the studio recording process. It is essential to register exactly who performed on a recording and accurately report this information to the phonogram producer and to the appropriate related rights CMO. It is also very important to inform the CMO if the performer's address or bank account details change. Many CMOs will now only pay out by wire transfer directly into a bank account. All related rights CMOs have problems paying out money to performers they cannot trace.

There are essentially three types of related rights income for the public performance of sound recordings:
1. Income when a recording is broadcast or communicated to the public by cable, satellite or the Internet.
2. Income from other public performances.
3. Income from home copying levies.

The first category is self-explanatory. It is the income paid out by broadcasters, cablecasters, satellite broadcasters and webcasters when a recording is played on their station or network. The second category is all other uses, such as when a recording is played in a hairdressing salon, shop, restaurant, factory, discothèque, club or at a sports event etc. The third category is discussed in the section on home-copying levies below.

Most countries in the developed world collect for the above types of related rights performance income, but some countries, such as Japan, have only legislated for broadcasting and communication to the public performance income for sound recordings and not for other public performance uses.

If an artist has his/her own record label or co-owns the label with his/her manager, they can of course collect both the performer's public performance in sound recordings income and the phonogram producer's income. In this case, it is very important for all the artist's recordings to be correctly registered with the related rights CMO both as a performer and as a phonogram producer.

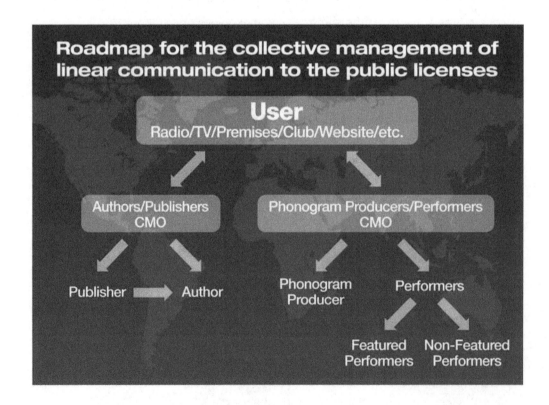

## 4.ix   Featured and Non-Featured Performers

There are two distinct types of performers on a recording. The principal performers are known as featured performers or featured artists. They are the artists that are credited as being the main performer(s) on a recording who are contracted to a phonogram producer or who have their own label. So Justin Bieber, Robbie Williams, PSY and Nicki Minaj are all featured performers. If a featured performer brings in extra musicians or singers to augment a recording, these so-called 'session' performers are referred to as non-featured performers. Equitable remuneration, as stated in the Rome Convention and the WPPT, is usually defined in many countries as 50% to the phonogram producer and 50% to the performers who performed on the recording, although in some countries different percentages apply. There will also be a further split of the percentage designated to performers between featured and non-featured performers. This can provide a very good income for a non-featured musician or singer who happened to be engaged to play on a recording that turned out to be a big hit with substantial radio play.

Different countries have different arrangements on the split between featured and non-featured performers. In the US for example, 95% of the performer money collected by Sound Exchange goes to the featured performers, whereas only 5% goes to non-featured performers via the musicians' unions AFofM (2.5% for musicians) and AFTRA (2.5% to singers). In the UK between 65% and 100% of the performer share goes to featured performers and up to 35% to non-featured, depending on how many non-featured performers (if any) performed on the recording. In the UK, if there were no non-featured performers, then the featured performer(s) would receive 100%. In France, related rights performer income is split at source, 50% to featured performers (which goes to featured performer CMO ADAMI) and 50% to non-featured performers (which goes to the non-featured performer CMO SPEDIDAM). Some other countries operate on a points system where points are awarded to a performance rather than dividing the revenue at track level, so that there is not an exact split between featured and non-featured performers, e.g. there might be one point awarded to each non-featured player but perhaps eight points to a featured performer. The total number of points is then calculated over an entire year. This system often favors non-featured performers, particularly if there was a large number of non-featured performers on a track, such as would be the case with an orchestra. If it was a 90-piece orchestra, each member of the orchestra might be given one point and the featured artist perhaps eight.

In some countries, studio producers can also qualify as non-featured performers if they directed the recording in the recording studio in a similar way that a conductor would direct an orchestra. A conductor of an orchestra may qualify as a non-featured performer or even a featured performer, even though he/she is making no audible sound. Rather, he/she is directing how the musicians play, which has a direct effect on a sound recording. If a studio producer directs a band or an artist in the studio, they may qualify in the same way as a conductor in some countries, although they will not receive income from other countries who do not recognize this right. If a studio producer makes any audible sound on a recording, then he/she would qualify as a non-featured performer in the same way that any other musician or singer would.

It is important that the appropriate related rights CMO is supplied with accurate information about who performed on a recording. This is sometimes referred to as 'performer line-up' information. This may become of great importance in the future, particularly for the income of non-featured performers. Related rights CMOs are constantly having to do forensic work to identify who the performers were on older recordings which still get played on the radio and in public places and therefore are still generating income.

## 4.x    Home Copying Levies

As we saw in the chapter on copyright, another income stream for authors, performers, publishers and phonogram producers that exists in many countries is that from home copying levies, which are sometimes referred to as private copying levies or blank media levies. These are levies that are applied to blank recordable media such as blank cassettes, CDRs, recordable audiovisual tapes, recordable DVDs and hard-drives of computers, which are intended to compensate the right holders for consumers copying copy-protected material in their own homes. Some countries also apply a home copying levy on recording hardware such as cassette recorders, video recorders, computers and DVD recorders etc. The levies collected flow to a CMO which could be a stand-alone home copying levy CMO, or one of the

existing authors or related rights CMOs, after which the income is distributed to the various right holders.

Most EU Member States have a system of home-copying levies which generate approximately US$1 billion per year for authors, performers, publishers and phonogram producers. The levies are usually set in the one to four percent dealer price range for media and/or recording equipment. Within the EU, the UK, Ireland and Luxembourg are notable exceptions where no home copying levies exist, and this considerably disadvantages authors, performers, publishers and phonogram producers in those territories. Even so, authors and performers in countries where the levies do not exist may receive home copying levies income in countries where they do exist, if their national CMO is able to claim it.

There is a school of thought which is critical of the concept of home copying levies. If, for example, someone purchased a blank CDR and used it to store personal holiday photographs, why should he/she pay a levy, the proceeds of which go to music authors, performers, publishers and phonogram producers? Many in the music industry would answer this objection by saying that home copying levies are rough justice, but that it is far better to have rough justice than to have no justice. In some countries, such as Germany, home copying levies provide a substantial income stream for authors and performers. WIPO publishes a free comprehensive International Survey on Private Copying each year which can be downloaded as a PDF from the WIPO website (www.wipo.int).

In the developing world, home copying income can account for over 50% of all related rights CMO income in some countries.

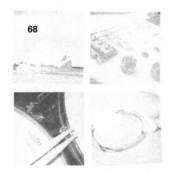

# CHAPTER 5
# A SHORT HISTORY OF THE MUSIC INDUSTRY

The following is a snapshot of the major events in the music industry over the past 4000 years, incorporating many of the landmark developments in law and technology described in this book.

The first evidence of musical notation was discovered in Iraq on a cuneiform tablet and is believed to have been written around 2000 BC. (It's ironic that, with Amazon's Kindle and Apple's iPad, tablets are very much back in fashion.) Musical notation as we know it today was first conceived in Italy by Guido d'Arezzo, a Benedictine monk who lived from 991 to 1033 AD. The Italian Benedictine monks continued to develop the concept of modern musical notation until around 1350, when it took on the form that we know today. Writing musical notation at that time was a laborious and time-consuming process, as each copy had to be individually handwritten. The first evidence of printing being used for music was in Mainz, Germany, in 1457, where the basic staves were printed but the musical notation still needed to be added by hand. The first full single-impression musical sheet music was printed in England by John Rastell in 1520. The printing of sheet music was a revolution in itself, which opened up the playing of music to the masses. The next major revolution came from Thomas Edison, Alexander Graham Bell and Emile Berliner, who between them developed the ability to record live performances. It was Emile Berliner's invention of the gramophone in 1887 that gave birth to the concept of performer's rights. The third revolution came in the 1990s when the MP3 compressed digital file was developed. It is this third revolution that we are in the midst of now and will be for well into the future.

As explained in the section on copyright on page 26, the first copyright law was The Statute of Queen Anne in 1710 in England. This was followed over the next 300

years by the international treaties, The Berne Convention, The Rome Convention, The TRIPS Agreement, the WIPO Internet Treaties and most recently the BTAP (Beijing Treaty on Audiovisual Performances).

| | |
|---|---|
| 2000 BC | First musical notation discovered on a cuneiform tablet in Iraq |
| 1020 AD | First modern musical notation conceptualized by Guido d'Arezzo, a Benedictine monk in Italy |
| 1350 | Italian Benedictine monks fully develop modern musical notation |
| 1457 | First printing of musical staves in Mainz, Germany (musical notation still had to be added by hand) |
| 1520 | First single-impression prints of sheet music by John Rastell in England |
| 1710 | First copyright law, The Statute of Queen Anne in England |
| 1847 | Ernest Bourget wins Les Ambassadeurs copyright case in France |
| 1851 | SACEM formed in France as the world's first authors' CMO |
| 1877 | Thomas Edison first records musical sounds on a phonograph wax cylinder in USA |
| 1886 | The Berne Convention – the first international copyright treaty for the protection of copyright in author's works |
| 1887 | Emile Berliner invents the gramophone with flat discs as the sound carrier (phonograms) in USA |
| 1893 | Emile Berliner forms the United States Gramophone Company (the world's first phonogram producer) |
| 1897 | Brittle shellac discs introduced as sound carriers |
| 1901 | Guglielmo Marconi from Bologna in Italy invents radio |
| 1907 | US inventor Lee DeForest commences regular radio transmissions using voice and music. |
| 1908 | Gramophone Company incorporates HMV (His Masters Voice) painting as the trademark for the company |
| 1926 | CISAC is formed as the international umbrella organization for authors' performing rights societies |
| 1926 | Scottish inventor John Baird demonstrates the first television transmission system in London |
| 1928 | 78 rpm (revolutions per minute) becomes international standard for flat disc records |

| | |
|---|---|
| 1929 | BIEM is formed as the international umbrella organization for authors' mechanical rights societies |
| 1936 | BBC commences broadcasting the world's first public television service in London |
| 1948 | 33.33 rpm long-play 12-inch vinyl albums first introduced |
| 1948 | FIM (International Federation of Musicians) formed as the international umbrella organization representing musicians' unions |
| 1949 | 45 rpm 7-inch vinyl records first introduced |
| 1957 | Stereo introduced |
| 1961 | The Rome Convention – the first international treaty for performers, phonogram producers and broadcasters |
| 1963 | 8-track cartridge cassettes and compact cassettes first introduced |
| 1970 | WIPO (World Intellectual Property Organization) formed |
| 1981 | MTV launched in USA |
| 1982 | Digital Compact Discs (CDs) introduced |
| 1982 | Modern Internet launched by ARPANET |
| 1983 | Illinois Bell launch first public mobile phone cellular service |
| 1990 | British scientist Tim Berners Lee invents the World Wide Web in Geneva |
| 1994 | TRIPS (Agreement on Trade Related Aspects of Intellectual Property Rights) agreed by WTO (World Trade Organization) |
| 1996 | WIPO Internet Treaties – WCT (WIPO Copyright Treaty) and the WPPT (WIPO Performances and Phonograms Treaty) agreed |
| 1999 | NAPSTER launched (first peer-to-peer digital file sharing service) |
| 2000 | Google search engine launched |
| 2001 | SCAPR formed as international umbrella organization for performers' related rights CMOs |
| 2001 | Apple introduces the iPod and iTunes |
| 2001 | Palm launch first smartphone in US |
| 2001 | BitTorrent peer-to-peer file-sharing program launched |
| 2003 | Apple launches iTunes store |
| 2004 | My Space launched |
| 2005 | Facebook launched |
| 2005 | YouTube launched |
| 2006 | Apple allow interoperability by facilitating MP3 conversion from their AAC files |

| 2006 | Google buys YouTube |
|---|---|
| 2007 | Apple launch iPhone |
| 2007 | Twitter launched |
| 2007 | Amazon launch Kindle tablet |
| 2007 | Deezer streaming service launched in France |
| 2008 | Spotify launched in Sweden |
| 2008 | Apple allows third-party apps for iPhone |
| 2008 | Android operating system launched for mobile |
| 2010 | Apple launches iPad |
| 2010 | Sony launch Music Unlimited cloud-based music service |
| 2010 | GoogleTV launched |
| 2011 | Amazon launch Cloud Player cloud storage music service. |
| 2011 | Apple launch iCloud and iTunes Match cloud storage services |
| 2012 | BTAP (Beijing Treaty on Audiovisual Performances) agreed |
| 2012 | Microsoft launch Xbox Music |
| 2012 | Google launch Google Play for the Android market |
| 2013 | Google launch Google Play Access All Music streaming service |
| 2013 | Apple launch iTunes Radio |

The main message that this short history shows is the exponential change from 2000 onwards. With every month that passes, some digital services will disappear and new innovative digital services will emerge to disrupt and change the digital ecosystem.

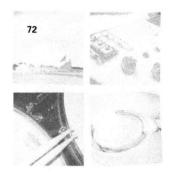

# CHAPTER 6
# ARTIST DEVELOPMENT AND ARTIST MANAGEMENT

## Choosing a Name

One of the first things an artist will have to decide is the name by which he/she wishes to be known. If the artist is a solo performer, or one who wishes to hire other musicians to accompany him or her, they may choose to use their own real name. Alternatively they may wish to make up a new 'stage' name under which they will be known. For example, Elton John's real name is Reginald Dwight, whereas Elton John is his stage name or artist name.

If the artist is a band, the name of the band needs to be chosen carefully. It is best to opt for a very unusual name, to avoid confusion with other existing artists. Searching using one of the Internet search engines is a good place to start. There have been many cases in the past where bands have had to change their name or contest their title in court as it came to light that there was another band in existence with the same name. For example, in the 1980s there was a very successful British band called 'Yazoo'. They discovered that there was already a band with that name in the US, so they changed their name to 'Yaz' for the US only, which served to avoid any legal action against them in that territory. It did, however, lead to considerable confusion globally.

If finances allow, it is a good idea to trademark the artist or band name as soon as possible, at least in the country of residence. This name can then be trademark-registered in other countries or perhaps worldwide as the artist or band becomes more successful. (See the section on trademarks on page 40.)

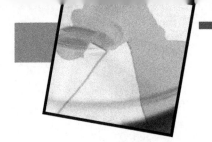

## Artist Management

As soon as an author or performer, or an artist who is both author and performer, starts to become successful, he/she will need to find a manager. A manager is someone who will look after the business side of the artist's career and will interface with all other parties involved in contributing to the artist's commercial success. Commerce and art do not always sit happily together, and it is the manager's job to provide that often difficult interface and make it work. Managers are the only group of people in the worldwide music industry who have to know about every aspect of the music industry. They are the ones who have to make the rules of copyright work on a daily basis and it is they who have to grapple with the rapid developments in technology and make sure, as far as possible, that the artist is paid correctly.

Let us consider the main aspects of management. As mentioned in the definitions section, an 'Artist' will be referred to as an individual principal performer or a principal group or band of musicians or singers.

## Artists seeking Management

As discussed in the chapter on building a team, in the early stages an artist will have to manage themselves until they reach the point where they need outside help. Alternatively it may be that a friend or relative of the artist or band takes on the management role at this early stage. Right from the start, an artist needs to begin creating a fan base. A fan base is a database of people who are interested in the artist and wish to find out where the artist is performing, and if and when the artist is releasing records etc. If a phonogram producer comes to see an artist play live and the venue is full, the artist stands a much better chance of being offered a recording contract, if that is the artist's aim. Phonogram producers want to sell as many records as possible, and if they see that an artist already has a substantial and enthusiastic fan base, they will be reassured that there will be a market for the artist's recordings. The leaps in technology haven't altered the starting point, which is pen and paper. At the first small shows in small venues, make sure someone with communication skills is out in the audience with a clipboard talking to individuals and gathering email addresses. Go to page 166 to find out how to build a fan base and develop it in the online environment.

When things start building, the artist should consider engaging a manager, but where does an artist find the right one? Having no manager is preferable to having a bad one, but a good, honest, hard-working and connected manager can make all the difference between success and failure. A good place to start is for the artist to find out who manages his/her own favorite artists, by searching online or by looking at his/her favorite artists' recordings. There are also lists of managers and their contact details in publications such as Pollstar (www.pollstar.com) and Billboard (www.billboard.com). The Music Managers Forums around the world would also be worth contacting (www.immf.com). It is worth asking other artists and people in the music business for recommendations. If an artist already has a music lawyer or accountant, these professionals can sometimes recommend a suitable manager, although it is important to meet several managers if possible. Yet another approach is to ask a family member or friend who has good entrepreneurial and administrative skills to be the manager. If this route is taken, it is really important that the relative or family friend should be prepared to learn and train in the complexities of the music business and never take his/her position for granted.

## A good manager should:

1. Be honest.
2. Be an enabler (he or she should be able to create opportunities that the artist would not otherwise have achieved alone).
3. Be a good administrator (he or she should be good at keeping accurate and up-to-date financial records and be effective in ensuring that income streams are maximized and that the artist is paid correctly).
4. Be a good communicator (relate well to other people and be good at networking).
5. Be a good negotiator.
6. Be a problem-solver.
7. Love the artist's music.

Problem solving is one of the most challenging of the above. Basically, a manager should never give up when there is a problem to be solved until perhaps all possibilities have been exhausted. By way of example, the author in his capacity as a manager was faced with a seemingly impossible problem in June 2012 when one of his artists' US visa was not granted some two weeks prior to a major US tour. It is

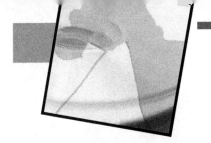

impossible to insure against visa failure, so he and the artist were staring at a huge financial loss if the tour had to be cancelled, not to mention the losses that would be suffered by all the US promoters. The paperwork received said that the visa would be considered again at some point within the next 90 days. The artist in question had been granted US visas many times before and had no criminal record. The situation had probably arisen due to someone else with a similar name being on the 'watch' list by US Homeland Security. Faced with this seemingly disastrous situation, the author/manager cold-called one of the senior US Senators in Washington, i.e. got a number from a Google search and rang it to see what would happen. Luckily everyone in the Senator's office seemed to be fans, which was a great first step. In the end the Senator made a call to the US Secretary of State, who at the time was Senator Hilary Clinton, who fixed the problem within a few hours. The artist's passport with the visa arrived on the morning that the artist and crew were due to fly out. A seemingly impossible problem had been solved by calmly taking the situation one step at a time... and maybe with a bit of luck too.

## Managers Seeking Artists

Let us now consider the issue from a manager's perspective. If someone wants to become a manager and they have good communication, administrative, networking, business and negotiating skills, how do they find an artist to work with? The first thing is to make sure the manager understands how the music industry works, by reading publications and books such as this one, or by participating in educational courses. No matter how experienced a manager becomes, it is always important to be updating and improving his/her knowledge by participating in training courses or simply by reading the latest books, magazines or obtaining information online. This applies to all professionals in all occupations.

Networking is the next important step. By networking we mean getting to know as many people as possible in the industry. This will include record companies, publishers, booking agents, promoters, journalists, film and advertising people, digital marketing people and collective management organizations amongst others. Knowing all the right people will help a manager open doors further down the road, and its importance cannot be underestimated. Such relationships can often result in recommendations from a record company, publisher, lawyer or accountant to an artist on the manager's behalf. In the modern era, many managers put too much emphasis on email and text. The author's advice for an up-and-coming manager is to get on the phone as much as possible and prioritize face-to-face meetings whenever it is practical to do so. Another way to find an artist is for a manager to simply visit clubs and small venues and to trust his/her own judgment to find an artist with real potential. Probably the most important thing is that the manager must love the artist's music and get on well with the artist or band on a personal level. Genuine enthusiasm is infectious and effective in moving an artist forward.

One way for a manager to learn more about artist management is to join one of the Music Managers Forums (MMF). These organizations are mainly concerned with artists' rights but also offer workshops and information for managers and self-managed artists. There are Music Managers Forums in Australia, Belgium, Canada, Denmark, Finland, France, Germany, Ireland, the Netherlands, New Zealand, Norway, Poland, South Africa, Sweden, the UK and the US. The international umbrella body is the International Music Managers Forum (www.immf.com).

## Short-Term Letter of Agreement

Let us now consider the situation where the manager or would-be manager has found an artist that he or she wishes to manage and the artist wishes to engage the manager. After the initial meetings and discussions, it is sensible for both the artist and the manager to put something down in writing to cover a temporary trial period to see if both sides can work well together. An example of a simple temporary letter of engagement is shown as Annex B on page 220. It is usual for such a short-term agreement to have a maximum term of six months, but it could be as little as three months. If, when the term of this temporary agreement expires, the artist and the manager wish to continue with the relationship, the manager or the manager's lawyer will need to present the artist with a long-form agreement.

## Long-Form Artist Management Agreements

Let us now consider moving on from the short-term letter of engagement to a long-form artist management agreement, which contains much more detail as to how the relationship will work in the longer term. At this point the manager and the artist

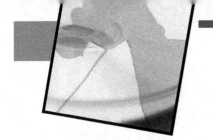 
could also consider alternative ways of working together, such as forming a company or partnership wherein the artist and the manager are directors or partners. (See Alternative Agreements below on page 81.)

It is best to think of longer-term artist management as a kind of marriage. It is essential that both sides get on with each other. The long-form artist management agreement should be the only time in the artist's career in which the artist and the manager sit on opposite sides of the table. Thereafter, they should work together as a team, with success being their common goal. When an agreement is reached, both sides should feel reasonably comfortable with it. If one side feels very happy and the other unhappy, it will not have achieved the balance needed for a good working arrangement.

The artist/manager relationship has to be based on trust and regular discussion on all the issues. It is important that the artist is told as much as possible, both good news and bad news, at the appropriate time (e.g. it is not a good idea for a manager to deliver bad news just before the artist goes on stage). The agreement itself should clearly lay down the ground rules, but there will always be unusual situations which will need discussion and which should be resolved within a spirit of common sense and compromise by all concerned. If there are any special arrangements made, they should preferably be made in writing and signed by both parties. From the manager's point of view, it is important that the conditions in the agreement fall broadly in line with industry norms in the country of residence, and are not unreasonable. If the contract as a whole is too harsh, a court may take the view that it is in restraint of trade. In other words, the contract is unduly restrictive from the artist's point of view.

Both the manager and the artist should clearly understand that time is valuable. The manager's expert advice, whilst not charged at an hourly rate as in the case of lawyers and accountants, clearly has a substantial value. If the manager is investing large amounts of time and/or money, he/she needs to be compensated for this risk in a way which is reflected in the commission structures. In the end the most contentious issues in these agreements are likely to be the post-term commission arrangements and the touring income commission arrangements. It is important for both the manager and the artist that a fair workable agreement is achieved in these areas.

It is important for a manager to try to provide high-quality management services to the artist. It is therefore a better idea for managers to focus on one or two artists than to represent too many and spread themselves too thinly, unless their businesses are structured with enough full-time staff to adequately administer a larger number of artists. Before drafting a long-form artist management agreement, it is a good idea to draw up a one-page 'heads of agreement' to establish the main points. Some of the factors that will have to be decided in a heads of agreement are as follows:

Term (how long will the agreement last?)

Territory (will it be worldwide or for just one or several countries?)

Commission rate (usually 20 percent but can be between 10 and 50 percent)

Commission rate for touring income (a rate lower than the commission rate)

Commission term (stated term plus a post-term period)

Commissionable income (what income is commissionable and what is not)

Scope of the agreement (the entertainment industry as a whole or just music?)

The manager's duties

The artist's duties

The manager's allowable expenses (an example of a typical expenses schedule can be seen in Annex B on page 221).

It is important that the artist receive independent legal advice, preferably from a lawyer specializing in the music business.

The manager and the artist should follow the standard industry practice in the country in which they are based. For example, in many countries the following types of income are not generally commissionable by the manager:

i) Recording costs (sums provided by a phonogram producer for making recordings).

ii) Video costs (sums provided by a phonogram producer for making promotional videos).

iii) Tour support (sums provided by a phonogram producer to cover losses on a tour).

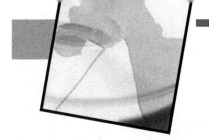

## The Importance of Independent Legal Advice

The important point with all these agreements is that the artist must have independent legal advice, preferably from a lawyer specializing in the music business or one who has some experience of music contracts. If the artist does not receive independent advice, the contract will be weakened considerably with the manager being open to a charge of undue influence. In some countries, such specialized lawyers simply do not exist. In such cases any independent advice is preferable to none. If it is financially viable, the artist and the manager could consider using lawyers in a different country where such specialization does exist. In this case it may well be that the contract would be governed by the law of the country in which the specialist lawyers work. Another advantage is that the foreign specialist lawyer may be able to assist the manager and the artist with opportunities in the country in which the lawyer is based. In making this decision, both the manager and the artist should decide where they think their music will find the biggest audience and consider engaging lawyers in that territory. By searching 'music business lawyer' plus the country of interest online, it should be easy to find the right specialist lawyers.

When an artist is starting out there is usually very little money available, and the prospect of incurring substantial legal fees is daunting. Most lawyers are aware of this and are often prepared to either charge a low fee or postpone payment until a recording or publishing advance is secured, in the hope that future work will be forthcoming. Sometimes the manager will be prepared to pay the artist's legal fees on the basis that reimbursement will be forthcoming when income starts to flow through. In either case, it is very important that the artist and the manager obtain a quote from their respective lawyers before work commences. It is essential that both the manager and the artist use different lawyers. If the artist is a member of a musicians' union, the union can sometimes provide legal advice for a comparatively low fee or free of charge. Information on musicians' unions worldwide can be obtained by going to the Fédération Internationale des Musiciens (FIM) website at www.fim-musicians.com.

This process of a verbal agreement, initially followed by a short-term trial period agreement, and then followed by a long-form agreement, is a fair and reasonable way to proceed. Many agreements have failed due to a manager being too demanding in the initial stages, perhaps by insisting that a full long-form management agreement is signed before starting work. An artist's lawyer might well advise the artist against this hasty and perhaps heavy-handed approach which could instill doubts in the artist's mind about the suitability and possibly the commitment of the manager. All these negotiations need to be handled sensitively and diplomatically so that both the artist and the manager retain their enthusiasm for moving forward together. It can be traumatic for the artist to have just met a suitable manager only to be thrown into heavy negotiations with that manager right at the beginning.

## Verbal Agreements

Some very high-level managers operate using verbal or 'handshake' agreements and seem to make them work. They may be so confident in their own abilities that they feel secure enough that the artist will not be tempted to go elsewhere. In the UK and some other countries, verbal agreements for services such as an artist management agreement are enforceable by law, whereas in the US such agreements have to be in writing.

The problem of course with a verbal agreement is that whilst it may work when things are going well, it can prove problematic if there is a dispute. In such a dispute it can often be one person's word against another's, especially if there were no witnesses when the verbal agreement was made. It is therefore advisable, if possible, to have reliable witnesses to such an agreement and to try and cover as many of the issues such as term, commission rates, what is commissionable, post-term commission arrangements, touring commission rates, reimbursable expenses etc. as clearly and as precisely as possible.

Another advantage of a verbal agreement is that it is more likely to be acceptable to the artist, at least in the initial stages, as the artist will not feel quite so committed. In general, even if at the very beginning the agreement is verbal, it is always better to agree a short-term letter of agreement as shown in Annex B on page 220 or a long-form agreement in writing as soon as is practicable. This allows both sides to know as clearly as possible what their rights and obligations are, although, as stated above, in a way that does not damage the spirit of the relationship.

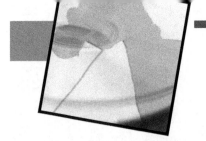

## Legal Limitations and Implied Terms for Verbal Contracts

A court may impose certain legal limitations on a relationship between an artist and a manager if there is a dispute and where there is no written agreement. Some of the implied terms a court might impose are:

1) The manager will not allow a conflict of interest to arise with the artist.

2) The manager will represent the artist with fiduciary care, i.e. the manager will diligently and honestly represent the artist and will not misuse confidential information regarding the artist or misrepresent the artist in such a way as to cause the artist damage.

3) The manager will keep accurate books of account in regard to an artist's income and expenditure together with all bank statements, invoices and receipts etc.

## Alternative Agreements

The problem with traditional artist management agreements from the manager's point of view is that they are service agreements or agency agreements, with no intellectual property being owned by the manager. They are therefore fairly weak agreements, with the manager always vulnerable to being dismissed. If the relationship breaks down, the only recourse that the manager has is either to come to a settlement with the artist or to sue for damages in the courts. No court will ever force an artist to continue working with a manager if he/she does not wish to. Rather they will award the aggrieved party damages based on the situation presented to the court. There is therefore a tendency for managers to look to other forms of agreements with the artist which involve some intellectual property rights, such as production agreements and publishing agreements. Let us now consider these alternative agreements.

## Production and Publishing Agreements as Alternatives to Management Agreements

There are two ways in which a manager can become a licensee or co-owner of the copyright or related rights created by the artist.

1.  Production agreements (where the manager pays for and licenses or co-owns the artist's recordings for a period of years).
2.  Publishing agreements (where the manager acts as publisher and licenses or co-owns the copyright in the artist's songwriting/compositions for a number of years).

The manager may agree with the artist to fill both of the above roles and will enter into two separate agreements: as a production company and as a publisher. It is essential that, if the manager becomes the production company and/or publisher, or both, he/she does not 'double dip', i.e. the manager should not apply management commission in these two areas. The manager could however have a third management agreement limited to live work and other income such as merchandising, sponsorship and branding. Provided the other work was not recording (making, distributing and selling records) or publishing (exploiting works), management commission could be taken.

In some countries, the above arrangement may be illegal as it may be considered a conflict of interest, but in the developed world this type of intellectual property licensing or co-ownership agreement with the artist is becoming more common. There are other business models being developed wherein the manager and the artist form a corporation and the manager is appointed managing director and/or Chief Executive Officer (CEO). The artist and the manager will be directors and shareholders. In this business model, all copyrights are owned by the corporation and income is split according to the shareholders' agreement. Yet another possibility is for the manager and the artist to form a partnership, administrated by the manager, where the copyrights are owned by the partnership.

In the production agreement business model, the manager may cease to be the manager of the artist's recording career in title, but may nevertheless provide management services without commission. The manager becomes the production company. The difficulty here is that the manager has to find the money to make an album, which can be a very high risk investment. Production agreements are typically 50/50 to 70/30 in the artist's favor. The production company makes the album and then licenses it to phonogram producers or distributors and aggregators around the world. The recording costs for the album are first deducted from any

incoming advances and sales income, together with any other allowable expenses, and the net is then split between the production company and the artist, according to the split agreed in the production agreement.

The advantage to the artist of a production company agreement is that the copyright in the recording will often be owned by the production company for a shorter period than would be the case with a direct signing to a phonogram producer. A phonogram producer will often insist that it owns the rights in the recording for life of copyright, which currently varies from 50 to 150 years from first release, depending on the country in which it was recorded. The term in a production company agreement might be for only 10 years. On termination, the rights in the recordings would revert to the artist (provided perhaps that the album costs have been recouped), which is attractive for the artist. In this way the production company can only license the recordings for 10 years to another phonogram producer, as those are the only rights it owns. This works to the advantage of the artist. Also, although the artist will have to split the royalties with the production company, the licensee phonogram producer will generally pay a higher royalty to a production company than to an artist signing directly, as it does not have to pay recording costs. The licensee phonogram producer also knows exactly what it is getting, as at least the first album is usually finished when it is licensed, minimizing the risk and saving A&R costs. The other significant advantage to the artist who signs to a production company is that the latter can protect the artist from unreasonable demands from the licensee phonogram producer and provide another tier of support to the artist in every area. In some cases, this could mean the difference between success and failure. (See the section on recording agreements on page 97.) If the manager takes this alternative route as the production company or as publisher, or as both, he/she may also provide management services, albeit without charging the artist any commission. The artist would then be free to engage another manager under a traditional management agreement for services at any time if they so wish.

If the artist enters into a publishing agreement with the manager, it may be possible to provide for the term of the publishing agreement to be for the duration of the management agreement plus, for example, 10 years. If the publishing splits were, say, 75/25 at source in the country of residence and 80/20 on receipts outside the country of residence, with no management commission payable, this could give the artist a net financial gain in percentage terms over traditional management arrangements and would give the manager greater security, i.e. if an artist were to enter into a traditional 75 percent at source deal with a major publisher, then a manager would expect to receive commission at perhaps 20 percent, leaving the artist with in effect 60 percent of at source income. If the manager sets up a publishing company, then the net pay-through to the artist would need to be higher than 60 percent at source for the artist to receive a higher overall percentage. Also, advances from third parties can be paid through to the artist if received by the manager's publishing company, provided that they can be identifiable as advances for the artist's works. Another advantage to the artist of this arrangement is that royalties are likely to be paid through more quickly than would be the case with an outside publisher. (See the section on publishing on page 107.)

In all these cases, it is important for the artist to try and retain ultimate ownership of his/her copyrights and related rights. This can be achieved by licensing these rights for a limited term, rather than assigning them to any production or publishing company or partnership that the manager may set up. As was stated in the chapter on copyright, from an author of performer's point of view, it is always better to license rights than to assign them.

# CHAPTER 7
# BAND AGREEMENTS

If the artist is a band or group of two or more performers operating under a band name, it is important to have a clear understanding of the rules under which the band will operate and what rights exist for the band members. It also helps to avoid arguments and misunderstandings within the band, and is particularly important in regard to who owns the band's name and what happens if a band member leaves or a new band member joins. If no band agreement exists and a band member leaves with no clear written agreement about who owns the name, it could be that the member leaving forms a new band with the same name, thus resulting in two bands operating under the same name, which can cause legal difficulties and public confusion. These agreements can also cover the way the different income streams are split amongst the band members and what happens if the band ceases to exist.

## Legal Status

The first thing to decide is what the legal status of the band will be. It could be a partnership or it could be that the band members form a corporation. Another possible structure is for one member of the band to employ the other musicians/singers in the band. The band members should take advice from their lawyer, accountant and manager as to which structure is best for them. If they choose to be a partnership, the band agreement will be the partnership agreement. If they decide to form a corporation or limited company, the band agreement will be the shareholders' agreement. Band agreements can be difficult and sensitive, so it is best to try and conclude an agreement as soon as possible once the band starts to become known. It is far easier to conclude such an agreement whilst everyone is on good terms with each other, rather than waiting until a dispute arises.

86

## Issues covered by Band Agreements

Here are some of the main issues that can be covered by a band agreement:

■ How will recording income be split?

■ How will public performance income in sound recordings be split?

■ How will the publishing income be split?

■ How will touring income be split?

■ How will merchandising income be split?

■ How will income from sponsorship or endorsements be split?

■ Who owns the band name and how can it be used if the band splits up?

■ What happens if one member leaves and what will the effect of this be on third party agreements?

■ What are the audit rights of the leaving member?

■ What are the liabilities of the leaving member?

■ What notice must a leaving member give?

■ Expected conduct of each band member.

■ Under what circumstances can band members be hired and fired?

■ What is the voting system for decision-making on behalf of the band?

■ On what issues does there have to be unanimous agreement from band members for a decision to be made?

■ How many band members need to attend third-party meetings before a decision can be taken on behalf of the band?

■ Who will be the signatories to the band's bank account and what will be the limit for which any single member can make payments?

■ What happens if a band member dies or is incapacitated?

■ Will there be a trial period for a new member joining the band?

■ Will the joining member be indemnified for liabilities that occurred before he/she joined?

■ When an individual member buys equipment with band money, is the equipment owned by the band or by the individual?

■ Will the individual have the right to buy any band equipment used by that individual from the band if he/she leaves, and if so, for how much?

■ How will band expenses be defined, and will they include a basic wage for each band member?

- Will members be able to work on outside projects if third party agreements such as the band's recording and publishing agreements allow?

- If outside projects are allowed, who keeps the income and what happens if the individual's absence affects the band adversely?

- If there is a dispute, what will be the mechanism for its resolution (e.g. mediation, arbitration or an alternative dispute resolution arrangement)?

- Will the band agreement be confidential?

- What will be the law that governs the agreement?

- How must notices concerning the agreement be given?

- Will there be an obligation for each individual to sign any agreement that has been agreed with a third party under the band's voting system?

A very common situation when the 'artist' is a band is that there will often be a situation where there are only one or two authors in the band, with the other members being purely performers. This can result in the author(s) receiving far higher income than the pure performers, which can often lead to bad feeling within the band. In extreme cases this can lead to a situation where the author is driving around in a Mercedes and the other band members still have to catch buses.

One of the bands that the author of this book managed found a way around this problem. The sole author in the band agreed that as long as a band member stayed within the band, he/she would receive a percentage of the publishing income, even though he/she did not actually write any of the band's songs. The sole author very generously agreed to split the publishing income four ways with the other three members of the band, i.e. each member received 25 percent of the publishing income after it had been received by the band's sole author from his publisher and the public performance collective management organization. The sole author took the view that the band was a vehicle for his works and that without the band his writing would stand little chance of success.

It is important in such a situation for all registrations with collective management organizations and publishers to be correct. In other words, the works should be registered accurately with the publisher and the appropriate CMO as to who actually wrote the work and not how the income is to be distributed. Once the author has received the income, then he or she can distribute it according to the band

agreement. In this particular case, it was agreed that if a band member who was not one of the authors left the band or was dismissed, he/she would cease to receive any of the publishing income from that point on.

## Dispute Resolution

If there should be a dispute between band members or between the band/artist and a third party, it is always recommended to try and settle the dispute by 'mediation'. This is the least expensive and the least stressful way of achieving a settlement. The mediator is a facilitator who will examine the evidence, listen to both sides and endeavor to facilitate a negotiated settlement between the parties which, if agreed, will be binding in law. The parties will normally provide the mediator with a short position statement in advance of the mediation meeting, together with any supporting documents. It is advisable to include a clause in all contracts that in the case of a dispute the parties agree to enter good faith discussions to settle disputes by mediation. It is also advisable, if possible, to name a mediator who would be acceptable to both parties in the clause. If this mediation process fails, the more expensive and stressful options of arbitration or litigation through the courts can be considered. The other advantage of mediation is that the dispute can normally be resolved (or not) in one or two days, whereas litigation through the courts can sometimes take months to reach a final judgment, and even then it is normally open to an appeal process.

It may be that some artist lawyers may not be enthusiastic about the concept of mediation, as lawyers make a lot of money from legal disputes. More enlightened lawyers, however, understand the value of mediation to their clients, which is making mediation a more popular and efficient method of settling disputes as time goes on.

# CHAPTER 8
## STARTING A RECORD LABEL – BECOMING AN INDEPENDENT PHONOGRAM PRODUCER

It may be as an artist, or as a manager, or as both working together that a decision is made to create a self-administered record label. If enough finance can be sourced to do this, it provides several major advantages. Firstly, it allows the artist to sell physical recordings at live performances, helping to build a fan base which, as has been stated throughout this book, is at the heart of artist development. It also allows the flexibility to sign to another phonogram producer when the time is right, if this is desirable, as the recording rights are owned by the artist or by both the artist and the manager.

Another advantage is that the unit income will be far higher for physical sales and/or digital downloads and streaming than if the artist signed to a conventional phonogram producer. Instead of receiving a royalty of perhaps 15 – 20 percent of PPD (the wholesale price), as is usually the case with a major phonogram producer, the artist receives 100 percent. Any manufacturing, packaging, marketing and distribution costs must be deducted from this 100 percent, but the net income per unit should be higher than would be received from a major phonogram producer. The other advantage is that the artist will have control over his/her rights. Also a third-party phonogram producer will usually require that the copyright is assigned to it for life of the copyright, which varies between 50 and 150 years, depending on the country in which the contract was signed.

The disadvantage of the artist becoming their own independent phonogram producer is that the artist will not be able to benefit from the financial and structural resources of a large third-party phonogram producer, particularly in regard to advances, recording costs, marketing, distribution and tour support. The one thing that well-resourced phonogram producers can offer the artist is money and marketing. It is far better to have 15 percent of US$500,000 (US$75,000) than 50 percent of US$50,000 (US$25,000). If the phonogram producer can achieve far higher sales, the more mechanical royalties will be payable for the underlying musical composition to the author and his/her publisher. If the artist is also the author, this can mean far greater income, and if sales are higher there may be much more radio play, so that the public performance income is also considerably increased on both the author's side and the performer's side. The most important advantage of all in signing to an established phonogram producer would be that the artist may reach and create many more fans, thus increasing the artist's fan base and social networking integration, which will mean playing larger shows and generating greater income from live work.

Here are the main issues to consider when starting a record label and becoming your own phonogram producer:

1. Choose a business structure. (This could be as a corporation/limited company, a partnership or a sole trader. The artist and/or manager need to obtain advice on this from an accountant or lawyer.)

2. Choose an original name for the label (do an online search to make sure that the name has not been used previously).

3. Create a business plan.
   Prepare a business timetable
   Prepare a cash-flow forecast
   Obtain several quotes for manufacturing records
   Obtain several quotes for preparing artwork
   Make an estimate for distribution costs
   Make an estimate for advertising and marketing costs
   Make an estimate for mechanical royalty payments
   Make an estimate for artist advances (if any) and royalty payments.

4.  Build a team

    The artist and/or artist manager/record label will need:

    A business bank account

    A music business accountant

    A music business lawyer

    A physical distribution structure

    A manufacturer

    An aggregator for online sales.

5.  Apply for a license from a mechanical collective management organization for each track released. The artist/manager/record label will need to apply for a license from the CMO in the country of residence that collects mechanical royalties on behalf of publishers and authors. It will be necessary to obtain mechanical licenses from the mechanical rights CMO for the works contained in the recordings, after which mechanical royalties will have to be paid to that CMO for every sound carrier, download or stream sold. In some cases, the mechanical rights CMO may insist on a mechanical royalty payment for every physical sound carrier manufactured rather than for every one sold. These royalties will then be passed on by the mechanical rights CMO, who will in turn pay through to the publisher, who will in turn pay through to the author(s) of the work. In some territories, such as the USA, it may also be possible to obtain a mechanical license directly from the author's publisher.

6.  Become a phonogram producer member of the appropriate related rights CMO that collects the public performance and broadcasting income for sound recordings. These CMOs collect income from radio and television stations, as well as other public performance uses when a recording is broadcast or played in public. As discussed in the chapter on collective management, in some countries there is a joint CMO which distributes to both performers and phonogram producers, and in other countries there are separate CMOs for each. It is important that phonogram producers and/or the performers supply the related rights CMO with information about the performers that played on a particular recording

and whether they were featured or non-featured. A phonogram producer receives income from these related rights CMOs, whereas with mechanical rights the phonogram producer will have to make payments to the mechanical rights CMO.

In the situation where the artist has written 100% of the work in a recording and has no publisher, it may be possible that the mechanical rights CMO allows the artist to bypass the mechanical royalties process altogether and self-administer the mechanical royalties, i.e. in this 100% case if the artist paid the mechanical royalty CMO $100 and the CMO's administrative costs were 15%, the CMO would pay back to the artist/author $85. If the artist can self-administer the mechanical royalty process, the artist would be $15 better off.

7. It may also be beneficial to join the trade organization representing phonogram producers in the country of residence. In some countries there are two such organizations, one which mostly represents the interests of the major phonogram producers and another which represents the interests of smaller independent phonogram producers. The international umbrella organizations for these two types of trade associations are IFPI (www.ifpi.org), which represents the major phonogram producers and others, and IMPALA (www.impalasite.org), which represents the interests of independent phonogram producers.

The above outlines the procedure for the artist and/or artist manager setting up as a phonogram producer even if it is only on a small scale. In the very early days it will probably be just a matter of manufacturing 500 CDs with a simple one-page printed insert, or by-passing the manufacturing process altogether and releasing online only. In either case, it will be essential to keep good accounting records and to join the appropriate CMOs, especially if the author of any of the works recorded and released is someone other than the artist.

# CHAPTER 9
## ARTIST & LABEL FINANCING – CROWD SOURCING

How does an artist or an artist and their manager working together find the money to start their own label and release recordings? For that matter, how do they finance the whole artist/management process? If money is scarce (and it usually is), as discussed in the previous section, it is best to release recordings for digital download or streaming only, at least to start with. After the recording has been completed, this is a very inexpensive process. As is stressed throughout this book, the online environment is providing a host of usually free tools that can be used to bring music to the world. Once an artist/manager has a computer and a broadband connection, they are in business. The main investment is time. Facebook, Twitter and YouTube are essentially free, as are most of the digital marketing and storage services, at least at the basic entry level. Provided an artist has a bank account or even just a PayPal account, it is easy to get an aggregator on board who will place and distribute their recordings on as many as 150 digital stores globally, including iTunes and Spotify, often at little or no cost. The aggregator will deduct a percentage for themselves and send through the remainder directly to the record label. Once a fan base has been created, it may be possible to raise finance by crowd sourcing.

The first band to do this was UK band Marillion. Marillion signed to EMI Records in 1982 and released their first album 'Script for a Jester's Tear' in 1983. They built up a loyal fan base both in the UK and around the world and continue to expand that fan base to the present day. By 1993 the band's US fans were becoming very disappointed that Marillion were not touring USA. The reason for this was that Marillion simply couldn't afford to do so. One of the American fans came up with the idea of raising money so that the band could tour. In 1996 some of the fans got together and opened a special escrow bank account and invited fans across USA to donate into the Marillion touring fund. Very quickly they raised US$12,000. At this point the band became involved and worked out that they would need to raise $65,000 to cover all costs. This was soon achieved and the tour happened in 1997. Each fan who had donated more than $10 was sent a special CD of live recordings. Those that had donated still had to buy tickets but they were just pleased that they had helped to make the tour happen. At this point the band realized the importance of building a database of their fans, and how immensely important it would be for their future not only in disseminating information via their website, but also as a possible source of funding for future projects.

In 2000 Marillion wanted to make a new album, but were unwilling to enter into another recording contract with a third-party phonogram producer who would make most of the profits from the sales. In order to fund the next album, Marillion decided to ask the fans for help. By this time the band had 6000 email addresses on their database. They wrote to all of them asking them if they would be prepared to purchase the album in advance. 5800 said yes and only 200 said no. This was the turning point. The band realized that their fans could fund the whole project by purchasing the album up to a year in advance of release. They decided that the first 7000 advance orders would have the fan's name printed in the album packaging, which the fans loved. They would also produce special limited edition deluxe packaging for those that had paid for the album in advance. Fans who had participated in advance purchase were also automatically entered in to a prize draw where they could win backstage passes, tickets to stand at the side of the stage during a show or win passes to see the sound-check. In the end the band sold 12,500 of the deluxe album package on advance order. This not only provided adequate funding to make and manufacture the album, but also paid for extensive marketing too. They repeated this process for their next album, entitled 'Marbles', in 2004 and this time achieved 15,000 advance orders at $35 per album. They reinvested heavily in PR, marketing and expanding their fan base still further by offering new fans a free CD entitled 'Crash Course', in return for their email address. For their next album, 'Somewhere Else', which they released in 2007, the band decided that they couldn't keep going back to their fans for finance so they took the conventional route and just paid for the album themselves and released it.

To the group's surprise, the fans expressed great disappointment that the advance purchase for premium product approach had been dropped. It was at this point that they realized that the fans really wanted to participate in the album process as it

made them feel a part of the Marillion community. They also preferred buying directly from the band as they felt the product was authentic. It made them feel like a partner to the band and a part of the creative process.

Throughout this whole process Marillion still used conventional distributors to sell the same albums in the stores in standard packaging, but they pioneered high value high price packaging for their core fans. The band also made it clear that there could be no artistic pressure or control concerning the album that fans had paid in advance for.

Many online services have launched who will help an artist raise finance by crowd-funding. These include Kickstarter, PledgeMusic, Sellaband, Ulele, Tunefund, Artistshare, Oocto and MyMajorCompany amongst others. As with all online services, some of these services will disappear and others will emerge. Kickstarter accommodates all creative start-ups and business projects. Most artists ask for around $5000 on Kickstarter in order to make an album or to fulfil some other musical project, and often achieve it if they are known. In 2012, American singer Amanda Palmer asked the public for $100,000 through Kickstarter to make her new album. 24,883 fans responded by donating a staggering $1.2 million which she used to make and market the album and tour. Those who pledge money on Kickstarter or PledgeMusic do not 'invest' in the project but rather 'back' the project in return for tangible items, bundles of items or experiences such as an album download, a ticket for the album launch, a CD with their name printed in the CD booklet, a signed poster, a day in the recording studio with the band or an album T-shirt – in fact, very much along the lines of the Marillion model.

Other artists have taken this concept a stage further and put a price-list on their website where fans can buy direct contact with the artist experiences, e.g. dinner with the artist, a weekend skiing, 30 minutes playing their instrument with the artist, artist to write a song with the fan's name in it etc. Other artists offer to write a song and record it customized to a particular fan's requests for a set fee. These are all ways of making a living from music, or at least getting started in doing so.

Another possible source of finance is that of venture capitalists buying into a management company or into an artist via the manager. The money they make available is used to develop the artist by way of recording costs, costs associated with live work, salaries to the artist and marketing costs etc. In return, the investment venture capital company will want a percentage of the profits or a percentage of the gross income from all income streams. Two of the venture capital companies in the music field who invest in artists are Ingenious and Icebreaker. Such investment can give the investor tax advantages in some countries.

# CHAPTER 10
## SIGNING TO A PHONOGRAM PRODUCER

Let us now consider the situation where a phonogram producer wishes to sign an artist with the intention of selling as many copies of the artist's recordings as possible. Traditionally this was the way for an artist to be successful, but as phonogram producers become far more selective as to who they will invest in, the crowd-sourcing model above is rapidly becoming the alternative financing model for many artists. It also allows the artist to have control of their own destiny and ownership of their recordings.

In the past, major phonogram producers (of which at the time of writing there were only three – Universal, Sony and Warners) would invest in an artist by providing advances, recording costs, marketing costs, tour support and distribution. The major phonogram producer would generally commit to making and releasing one album with the artist but would want options on as many as eight further albums. The other important feature of these investment-type recording agreements is that the phonogram producer will generally demand that all recordings made under the agreement be assigned to them for the life of copy protection, i.e. assignment will be sought for the full period of related right copy protection for sound recordings in each territory covered by the agreement. This means that the artist will earn royalties from any sales during the period that the recordings enjoy protection, but he/she will never own their recordings. The major phonogram producers will argue that they need this assignment to justify their investment in the artist, which is highly speculative. From the artist's perspective, this may appear to be unreasonable, as in many countries the artist invariably pays all the audio recording costs and usually 50 percent or even 100 percent of any video production costs from his/her audio royalty account. This concept of the artist having to pay all the recording costs but never owning the recordings is one that is constantly questioned in the music industry.

The way for an artist to avoid this dilemma is to enter into a limited assignment of perhaps 10 – 25 years rather than for life of copy protection or, better still, to license his/her recordings to the phonogram producer for a limited term. The licensing approach is far better from the artist's point of view and is becoming far more common, particularly in the case of the smaller independent phonogram producers who will often enter in to an agreement wherein the artist receives 50% of net receipts. Net receipts are usually defined as the balance left after all identifiable costs in the recording, manufacturing and marketing of an album have been deducted from the gross income. It is important to remember that if the artist licenses his/her recordings to a phonogram producer, he/she retains ownership of the related rights in the recordings.

The advantage of signing to a major phonogram producer is that they may be prepared to spend larger sums of money on marketing campaigns for the artist, such as television and radio advertising, pluggers (people who work to get an artist's records played on radio and television), in-store campaigns, print and online advertising, social media integration and digital marketing campaigns. They are usually also prepared to spend larger sums on recording costs (even though these will usually be recouped from the artist's royalty account), tour support (providing money to cover any loss on a tour, again usually recoupable from the artist's royalty account) and video production (even though usually 50 percent of these costs are recouped from the artist's audio royalty account and the other 50 percent from the artist's video account). Whilst the artist may receive lower royalties per unit sold than can be paid by an independent phonogram producer, and certainly less than if the artist has their own label, he/she could well be better off, purely because of the greater scale of sales that a major phonogram producer may be able to achieve. As mentioned earlier, it is far better to receive a smaller percentage of a large sum rather than a large percentage of a much smaller sum, and this is something the artist and the manager will have to consider before committing to a recording agreement.

The new digital royalty structures being offered by major phonogram producers to performers have been controversial, as digital downloads and streaming increasingly replace physical sales. With digital downloads and streaming, the phonogram producer has no manufacturing costs, no physical distribution costs such as shipping

by road, rail or air, no faulty returns and no packaging costs. Despite these savings, the major phonogram producers have continued to set performers' royalty rates at the same or a similar level as the royalty rate for physical product. This has given some independent phonogram producers a competitive edge. If they are offering 50% of net receipts on digital, that is far more attractive for artists than the royalty rates usually on offer from the majors.

An additional advantage of signing to a smaller 'independent' phonogram producer is that they are usually much more open to entering into a licensing agreement rather than an assignment agreement. The recording agreements are also often considerably more favorable to the artist than can be negotiated with a major company. For example, a typical independent deal might be a licensing agreement for anything between three and 15 years, after which the rights in the recordings will revert to the artist and he/she will be free to either negotiate a further term with the same phonogram producer, negotiate a new agreement with another phonogram producer or release the recordings on his/her own label. The disadvantage with a licensing agreement is that often the artist has to pay for the audio recording costs, i.e. the artist has to supply the phonogram producer with finished recordings. This can sometimes be financed from the advance that the independent phonogram producer pays. In any case, due to advances in home recording technology, it is far less expensive to record an album than it was in the past.

As we have seen above, it is important to consider carefully the royalty structures of a recording agreement. In the past, major phonogram producers developed very complicated royalty payment structures for physical sales of recordings. These would usually be calculated on a royalty base rate which might increase at certain sales figures and with future albums if the options on them were taken up. These royalty rates could be based on the Published Price to Dealers or Dealer Price (PPD) or on the Recommended Retail Price (RRP), which is sometimes also called Suggested Retail List Price (SRLP). This often resulted in misunderstandings between artists, one of which was paid on a royalty rate based on PPD and another signed to a different company, which based its royalties on RRP. The PPD royalty would always be higher than the RRP royalty for the same amount of income per unit sold. All sorts of deductions are applicable to this base royalty rate. There is usually a 'packaging' deduction which is typically 25 percent for CDs. This means that the royalty is instantly reduced by 25 percent. Some phonogram producers have even substituted the packaging deductions for digital downloads and streaming (where there is no packaging) with 'new technology deductions'. There will also typically be reductions for sales to libraries, the armed forces, record clubs, mail order, sales at budget and mid-price (rather than full price), sales that involve special packaging, and sales when a recording is included in a compilation album.

In 2002, BMG, before they merged with Sony, spent a lot of time attempting to reform these royalty structures into one simple royalty payment which they set at 15 percent of PPD for every record sold. This royalty rate had no packaging deductions or any other deductions, which meant a much more streamlined and efficient accounting system for the phonogram producer, and one which was also easier to understand by the artist and manager. This was a really sensible move for both parties, but the majority of major phonogram producers still use the old complex royalty contracts, which can sometimes run to over 100 pages.

Before a long-form recording agreement is negotiated, the phonogram producer will usually put forward a suggested heads of agreement, which is a brief summary of the main points in the agreement, to start negotiations. An experienced manager will negotiate this directly with the phonogram producer and then bring in a lawyer for the long-form agreement, which will include all the so-called 'boiler plate' legal text. An inexperienced manager or an artist without a manager would be advised to enlist the services of a lawyer as soon as the heads of agreement are received. An experienced manager may approach it the other way around by issuing the phonogram producer with a suggested heads of agreement. Here are the main issues to negotiate at this point:

1.  Type of agreement: license or assignment.
2.  Territory: This could be one country, a group of countries, a continent, several continents or worldwide. Sometimes the world is extended still further to include the 'solar system' or even 'the universe'. (The rationale for this is that if sales were via satellite they wouldn't actually be on a territory on earth.)
3.  Term: The length of time that the phonogram producer will have to exploit the recordings covered by the agreement. This could be anything

from three years to life of copy protection available in law in each part of the territory.

4.  Albums: The number of albums in the agreement: usually one or two, with options for more. Sometimes it is possible to negotiate guaranteed releases on the first two or even three albums. It is in the artist's interest to have as few phonogram producer options in the agreement as possible.

5.  Advances: The amount of money the phonogram producer will pay to the artist in advance of an album being made. This could be in addition to recording costs, or it may include recording costs. Advances are usually fully recoupable from royalties. The phonogram producer will usually be obliged to pay additional, increasing advances at each option point if each option is taken up. Sometimes the advance payable on option albums is linked to sales of the previous album. Also included here could be how the advances are to be paid, e.g. 50 percent on signature of the recording agreement and the remaining 50 percent on delivery of the album.

6.  Recording Costs: A sum of money for making the first album, recoupable against royalties, which is usually increased for successive albums if the options are taken up. This is sometimes included in the album advance. (In some countries, like France, recording costs are not recoupable from royalties, but royalty rates are lower to compensate the phonogram producer for this.)

7.  Royalties: The royalty rates payable by the phonogram producer for sales of full price albums, double albums, mid-price albums, budget price albums, singles, extended play singles, albums sold as part of a TV or radio advertising campaign, through a record club, by mail order, as sales to libraries or to the armed forces, for export, as sales in certain foreign countries included in the territory etc. There will also be royalty rates for sales of digital downloads, telephone ring tones, real tones and ring-back tones and for sales from streaming. A manager/artist should pitch the download and streaming digital royalty rates much higher than the physical royalty rates as a first negotiating position. The income split for master re-uses where a recording is synchronized with visual images in a film, TV program or an advertisement should also be negotiated here.

8. Artistic Control: The uses of the recordings for which the phonogram producer needs approval from the artist, and also whether or not a recording delivered by the artist can be rejected as technically or commercially unacceptable by the phonogram producer. Also as to whether or not the phonogram producer or the artist has the final approval over artwork, biographies, photographs, videos, choice of singles, song sequence on albums, branding etc.

9. Accounting: How often the phonogram producer is obliged to send royalty statements to the artist and when royalties (if any) are payable.

10. Audit: How often, under what circumstances and in what parts of the territory the artist can send an auditor in to the phonogram producer's business or that of the phonogram producer's licensees to check on whether royalties have been accounted and paid correctly. In regard to the audit rights, the artist not only needs to be able to audit the phonogram producer in the country of residence, but also to audit his/her foreign licensees or sister corporations in other countries if those countries are included in the territory. This is unfortunately very difficult, but if not achieved it leaves a large area of unaccountability in the agreement.

Another approach is to sign a different recording licensing agreement in each part of the world. This makes for a lot more work on behalf of the artist and manager, but some artists have done it very successfully. A typical arrangement here might be one agreement for Europe, another for North American Free Trade Association (NAFTA) members (the US, Canada and Mexico), another in Japan and another in Australasia (Australia and New Zealand).

## Advances and Recoupment

The very important concept of recoupment is one that needs to be clearly understood. If an advance is recoupable, it means that as royalties come in they are first offset against the advance. For example, if the advance and other recoupable costs are US$50,000 and after the first accounting period the royalties payable to the artist are US$60,000, the phonogram producer will pay US$10,000 to the artist. In this example, the advance and other recoupable costs have been fully recouped in the first accounting period. If, however, the royalties payable for the whole term of

the agreement in this example were only US$35,000, then US$15,000 of the advance and other recoupable costs would remain unrecouped. It is important to realize that unless the agreement states anything to the contrary, the sum of US$15,000 does not have to be paid back by the artist to the phonogram producer in this example. The advance and other recoupable costs are an amount of money paid out by the phonogram producer at his/her own risk, and are not repayable by the artist except from royalties earned.

## 360 Degree Agreements

As phonogram producers' turnover and profits have been declining due to the problems that exist with unauthorized file-sharing, many have been looking to participate in some of the other income streams available to artists. These are fast becoming the norm and are referred to as 360 degree agreements. In addition to recording income, phonogram producers are demanding participation in other income such as publishing income, income from live work, merchandising income and income from branding and sponsorship etc. One of the landmark 360 degree agreements was that negotiated by EMI with the artist Robbie Williams. In this contract, EMI not only acted as the conventional phonogram producer, but also as publisher, and participated in income from live work. The US band Korn also negotiated a similar agreement. The attraction for the artist is that phonogram producers are usually prepared to pay much higher advances for this type of agreement. In geographical areas where piracy is a major problem, such as Africa, Asia and Latin America, this type of agreement is normal. Artists and their managers should think very carefully before entering into this type of agreement, as it may be much more advantageous to manage these other income streams themselves.

## Website and Fan Database Ownership

Some phonogram producers will try to insist that they own the artist's website and/or the artist's fan database. Managers should resist this if possible or should at least make sure that the artist co-owns or at least has access to the database at all times. If the artist is dropped by the phonogram producer and the artist loses access to their fan database, this will be a complete disaster for the artist. The fan database is the most valuable asset the artist will ever have.

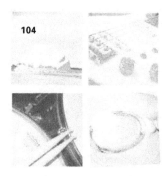

# CHAPTER 11
# STUDIO PRODUCER AGREEMENTS, RECORDING, SAMPLING & MASTERING

As mentioned in the definitions section, the person whose job it is to supervise the studio recording is often referred to as a 'producer'. In order to distinguish this role clearly from the phonogram producer we will use the term 'studio producer'.

A typical arrangement for a studio producer agreement is for an advance to be paid to the studio producer for each track to be recorded, against a studio producer royalty of 1 to 6 percent of PPD, depending on the status of the studio producer. In most recording agreements, the phonogram producer will pay the advances to the studio producer. Advances paid out to the studio producer, and any subsequent studio producer royalties paid out by the phonogram producer, will be regarded as recording costs, which will normally be recoupable against the artist's royalties. It is therefore important for an artist or manager to monitor these deals carefully, as they will directly affect the income the artist eventually receives. For example, if the artist is receiving a royalty of 20 percent of PPD and the studio producer's royalty is four percent of PPD, the artist will actually end up with a royalty of 16 percent of PPD. Sometimes the studio producer will be paid a royalty from the first record sold, and in other agreements the producer will only start to earn royalties after recoupment of recording costs associated with the tracks that the studio producer produced. The choice of a studio producer is an important decision. How a track is recorded, mixed and edited can make a considerable difference to the level of success the track achieves. Some producers will be more focused on the creative recording process and will insist on a separate engineer to supervise the technical side of the recording. Other studio producers prefer to both produce and engineer the tracks themselves. It is also quite common to engage a specialist mixing engineer to do the final mix of the track. One of the most famous specialist mixing engineers is Bob

Clearmountain, who is based in Los Angeles and mixes many of the top recording artists such as Madonna, Bruce Springsteen, Rufus Wainwright, Ziggy Marley and Ricky Martin. An experienced mixing engineer will also justify his/her own royalty, usually in the region of one percent of PPD (or 'one point', as it is often called).

Studio producer agreements also often oblige the studio producer to complete the appropriate forms confirming who played what instruments and who sang on a particular recording. This is particularly important for the performers who participated on the recording, as it will (in many countries) entitle them to public performance income when, and if, the recording is later played on the radio, television or anywhere in public.

Another aspect of studio producer agreements is that the studio producer is obliged to declare to the phonogram producer if any 'samples' have been used in the recording. As we have seen in the copyright chapter, a 'sample' is when a section or part of an already existing recording is used as part of a new recording. This obligation is nearly always found in the main artist recording agreement with the phonogram producer, so both the artist and the studio producer have a legal obligation to declare and possibly clear any samples. In such a case, permission has to be received from both the right holder in the original recording that has been sampled and the author/publisher of the original work contained in the sample. A middle way is to make a new recording of the sample, which means that permission is then only required from the author/publisher of the work contained in it. Specialist companies exist such as Replay Heaven (www.replayheaven.com) who, for a fee, will recreate a recording which is astonishingly close to the original. The sample clearance process can be an expensive and time-consuming procedure. It is therefore advisable not to use any samples of other recordings or works if at all possible.

As time goes on, recording equipment is becoming less and less expensive, and this has resulted in many artists buying and setting up their own studios rather than hiring a recording studio. There have been examples of phenomenal recordings being produced in artists' bedrooms using fairly inexpensive recording equipment and computer software. This also gives the artist or band the advantage that several albums can be recorded once the initial equipment has been purchased, thus providing a substantial saving on recording costs. It may also be worthwhile for several artists or bands to get together to purchase recording equipment which they can then share to produce recordings, which will provide a further cost saving.

The final stage in producing a recording is known as 'mastering' and is the process of taking the finished and mixed recording and enhancing the sound of the recording prior to manufacture or digital release. There are specialist mastering engineers who can provide this service, or special mastering software can be purchased, allowing an artist or a studio producer to do the mastering themselves. Probably the world's most famous mastering engineer is Bob Ludwig of Gateway Mastering (www.gatewaymastering.com) who is based in Portland, Maine, in the US. If an artist wants the very best he is the man to contact, but good mastering studios are to be found in almost every country in the world.

In some jurisdictions such as the UK a studio producer may qualify as a non-featured performer if he/she has directed proceedings in the recorded studio in the same way that a conductor will direct proceedings while an orchestra is performing. An orchestra conductor qualifies as a non-featured performer even though they make no audible sound on a recording in many jurisdictions, and if the studio producer fulfils a similar role in the recording studio he/she would also qualify in the same way.

# CHAPTER 12
# MUSIC PUBLISHING

An artist who is an author will need to consider finding a publisher at some point. In the early stages of an artist's career, publishing income can be achieved by simply joining the appropriate mechanical and public performance CMO and registering the works with them. Generally speaking, these CMOs will not pay advances but will simply pay royalties to the author as they are collected. The CMO will deduct their administration fees from the gross income and pay through the balance to the author. These CMOs tend to be passive inasmuch as they will try to collect all income due, but they will not usually reach out to the market and try to create new uses for the author's works.

A publisher will often pay a lump sum advance to the author, in return for an agreement where the author will be tied to the publisher for a period of years or for a number of albums. Usually, everything the author writes within the term of the publishing agreement will be administered exclusively by the publisher, who will also usually agree to reach out to the market and try and create new uses and opportunities for the author's works such as covers, audiovisual uses, the publication of sheet music etc. The publisher may also be able to help the artist and the manager to obtain a recording contract. Hence, if the author signs to a publisher he/she can expect to receive mechanical and public performance royalties as well as a service whereby the publisher seeks new uses for the author's works in order to generate more income. In return for an advance and for these services, the publisher will want to take a larger share than is the case if the author receives income directly from a CMO. In the early days of an artist's career there is usually very little money available, so a publishing advance can really help the artist to get started.

The following are the main deal points of a publishing agreement:

**Term:** The time period wherein the agreement is effective. This could be a specified period of time, a number of albums or a combination of both. All works written by the author during the Term and sometimes also written prior to the start of the Term are controlled by the publisher for the Rights Period (see below).

**Options:** The point in time in the agreement when the publisher has the right to decide whether to continue with the agreement and pay a further advance or to terminate the term of the agreement.

**The Rights Period:** The period of time in which the publisher has the right to collect publishing income for works controlled during the Term.

**Royalties:** The different royalty rates for mechanical income, public performance income, covers, synchronization licenses, sheet music sales etc. payable to the author.

**Royalty Basis:** 'Receipts' or 'at source'. 'Receipts' means the amount received by the publisher after costs, including the sub-publisher's commissions etc. 'At source' means the actual gross amount paid on behalf of the author's works from the CMO or phonogram producer to the publisher in each part of the territory. From the author's point of view it is far better to be paid 'at source'.

**Minimum Commitment:** The minimum number of works required to be released or written by the author within each option period. If the option period is based on an album being released, there may be a provision that there must be a minimum percentage of works written by the author on the album. This is often in the 70 – 90 per cent range. If the author does not manage to achieve that percentage, the publisher may be able to reduce the advance on the next option period pro-rata or to extend the current period.

**Advances:** The lump sums payable to the author on signing the agreement and at the points any options are taken up by the publisher. These sums are recoupable from royalties.

**Territory:** The geographical area in which the publisher is entitled to collect publishing income. This is usually the world, but it could be limited to certain countries or continents.

In regard to royalties, it used to be the case, and still is in some countries, that the publisher would take 50 percent of all income received on a 'receipts' basis and pass on the remaining 50 percent to the author. The publisher would also often demand that the term was for the life of copyright which, as we saw in the section on copyright and related rights, could be as long as 150 years. Since the 1980s things have changed

considerably in the author's favor. A typical deal might be 75/25 at source for mechanicals and performance with other rates for synchronization and other income. In this typical percentage, 75 percent of the at source income goes to the author and 25 percent is retained by the publisher. A typical term might be for one album cycle (perhaps 18 months) and thereafter one, two or three options which will extend the term if they are taken up. Each option period would cover another album or a minimum number of new works and would attract a further advance. The rights period could be anything from five to 25 years but should not extend beyond that.

Some publishers will offer an author a mini/max advance structure on options. This will state a minimum guaranteed advance if the publisher picks up the option for the next album or the next writing period. There will, however, be a formula based on income or sales for the previous period (sometimes referred to as 'pipeline' income) which could result in a larger advance being paid. No matter what the figure the formula produces, the larger advance can never exceed the maximum advance stated in the contract. Another legal mechanism sometimes found in publishing agreements is a 'first and last matching right' clause. This is normally where there is an obligation for the author and the publisher to have a 'good faith' negotiation about an option for the publisher to continue publishing the author's works for a further album or period. If the negotiation fails, the author will be free to try and secure a publishing agreement with another publisher. When the best offer is received from another publisher, the author will be obliged to declare this offer to the original publisher. The original publisher will then have the right to match this external offer and continue publishing the author.

Some of the top global music publishers at present are Universal Music Publishing, Warner/Chappell Music, Sony-ATV Music Publishing and BMG Rights Management, although acquisitions and ownership are constantly changing. Kobalt Music Publishing arrived on the scene in 2000 with a slightly different business model. Kobalt rarely pays advances but offers a higher royalty of 85-90 percent of income received at source. They will also account to the author every three months instead of every six months as is the case with some of the major publishers. This arrangement is very attractive to more established artists looking for a new publishing deal, but is more difficult for a new author who will probably need a substantial advance to get started.

These are the main duties of a music publisher:

1. To negotiate, organize and issue licenses for the author's works and make sure the creator receives as much remuneration as possible for a particular use.

2. To issue or authorize the issuing of mechanical licenses via a CMO to phonogram producers who want to use the author's work on a recording.

3. To issue and try to acquire 'synchronization licenses' where the author's works are synchronized with visual images (i.e. films, television advertisements and video games).

4. To obtain 'covers' for the author (i.e. to persuade and suggest that other performers make recordings using the author's work).

5. To correctly register all the author's works with the appropriate authors' public performance and mechanical CMOs.

6. To administer printed music sales and online digital sheet music of the author's works or to license this to third parties.

7. To collect the above income on behalf of the author throughout every part of the territory. If the territory is the world, the publisher will have offices or sub-publishers in every part of the territory or may collect directly from the local CMO in a particular part of the territory.

8. To accurately account to the author at least once every six months, providing detailed statements and payment (if any is due).

Publishing income is very important for an all-round artist who writes and performs his/her own material. It can be the only income stream that an artist has to live on in the early days. It is generally easier to recoup publishing advances than it is to recoup recording advances, as there are normally no deductions other than advances and the publisher's share of the income, whereas in recording agreements there are many deductions such as video costs, recording costs and tour support in addition to advances. Most authors' public performance CMOs will only pay 50 percent of the income payable to the publisher, with the other 50 percent going straight to the author's bank account. If the royalty rate for public performance in the publishing agreement was 75/25 at source, the publisher would actually take 50 percent of the publisher's share, i.e. 50 percent will be paid directly from the CMO to the author and 50 percent directly from the CMO to the publisher, the latter being defined as the 'publisher's share'. In order to arrive at the 25 percent at source payable to the

publisher, the publisher will take 50 percent of the 50 percent received from the CMO, resulting in 75 percent being paid to the author overall. This system greatly helps the author as, in addition to the publisher's advance, the author knows that 50 percent of public performance income will be received even if his/her account with the publisher is unrecouped. This helps the author's cash flow. As mentioned previously in the section on Authors Public Performance CMOs, it is also important to be aware that in many countries income is collected from the promoter of live events by the authors' public performance CMO. This could be anything from 1-17 percent of the gross income from box office ticket sales. Some of these authors' CMOs are sophisticated enough to ask the promoter for details of every work that was performed at a particular concert. If this form is correctly completed, the money collected will eventually be paid to the authors of the works performed. The artist or the artist's manager should make sure these forms are completed accurately as, if the artist is an author, this will provide a further publishing income stream for the artist which can be substantial. So much artist money has been lost due to managers and artists not submitting set lists of live performances to promoters and CMOs following a show or a tour.

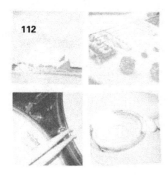

# CHAPTER 13
# MUSIC IN FILM, TV, ADVERTISING AND VIDEO GAMES

Let us now look at the use of music in film, television advertising and video games. This audiovisual use of music is becoming increasingly important to performers, authors, phonogram producers and publishers as income from the sales of recordings has diminished. As an example, the author of this publication secured the use of one of his artists' songs in an advertisement for an automobile manufacturer in Japan. The artist was the sole author of the work. He and the artist's publisher negotiated a synchronization fee of US$70,000 for the use of the work in this advertisement. The car company wanted to save money and/or put its own creative style to the song, so they decided to make their own recording of it. By doing this they did not have to pay the artist's phonogram producer or the artist for the recording rights. The automobile manufacturer paid local Japanese musicians a one-off session fee to make the recording of the work, thus creating a new recording with its own separate copyright protection. In a case like this, the rights in the original recording are irrelevant and do not apply. The new recording was owned by the automobile manufacturer and so no related rights income flows back to the original phonogram producer or the original performers who played on the original recording. The automobile manufacturer did, however, have to pay the author's publisher (and therefore the author) for the use of the work and this is the use the one-time synchronization fee of US$70,000 covered. But that was only a part of the income that this use generated. There was also the right of public performance/broadcasting in the work which was collected by the Japanese authors' CMO, JASRAC, based on the amount of public exposure this advertisement received. The advertisement was shown on every major Japanese commercial television station several times a day for a year, which generated a very substantial amount of public performance income. The result was a pay-through to the author after CMO deductions and the publisher's share of over US$450,000 in public performance income. So, with

the initial synchronization fee of $70,000 (less the publisher's share), the total income payable to the author was over $500,000. A further bonus was that the song title appeared on the television ad in the lower right-hand corner so that the viewers could easily find it and purchase it on one of the digital download sites or stream it from one of the streaming services if they wished.

Many audiovisual uses of music generate a very small amount of income, but as can be seen by this somewhat exceptional example, it is very important for the publisher and the manager to devote a considerable amount of time trying to get the artist's music used in audiovisual media. In addition to the financial rewards, any audiovisual use of the artist's music, whether the artist is the author or not, can be very helpful to his/her career development. It provides mass exposure of the artist's music, which can often lead to increased record sales and generally elevate, or, in the case of an unknown performer, sometimes launch an entire career.

One unusual aspect of the audiovisual use of music is that this is one of the only areas where the copyright in the work and the related rights in the sound recording are usually regarded as being equal in value. When a fee is agreed with the user for either the synchronization fee for the work, or for the master re-use fee for the sound recording, it is best to try to agree the fee on a 'most favored nations' (MFN) basis. This means that if the other copyright/related rights fee is greater than that agreed, it is automatically increased to the same figure as the other copyright or related rights fee. For example, if a publisher agrees a synchronization fee of US$10,000 and the phonogram producer agrees a master re-use fee of US$8,000 on a most favored nations basis, the master re-use fee would automatically increase from $8000 to US$10,000 to equal the amount of the synchronization fee agreed by the publisher. The most favored nations arrangement always equalizes at the higher figure, not the lowest.

## Music in Films

Since the dawn of audiovisual films when sound was first successfully synchronized to moving images in the 1920s, music has been an essential ingredient in their production. It has the ability to enhance a mood or a piece of drama on the screen, which heightens the desired effect to the viewer. There are several ways a film producer will approach this in conjunction with the film director. It usually involves engaging an author to compose an entire score for the film, but increasingly this will be interspersed with existing recordings and/or works which are often recognizable by an audience, or which have enhancing lyrics or mood, thus heightening the effect of a scene in the film. A moviegoer, staying in a cinema when a film is over, will see a long list of credits including details of all the works and recordings that were used in the film. Typically such credits show who wrote the work, who performed it, who the publisher is and who owns the rights in the recording. These credits will also state who the music supervisor was and who the score composer was for the film. (The author of this book has often experienced pressure to leave from cinema cleaners, as he stayed right to the end of the credits for a film, often taking notes.)

If a publisher or manager can achieve such a use of one of the artist's existing recordings, this opens up several income streams. In the case of a major movie these are:

1.  A synchronization fee payable from the film company to the author's publisher (or the author if they don't have a publisher) who will in due course credit the author's royalty account according to the publishing agreement.

2.  A master re-use fee payable from the film company to the artist's phonogram producer, who will in due course credit the artist's royalty account according to the artist's recording agreement.

3.  Mechanical royalty income to the author's publisher/author if the song appears on a soundtrack album of the film. Also mechanical income if the film is released as a DVD, download or stream (unless mechanical income is agreed as a buy-out in the synchronization license agreement)

4.  Recording royalty income for the artist and for the artist's phonogram producer if the song appears on a soundtrack album of the film.

5.  Public performance income for the author and the author's publisher in countries where such rights exist, when the film is shown in public cinemas.

So how do artists get their music into a major film? The best method for a manager is to be on good terms with the artist's publisher's film and television music coordinator. This is the publisher's representative who will meet with film music supervisors and suggest suitable works for inclusion in a film. The problem here is that if the author is with one of the major international publishers, the publisher's music coordinator will approach the film's music supervisor, often representing over

a million works, so in that situation the chances of any real representation for the author are very low. It is therefore essential that the manager, as well as the publisher, take a pro-active role in seeking to acquire audiovisual placements. This can also be to the financial advantage of the artist and manager, especially if the manager has insisted on different rates in the publishing and recording agreements when a synchronization or master re-use license is obtained by the artist and manager, as opposed to when it is obtained by the publisher or the phonogram producer, e.g. if the publisher obtains the synchronization, the income split in the agreement might be 65 percent to the artist and 35 percent to the publisher. If the manager and artist obtain the synchronization, the income split may be increased in the artist's favor to perhaps 75 percent to the artist and 25 percent to the publisher. The same increase is often negotiated in recording agreements where the split could be 50 percent to each party on master re-use fees, which could increase to 60 percent to the artist if the artist/manager procures the master re-use.

The first step for the manager or artist is to find all the information on who the independent music supervisors and the major film company music departments representatives are. All the US, Canadian and some European information can be found in a yearly publication called The Film and Television Music Guide, available from The Music Business Registry in Los Angeles (www.musicregistry.com). Another way to keep up-to-date with which films are in production and who are the music supervisors appointed for them is to look at the Hollywood Reporter, a weekly publication carrying all the latest information (www.hollywoodreporter.com). It is also possible to subscribe to the IMDbpro database (http://pro.imdb.com) which carries details of films being made and at what stage they are in the film cycle. IMDbpro usually offers a free two-week trial.

One thing is certain – unless an artist or the artist's manager is standing at the bus stop, they are never going to get on the bus. In other words, unless the music supervisors have an artist's music nothing is ever going to happen. The author of this publication has found that going to Los Angeles and meeting as many people involved with music in films as possible has always paid off, and if an artist or the artist's manager can afford do this, it is strongly recommended. If that is not possible, the next best thing is to alert music supervisors to an artist's music via email. See the tips section at the end of this chapter to find out how to do that.

It might be that a music supervisor has an emergency wherein they have to replace a piece of music quickly because the original piece of music cannot be cleared. If they have recently listened to a piece of submitted music it may just be what they need. Whilst the vast majority of global film releases come from Hollywood, there are of course very active film industries in other countries such as India (Bollywood), France, Germany, Australia, New Zealand and the UK, all of which should be targeted for possible synchronization and master re-use if it is felt that the artist's music might be suitable.

When negotiating synchronization licenses it is important to note that they are often based on a buy-out of mechanical rights when the film is later sold to the public as a DVD, download or stream. If this is not the case the film company will need to acquire mechanical licenses for every work in the film if they want to sell copies of the film to the public. In practice there are often a series of options in a synchronization license so that an additional payment is made from the film production company if the film is to be sold as a DVD, stream or download. There may also be territorial options. For example, the synchronization license may be for US only. If the film company want to extend this to worldwide exploitation a further payment will need to be made. Whilst mechanicals can be included as a buyout in these synchronization agreements public performance is generally not included. So in addition to the synchronization fee an author/publisher can look forward to further income when the film is shown in cinemas and later on television and on-line. The exception to this is the US where no public performance payments are made when a film is shown in a US movie theatre. Public performance payments are made, however, if the film is shown on US television.

## Music in Television

Music in television productions is another important income stream possibility for authors and performers, although the synchronization fees payable are usually much lower than those for films. In many countries there are industry agreements based on blanket licenses which allow TV stations to use music for certain set fees based on the time of day the broadcast takes place, the number of minutes used and other criteria. CMOs will also have agreements in place in regard to their rates for the public performance of the music. In the US, the system used for music in television is much the same as that for films, i.e. a synchronization fee and a master re-use fee

are negotiated in each case. The major difference in the US is that, whereas there is no public performance right for films shown in movie theaters, there is a public performance right when music is used for television. So when the Rembrandts' song 'I'll be There for You' was chosen by American TV network NBC for the signature tune of their highly successful series *Friends*, the synchronization fee would have been insignificant compared to all the public performance income that must have been generated over the years. Again the artist's publisher's film and TV representative will be the one with whom to stay in contact, but the manager should also be independently pro-active wherever possible.

## Music in Advertising

Placing music in advertisements can also be very financially rewarding, as was seen in the example at the beginning of this chapter. Japan is particularly strong in this regard and it is a very good way to break into the Japanese market. Unfortunately, many Japanese corporations are only too aware of this and may ask a new up-and-coming artist to waive the public performance income if his/her song is to be used on national television for a particular product. As can be seen by the earlier example, it can be a difficult decision to make. This is again a function of the artist's publisher's and phonogram producer's film and TV coordinator, but it may be that the artist's publisher and/or phonogram producer has a member of staff who works on advertising uses only.

Most of the major advertising agencies have music departments, and again, unless advertising agencies are aware of an artist's music, they are never going to place it, so the manager should make sure that as many agencies as possible are aware of the artist's material. Artists such as Groove Armada, whose track 'Shakin' that Ass' was used extensively on the Renault Mégane television commercials internationally, have reaped enormous rewards from this use. It was also estimated that Sting's track 'Desert Rose', used in a TV advertisement for Jaguar cars, resulted in Sting selling over 2 million additional albums: so uses in advertising can be very beneficial.

## Music In Video Computer Games

Music in video games is an area that is becoming increasingly significant, not so much for the amount of income that such uses generate, but more for the marketing and career opportunities that they can create. The biggest computer games software companies in the world are Electronic Arts, Activision, THQ and Ubisoft. Electronic Arts, based in Los Angeles, is responsible for such successes as The Sims, FIFA World Cup, Need for Speed, NFL Live, NBA Live, Medal of Honor, Command and Conquer, SimCity and Harry Potter. Sometimes the games are adapted for each country, at least in the packaging, but they can also be adapted so that the entire game is in the local language. Games are also designed for specific platforms such as PC, Mac, Xbox, Playstation Wii, Nintendo, iPhone, iPad, Facebook and Android. Music included in such games has enabled unknown artists to obtain major recording and publishing contracts and to sell thousands, if not tens of thousands of recordings.

The fees payable are usually 'buy-out' fixed synchronization and master re-use fees in the US$3000-US$15,000 range 'per side', with no royalties payable. The term 'per side' means that there would be roughly US$3000-US$15,000 payable to the author(s) either directly or through their publisher, and the same fee payable again to whoever owns the copyright in the sound recording. The author's rights are one side and the recording/performers rights are the other side. A 'most favored nations' arrangement usually operates where the fee payable for the work will be the same as that paid for the use of the recording. Most of the large video computer games companies work on this buy-out only basis, but some smaller companies, and companies which produce music-based video games such as Guitar Hero, will pay an advance against royalties.

Many artists and managers overlook this hugely important use of music, but they do so at their peril. Some in the music industry regard music in video games as the 'new radio', especially as it seems to be getting increasingly difficult to get new music broadcast on traditional radio in many countries, particularly in the US. Many young people are spending countless hours each week playing video games and hear more music on video games and YouTube than they do in any other way.

## Library or Production Music

Library or production music is usually created by specialist library music companies who are often linked to one of the major publishers. An author is asked to write music for specific audiovisual moods or types of use such as 'high drama' or 'tranquility' or 'travel music'. The

library music company will pay for the recording of the work either using session musicians or the artist's own recording facilities and will own the copyright in the recording as well as the work. A film company, television company, advertising agency or website designer can then use this music in return for certain set rates. The music has already been cleared so it is easy for the audiovisual music supervisor to use. Compensation to the author for production music is usually 50 percent of any fees received and 50 percent of any associated public performance income. The rates for library music are sometimes set and administered by a CMO that collects mechanical royalties on behalf of publishers and authors. The license that such a CMO will issue will cover both the clearance in the rights of the recording and clearance in the rights in the work. The rates will vary depending on the number of minutes of music used and the type of use.

## Commissioned Music

When a film company, television company or advertising agency want a completely new piece of music for a particular use, they will often commission an author to write something specifically for a particular use or scene. In the case of a major film or television production, an author might be asked to write the entire film score. There are relatively few top major film score composers, such as Hans Zimmer, Howard Shore and David Arnold, who are regularly employed in this way and it is often difficult for a new composer to break into this field. Film companies tend to play safe and use tried and tested composers who they know will deliver. If this is an area an author wishes to explore, it is important to create a showreel and engage a specialist composer agent such as Gorfaine/Schwarz (www.gsamusic.com), Soundtrack Music Associates (www.soundtrk.com) (both of which are based in Los Angeles) or Air-Edel (www.air-edel.co.uk), who are based in both London and L.A. A full list of composer agents and many other categories of music in the film business is available in the above-mentioned Film and Television Music Guide (www.musicregistry.com).

## Tips for placing music in Film, TV, Advertising and Video Games

In the digital era, the best way to present music for these audio-visual uses has changed considerably. Here are some tips as to the best way to make a successful connection with an artist's music.

1. Make a high quality recording. Never send in a demo. Music supervisors expect a great sounding, well-mixed and well-produced recording.

2. Do your homework. Find out as much information as you can and only submit music that might be suitable for a particular production. If it is a series, check the credits of previous episodes or games and see what music was used.

3. Build personal relationships with a few key supervisors, if possible. Encourage them to send you 'briefs' when they are looking for music for projects. When sending music for a brief, only send relevant music.

4. When submitting music, never use email attachments, as it can clog up music supervisor's email boxes. Use a link to an MP3 via streaming services such as SoundCloud, YouSendIt or DropBox. Always allow the music supervisor to be able to download the track with one click if they want to. Don't use services where they have to give feedback in order to download the track.

5. It is absolutely KEY to include your contact details in the metadata when sending a link to an MP3 file. Metadata is the title of the file. MP3 files on a link or flash drive mean you can control the quality of your data. Be sure your email address is easily visible when the MP3 is imported into iTunes. Include your contact email address after the artist's name in brackets in the metadata.

6. If you control both the recording and publishing, make this very clear. Use the words 'ONE STOP SHOP'. This is very appealing to supervisors, as they will know they can clear the track quickly and probably for a lot less money than a track signed to a large publisher or phonogram producer. Independent artists are very appealing to music supervisors, especially in the USA where it can be expensive to use music from major phonogram producers and publishers. They will often look for an 'indie' replacement for a song they cannot afford from a major publisher or phonogram producer. In a high-end TV show, it is often the case that they will have a budget for one or two 'big' songs which could cost them US$15,000 a side or more. They will then look for additional songs for a fraction of this fee to fill the show.

7. NEVER send music supervisors any music that contains a sample, unless it is totally cleared. This is fundamental. If you send them a track which they

push through with a director and it then transpires that there is an uncleared sample in the track, they will never take your music seriously again.

8. Don't expect instant reactions from supervisors. They are very busy. They are sent hundreds of hours of music every week. Never send links to more than two tracks with any communication.

9. Don't contact music supervisors too often. If you do, they will designate you to their junk filter.

10. As well as sending music to music supervisors directly, it is important to work blogs and radio stations such as the eclectic KCRW in Los Angeles. Music supervisors tend to listen to this station and some are also KCRW presenters.

11. As well as representing the music yourself, there are also numerous agencies that will represent your music for you. As with everything, some agencies are better than others. It is wise only to use one agent. If a supervisor is being presented with music from several different reps at once, it will confuse them and this can be detrimental. Agents' fees of 20-25% of income they source are reasonable. It is important to try an agent out on a few tracks before committing a whole catalog. Also ask the question of how a deal signed to an agent could affect an artist's ability to sign a larger publishing or recording deal in the future. Decent agents are usually based where the media is created in L.A., New York and London, where they live the scene. Try to get a clause in the agent's agreement that if they don't get any placements within six months (for example), you are free to go elsewhere.

12. To get noticed by a music supervisor, make sure your music is available on services such as Spotify and YouTube. Many music supervisors spend a lot of time on YouTube, so if you are able to make a decent video that is always a plus. Don't be afraid to send credible cover versions of well-known songs – music supervisors will often look on Spotify for covers if they can't afford the original.

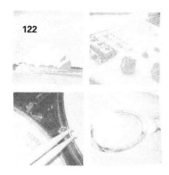

# CHAPTER 14
# LIVE WORK, TOURING AND MERCHANDISING

As we have seen in the section on artist management, live work is becoming more important as an income stream for artists. Whilst the Internet is throwing up some serious challenges to the traditional income streams for sales of recordings, live performances will always be unique and hold a special value for fans. It is impossible to experience the real effect of a live performance unless one is actually present at the time, and whilst there will always be DVDs and audio recordings of an artist's live performances, these will never compare with actually being there. If an artist becomes very popular with just one or two big hit recordings, he/she can continue to earn a good living as a live performer from the public awareness of those hits for the rest of his/her life. For example, The Searchers, who were a very successful British band in the 1960s, still continue to play over 100 shows per year worldwide to an audience now mostly in the 50 – 75 age group. In the early 1960s this audience was in the 10 – 25 year range, but they have stayed loyal to the bands they loved when they were young. The artists and the audience have grown old together, allowing the artists to continue making a good living from live work alone. The most extreme example of this is the Rolling Stones, who still write and record occasionally, but now have little success in terms of record sales. Their touring career, however, is another matter. Their 2005/6 world tour was estimated to have grossed over US$400,000,000 with tickets on sale at up to US$400 each. Mick Jagger, Keith Richard and Charlie Watts, the three original members of the band, are now all in their sixties, and with every world tour the worldwide audience wonders: 'Will this be the last ever Rolling Stones tour?' Many other artists who had hits years ago such as Crowded House, The Zombies, Paul McCartney, Van Halen and The Eagles have dusted off their guitars and gone back out on tour with great success.

No matter what kind of music an artist chooses to play, it is immensely important to work hard on live performances both in terms of improving musical skills and visual

presentation. The live performance has to impress the audience whether by sheer spectacle, musical excitement, musical brilliance, by moving the audience emotionally or by making the audience dance. If an artist can impress an audience and make the live performance experience a good one, the audience will grow and this will enhance all the income streams mentioned elsewhere in this book.

## Getting Started as a Live Artist

The best way to establish oneself as an impressive live performer is to spend a lot of time practicing and rehearsing. It is said that every great musician or singer has to put in their 10,000 hours of practice to become truly proficient. A performer who plays a musical instrument should learn from other players, study videos of favorite players, take lessons, and play and practice as much as possible every day. Even the most accomplished musicians need to practice extensively every day if they are to remain at their best. If the performer is a singer, no matter how good or successful, it is essential to take regular voice lessons.

The other facet of performing live is stage presentation. One very good way to perfect this is to rehearse in a room that has a wall of mirrors, so the artist can see what he/she looks like while performing. In this way it is possible to try out new things and develop moves that add to the overall live experience. If the artist is a band, they can see how the members of the band interact with each other on stage for maximum effect. Clothes, hair and make-up can also be important in creating the right look. Never underestimate the importance of presentation. Whether it be outrageous, cool, sexy or ultra-smart, image can greatly affect how impressive an artist's performance is for an audience. No matter how successful an artist becomes, it is important to always be thinking about new ways to present the music to an audience so that the artist's style constantly evolves.

## Sound and Lighting

Even at the earliest small shows, it is essential to make sure that the PA sound system and the lighting at the venue are adequate. The author of this book has often been at small live performances where there was no direct lighting at all, which is very frustrating for both the artist and the audience. Try to persuade venue owners to invest in some stage lighting, no matter how basic. Alternatively, the artist can invest in two or three lamps on stands which they can take around with them. As soon as possible, try to find someone who is interested in lighting to come to shows and direct the lighting. If the venue already has built-in stage lighting, it will be important to set and focus the lights during the sound-check.

Sound is also of great significance and can make the difference between a successful show and a disastrous one. First of all, it is essential that the band can hear what each member is playing and singing. A good monitor system (sometimes called 'fold-back') is therefore fundamental to the band playing well together. Most small venues use conventional wedge monitors, but increasingly bands are using IEMs (in-ear monitoring). IEM systems are radio wireless systems where each musician/singer has a small beltpack receiver which is connected to in-ear headphones, with the monitor feed coming from a transmitter at the side of the stage. The monitor mix will be a separate mix from a mixer usually positioned at the side of the stage, or it can be from a combined front of house mixing desk and monitor desk. If a radio system is being used for either radio mics or IEM systems or both, it is essential to make sure the venue (or the artist if it their own system) has the appropriate local radio frequency licenses cleared in advance of the show. There is nothing worse than a taxi-driver suddenly speaking through the PA system in the middle of a song because he/she is using the same frequency as the band. (The author of this book has actually experienced that happening.)

The artist should try to find someone who is interested in mixing sound as soon as possible and ask them to mix the band's front of house sound (and monitors if appropriate) at each show. If a sound-check is possible, always make sure that everyone arrives at the venue in good time to have a proper sound-check. At festivals this is often not possible, with only a short 'line-check' being permitted immediately before the artist goes on stage, but at normal indoor venues a sound-check should always be possible.

## How to Get Live Work

In the early stages, an artist should try to get on as many live shows as possible, no matter how small the potential audience. The artist should play live at parties, bars,

malls and clubs – in fact, anywhere there is an audience. When UK band The Police played their first ever show in the US, it was at a small club called The Last Chance in Poughkeepsie in upstate New York. There were only three people in the audience, but they still performed with complete conviction, as if the venue had been full. As most people will know, The Police went on to become one of the most successful bands in the world in the 1980s, and after they split in 1984 their lead singer, Sting, went on to have a hugely successful career as a solo artist. Similarly, U2 played over 250 shows in their first year perfecting their songs and stagecraft. The important thing for artists is to play every show as if their lives depended on it, no matter how big the audience. With regular rehearsals and hard work, an artist's live performance will hopefully become something that audiences will want to see, and then everything can build from there.

As can be seen in the chapter on building a fan base, the fan base is central to building large audiences at live shows. If the plan is to invite publishers and phonogram producers to a show with a view to signing a publishing or recording agreement, it is advisable to pick a really good venue with a good PA and lighting system where the conditions for performing will be at their best. The fans on the database should then be informed that this is a special show and it would be very helpful to the artist if they attended.With any luck, the place will be packed, which always impresses.

To find bookings it will be important to write an interesting and lively biography of no more than two pages. This should include a brief history of the artist's career to date, including any notable achievements in the media, live performances and any other notable events. It should also make clear the type and genre of music played. Don't be shy about using humor in the biography, as it always attracts attention, especially if it is genuinely funny. Good photographs are very important, especially the main photograph on the artist's website landing page. To start with, try a photographer who is one of the artist's fans or a local photographer who is enthusiastic about the project. Most amateur photographers are only too pleased to take photographs of an artist or band at very little or no cost. If that doesn't work, it is well worth investing in a professional photographer who will provide first class photographs.

With a good entertaining biography, photographs and links to the artist's best recordings, the manager or artist will have created the artist's first DPK (Digital Press Kit), also sometimes referred to as an EPK (Electronic Press Kit). An EPK must be downloadable from the artist's website or other online platform by sending the potential recipient the appropriate link. An EPK could feature a video interview with the artist, as well as links to downloadable high resolution photographs, a text biography, live video of the artist performing and any other relevant audio or audiovisual information.

One online service which is designed to assist artists get gigs (shows) is Boston-based Sonicbids (www.sonicbids.com). Sonicbids is a social music marketing platform that connects bands, promoters, consumer brands and music fans. Since its inception in 2001, it claims to have connected more than 350,000 bands with 26,000 promoters in over 100 countries. Sonicbids will get an artist's EPK to promoters and brands. There is a free two-week trial and then there is a subscription of about $7 per month.

However an artist achieves a booking for a live performance, when the booking is confirmed, it is always best to get the agreement in writing and signed by the promoter. As soon as fees start to grow, it is also a good idea to insist on a non-returnable deposit of normally 50% of the agreed fee payable in advance. The artist or artist manager should make sure a link to their EPK is sent to local radio and TV stations, as well as newspapers and magazines in the area of each live performance. The artist or manager should follow up by telephoning and trying to persuade the media to do a phone interview or an in-studio interview or performance, in order to boost ticket sales for the show. As an artist becomes more successful, a publicist could be engaged to handle this media interaction on behalf of the artist, but in the early stages either the manager or artist or both will have to do it themselves.

## Street Performances and Busking

Some artists start off by playing on the street, which can be an excellent way of perfecting the art of playing live. It also gives very direct contact with an audience and the artist will be able to see what causes a member of the public to stop and listen, as opposed to just walking by. Of course the income is usually a hat or a

guitar case into which those listening can throw coins or even notes if they are particularly impressed. This will give an artist great insight into what works and what doesn't. Feedback is immediate. If people like it, they donate, if they don't like it, they don't donate. It also should give an artist confidence in their ability to perform. If they can have the confidence to play on the street, they can have the confidence to play anywhere. For best results, it is better to pick a spot where audiences can gather without causing a traffic jam. In many cities like London there are specific sites in underground train stations and other places that the city authorities designate as places that performers can play. It is usually necessary to obtain a license in order to perform in one of these designated places. One of the best attended festivals for buskers is the Buskers' Festival, which takes place in Ferrara in Italy every August. In certain circumstances, the income that can be received from busking can be substantial. The following is a first-person account of such a case:

> Let me give an example of a street performer I saw in Florence, Italy. This performer had a small portable PA, a mic stand and mic and a pedal board for guitar effects. He played guitar and sang completely live. In other words there were no backing tracks or drum loops. He was very good and played familiar songs like Pink Floyd's 'Wish You Were Here' and U2's 'Where the Streets have no Name'. He also played a few of his own songs that he had written. I was impressed, so I threw a few euros into his guitar case.

> It was then that I noticed a stack of his CDs with a notice saying 'serve yourself – €10 each.' I listened for a while and decided that I was sufficiently impressed to buy one of the CDs. I put €10 into the guitar case and took a CD. Over the next 15 minutes I counted 10 other people buy his CD and several others threw money into his guitar case as I had originally done. The CD was a blank recordable CDR with nothing printed on the CD itself and a simple black and white one page paper insert with a picture of the artist in a very basic standard plastic jewel case. Now let's do the math on this. The CDs could have cost no more than €1 to manufacture. If he sold 10 in 15 minutes that would be 40 in one hour. If he makes €9 on each one that's €360 in one hour. Let's suppose he busks for two hours every

afternoon and two hours every evening, 6 days per week. He takes
4 weeks holiday each year so he works for 48 weeks per year. That's
€360 X 4 hours X 6 days X 48 weeks. That totals €414,720 per year
before tax which equates to around US$545,000. That's over twice
what the British Prime Minister earns. OK, maybe that's a little
extreme. Maybe in the following hour he didn't sell that many. Even if
it was only 25% of the figures I have given, he would still earn
US$136,350, which isn't a bad annual income for a young musician.
Of course, as we have seen in the copyright chapter, he would have
to pay mechanical royalties to Pink Floyd, U2 and the other authors
whose songs he had covered on the CD, but I'm sure the donations
he received would more than cover that cost. I have to emphasize
that this guy was very, very good and he performed very well. How to
make a living from music?

## The Next Stage

Let us now consider the situation where an artist is attracting good-sized audiences
at live shows and things are building. As has been touched on in the section on artist
management, this is the time the artist should consider finding a manager if this has
not already been done.

## Booking Agents

The manager will then need to find a booking agent, unless they feel capable of
taking on this role themselves. A booking agent will be the interface between the
manager/artist and promoters who are interested in presenting live shows. A good
booking agent who is prepared to work hard to get an artist live work can be a very
important part of the team. Interestingly, finding the right booking agent is one of the
most difficult things for a manager. Booking agents tend to be very particular about
whom they represent and they will want to be convinced that it will be worth their
while. A booking agent will typically take 10 percent of the gross fee negotiated for
an artist to play a particular date. It is often the case that initially the booking agent
may wish to take 15 percent of the fee up to a certain level. When that level is
reached, the commission will reduce to 10 percent. In return for the commission

agreed, the booking agent will find live opportunities, negotiate fees and issue contracts on behalf of the artist. The fee for a performance could be a straight guaranteed fee or it could be a guaranteed fee against a percentage of box office ticket sales. For example, the fee might be US$1000 guaranteed or 70 percent of the gross ticket sales (less any sales tax or VAT), whichever is the greater. If the after tax gross ticket sales were US$1400, the artist would receive the US$1000 guarantee only, as 70 percent of US$1400 is US$980, which is less than the US$1000 guarantee. On the other hand, if the gross ticket sales were US$3000, the artist would receive a fee of US$2100, as 70 percent of US$3000 is US$2100, which is higher than the US$1000 guarantee. The difference between the guarantee and the percentage is often referred to as the 'overage'. In this example the overage was US$1100.

It is often the case that there will be different booking agents in different territories, but some of the larger booking agencies, such as William Morris, CAA or The Agency can operate on a worldwide basis. Sometimes an artist will have one booking agent in Europe and another in the US. The rest of the world might then be divided between these two agents, depending on who has the best contacts. The US agent may also want to book the other American territories including Canada, Mexico and Latin America, for example, whereas the European agent may have better contacts in Australia and Japan.

As the music industry has evolved, it is unusual for there to be a booking agency agreement with the artist. In some countries it is actually illegal. This means that the booking agent has to work hard to retain successful artists, as they are always free to move on to another agent if they wish.

360 degree recording agreements typically include that a percentage of the gross income on live work (usually 10%) goes to the phonogram producer. Some managers have therefore been insisting that booking agents take a 9% commission rather than the normal 10% in situations where the phonogram producer is taking 10% of the gross, i.e. the booking agent is obliged to take 10% of 90%, which equates to 9% of the gross.

## Tour Managers

As audiences increase in size, the manager will need to engage a tour manager unless wishing to take this role on him/herself. A tour manager is responsible for all the day-to-day running of a tour, including the coordination of travel and hotel arrangements, keeping good financial records of expenditure, looking after the artist and interfacing with promoters at the shows. It is essential that good financial records be maintained on tours, and a good tour manager will have a spreadsheet system in place which can be emailed back to the manager on a daily basis. This computer spreadsheet will show all income received on the road, together with all expenditure and the balance of cash in hand. This should be backed up by a tour envelope system as shown on page 138.

### Building a Touring Team

In addition to the tour manager, the manager may need to engage additional road crew as the artist becomes more popular and is able to do bigger shows. This could include:

1. A front of house sound engineer who is usually positioned at the back of the venue (the end opposite to that of the stage) and who mixes the sound that the audience will hear.

2. A monitor engineer who is usually positioned at the side of the stage and who will mix the sound on stage so that the performers can hear each other and play in time and in tune with each other.

3. A lighting engineer who will set the lights and direct the stage lighting and visual special effects.

4. On-stage roadies who supervise and set up the on-stage equipment.

5. Drivers for buses and/or trucks for the equipment.

6. A production manager who supervises all aspects of the on-stage equipment, the PA and lighting systems, especially if they are being transported with the artist from show to show.

7. A travel agent

8 A visa/work permit agent

9. A freight/shipping agent

10. A wardrobe assistant

11. A choreographer

(See Team Chart on page 24.)

## Visas and Work Permits

For any live work outside of the artist's country of residence, a visa or work permit is often required. The process involved in obtaining these can take up to four months in some cases, so it is essential for the manager or artist to deal with this issue as soon as foreign dates are confirmed. There have been numerous foreign tours that have been cancelled due to insufficient paperwork or visa denial, which is a disaster for the artist and very embarrassing for the manager. Visas and work permits need to be a top priority for any good manager and the progress of these documents needs to be monitored on a daily basis. If the artist or any member of a band has a criminal record for drug possession or anything else, this can be a major problem in securing visas and work permits, so before engaging a new band member it is worth checking these issues. Obtaining visas to perform in the US is becoming increasingly difficult. There are also substantial government fees attached to a successful US work visa. A scheme also exists that, for an extra fee, an artist's visa can be fast-tracked through the system, but even this process can take up to two months to complete. If the manager feels uncomfortable about interfacing with consulates and embassies for such documentation, there are several specialist visa agencies that can be used to obtain visas on behalf of artists. US visa agencies specializing in US work visas include EVC-Entertainment Visa Consultants (www.entertainmentvisaconsultants.com) and Traffic Control Group (www.tcgworld.com). There is also a separately owned Traffic Control agency in London, specializing in European work visas and embassy interface for UK artists (www.trafficcontrolgroup.com).

These are just three examples, but an online search will throw up several examples of other such agencies based all around the world. It should be noted that no visas or work permits are required if the artist is resident in the EU and wishes to perform in another EU member country.

## Freight Agents, Shipping and Carnets

If equipment is being shipped from one country to another, it is often the case that temporary import documentation is required, which is known as a 'carnet'. If an artist is based within the EU and wishes to perform in another EU member country, carnets are not required. If, however, the artist is based in Italy and wishes to perform in Norway (which is not a member of the EU), then a carnet would be required. Similarly, if the artist is based outside the US and wishes to perform in the US, a 'carnet' is required listing every piece of equipment that is being temporarily imported, together with serial numbers and other details.

Specialist freight agents such as Rock-It Cargo (www.rock-itcargo.com) or Sound Moves (www.soundmoves.com) will, for a fee, do all the necessary paperwork, including obtaining the correct carnets and customs clearances and shipping the artist's equipment to specific destinations worldwide. Rock-It Cargo have offices in the UK, Germany, US, Japan, China and South Africa and are the biggest freight operators in the music sector. Other music freighting companies include Soundmoves (based in the UK and the US with offices in France, Belgium and Japan) and Showfreight (based in Australia http://www.showgroup.com.au). If equipment is moved by road, it should be noted that some countries have restrictions on vehicles over a certain weight travelling on Sundays and national holidays. A special permit can usually be obtained if it is essential to transport the artist's equipment in a large vehicle on these days, but this needs to be organized well in advance.

## Travel and Hotel Arrangements

The manager will also need to coordinate travel and hotel arrangements, usually with a travel agent and the tour manager. Sometimes the manager will delegate everything to the tour manager, but the manager should still monitor the costs and logistics of all the arrangements. It is always a good idea to start early when leaving for the next show in the next town or city, to allow for unexpected factors such as a vehicle breakdown, heavy traffic or bad weather. If there are two hours in hand, this can make the difference between being able to perform or not, or maybe having to do the show without a sound check (which is never a good idea).

Similarly, it is always better to take earlier flights so that if by chance one flight is cancelled there is still a chance to catch a later flight and reach the destination in time. Before flying, it is important for the tour manager to check well in advance the check-in luggage allowances and the cost of any excess baggage. It may be more

economical to ship any excess baggage or equipment separately. Each member travelling should be informed of luggage weight and size restrictions so they can pack accordingly. The tour manager should always go through airport security and passport control last, so as to be able to manage any problems that a member of the band or crew has ahead of him/her.

If the artist or manager are booking hotels themselves, there are some excellent aggregator hotel booking sites such as 'Trivago' and 'Trip Advisor' which will provide all the hotel options in a particular city and will also advise which booking operator has the best rate for a given hotel on a certain date. In the US the Hotel Planner site specializes in special low rates for group bookings and invites hotels to bid for the booking after the hotel requirements have been submitted.

One form of transport in the early stages is what is known as a splitter bus. This is a medium-sized bus that has seating for the artist's entourage at the front and a separate area at the back for the artist's stage equipment. Another way of doing this is to use a seated bus that tows a trailer containing the artist's stage equipment. When the artist becomes better known, it may be that the use of a full-sized tour bus becomes feasible. These are custom-made buses which have one or two lounges, onboard toilet facilities, kitchen facilities and on-board sleeping facilities. The artist's entourage can sleep through the night whilst the bus is travelling from one city to the next, which is convenient and can save hotel costs. It is also possible in some cases for these luxury buses also to tow trailers containing the artist's stage equipment. It may be the case that the artist needs to do radio and television promotions on show days. Unless he/she is some kind of super-being it is best to pace this as carefully as possible. If an artist has not had enough sleep and does too much promotion, the show that night could be adversely affected. It is not a good idea either for an artist to have to sing early in the morning on radio or television. The human voice does not warm up until around midday. Singing live on radio or TV before that time can do the artist more harm than good.

## Insurance and Force Majeure

The manager will need to make sure that adequate insurance has been taken out prior to the start of every tour or live date. The artist's equipment should be insured on a permanent basis when located at the home base and also against damage or loss during touring periods. The manager or tour manager will need to inform the insurance agent every time the equipment is taken outside the artist's home country, so that adequate insurance is in place.

Travel insurance (including emergency medical expenses and personal luggage) should be in effect for any overseas travel, and the manager should establish who will be provided with such cover and who should arrange their own. An increasing number of countries require proof of such insurance when applying for visas. The artist should also hold Public Liability Insurance in each territory being toured by the artist. This public liability insurance has different titles in different countries and is often referred to as 'Employer's Liability' or 'Worker's Compensation'. In most countries, public liability insurance is a legal requirement and protects the artist if a band/crew member is injured and the artist is legally liable for such injury. Some countries have special insurance and employment requirements which must be checked prior to a tour commencing, e.g. to work in the US a Worker's Compensation certificate is necessary for any US workers employed on the tour. Public liability or General Liability usually provides cover for up to US$5,000,000 against damages if a member of the audience should be injured or even die at a concert and the artist is brought into any legal action – regardless of whether or not it is eventually found to be the artist's fault. Promoters and venues will also have their own Public Liability Insurance, but this will not cover the artist's Public Liability insurance risks. Although the amount insured is high, the cost of the insurance is a tiny fraction of the risk cover.

Cancellation insurance is also possible and advisable on tours and live work, although it is not a legal requirement. The cost is a small percentage (usually about 2% of the fee for each show) which is payable to the insurer. With cancellation insurance, if any essential member of the artist's entourage falls ill and is unable to perform, or if the show has to be cancelled or rescheduled for many reasons outside the control of the artist and the manager (such as transport failure/delay and adverse weather), the insurer will compensate the artist for the full fee or show costs, whichever is higher, even though the concert did not take place. This cancellation insurance can also cover the eventuality of a member of the artist's family falling seriously ill, resulting in the artist having to return home and thus causing the show or shows to be

cancelled. In order to claim from the insurer, it is vital for the tour manager to get a medical certificate if the artist or a close family member falls ill which results in a cancellation.

There are certain situations, however, that cannot be insured, including visa failure, lack of ticket sales resulting in cancellation, any financial cause or breach of contract. If a promoter cancels a show for commercial reasons such as lack of ticket sales, it would be down to the manager and the booking agent to insist that the promoter still pays the full fee for the show. If this payment is not forthcoming, it may be necessary to take legal action against the promoter in question. It is important to make sure that the promoter has signed the show agreement and paid the appropriate deposit as soon as possible after the date has been confirmed. It is quite usual for the promoter to have to pay the deposit (perhaps 50% of the contracted fee) some months prior to the show date and the balance of the contracted fee a few weeks prior to the show date, particularly for international festivals. Cancellation insurance can also be extended to insure the booking agent's commission and loss of income from merchandising sales if a date is cancelled. If the booking agent's commission is insured, there should be an arrangement made with the booking agent that they will pay 10% (or the appropriate percentage) of the cancellation insurance costs. That way, if a date is cancelled due to reasons beyond the control of the artist, both the artist and the booking agent will still receive their full fees.

Another key factor here is the so-called 'force majeure' clause in the show agreement. Force majeure means 'superior force' and defines under what circumstances the promoter would be excused from paying the artist. This might include such reasons as 'Acts of God' (such as hurricane, flooding, earthquake, volcanic eruption etc.). The artist should always try to get the following wording at the end of the force majeure clause: 'Notwithstanding the above if the artist is ready and willing to perform, the promoter shall pay to the artist the full contracted fee.' Sometimes if a Force Majeure situation arises resulting in cancellation, the outcome may be that the promoter and artist agree that the date will be postponed to a later date, and cancellation insurance can often cover and pay the rescheduling costs. There are several specialist music business insurance agents such as Robertson Taylor Insurance Brokers who have offices in Los Angeles, Las Vegas, Nashville, New York and London (www.robertson-taylor.co.uk), and AON who have offices in most countries (www.rewritinginsurance.aon.co.uk/entertainment-and-media-insurance.aspx).

## Security

In cases where an artist has a fanatical following, such as is the case with some young boy bands who attract large female audiences, security could be a major issue. This could also be the case if the artist sings songs with a strong religious or political message. It is the manager's job to ensure that the artist and the artist's possessions are secure at all times and special arrangements will need to be made, particularly in getting to and from the venue or to and from TV and radio stations. The venues themselves can often assist with this, but it may be necessary to employ a special security person who accompanies the artist at all times. If there is political unrest or some other security risk, it may be that further special security measures are required. If there are a large number of fans at the stage door, the festival entrance or the artist's hotel, it may be necessary to arrange that the artist enters the venue or the hotel using an unusual entrance.

Stage security may also be necessary, with a security person positioned at each side of the stage to protect the artist if any members of the audience take it on themselves to try and get on stage during the performance. Similarly, dressing room security is important, especially if valuable equipment or personal possessions are left there. This could be just a matter of the tour manager making sure that each dressing room is lockable and that he has the appropriate keys or that a dedicated security person is positioned to guard the dressing rooms. In extreme cases, the artist could come off stage, jump straight into a car and be away from the venue before the audience has stopped applauding so as to avoid any problems. The Beatle Ringo Starr, who still tours from time to time, continues to follow this procedure which The Beatles perfected in the 1960s. He and his band will come off stage, get straight into a waiting limousine, drive to the airport (often accompanied by police outriders), and board a private jet bound for the next city. They then check into a hotel in the next city that same night. That's as expensive as it gets.

## Accounting

One of the primary duties of a manager is to ensure that the artist gets paid properly and that expenditure is kept under control. This is largely the responsibility of the tour manager on the road, but for important tours, a specialist tour accountant may

be engaged who will be on the road with the artist and who will make sure that the correct amounts are being paid by the promoter for each show and that all outgoings are kept within budget. It is particularly important that the manager, tour manager or tour accountant monitors shows where a percentage of the gross ticket sales are a factor in the fee payable. These deals can often be quite complex and will include evidence and verification of all the promoter's expenditure, including advertising, staff costs, public performance fees, venue hire etc.

As has been mentioned earlier, the most important issue with all tours, no matter how small or large they are, is to keep accurate financial records on a daily basis, preferably on a computer spreadsheet. This will make for efficient accounting at the end of the tour, which is in everyone's interest. A truly professional tour manager or tour accountant will email a spreadsheet of daily expenditure every day to the manager, showing all expenditure and income together with the balance of cash in hand at the end of each tour day. This would also be accompanied by a separate spreadsheet analyzing daily merchandise sales. Many tour managers use a tour envelope system wherein all expenditure receipts and income are recorded on the face of the envelope and the receipts are placed inside the envelope. See an example of such an envelope on page 138.

## Per Diems

When an artist is touring, it is industry practice to pay each member of the band and the crew a 'pd' (*per diem*, which is Latin for 'per day'). This will be a daily cash allowance for food and other daily expenses which a member of the touring party will need when on tour. This pd allowance is payable in addition to the agreed daily or weekly fee for any member of the band or road crew. The pd rate will vary depending on which country is being toured, e.g. the pd rate in Japan will be considerably higher than the rate for Europe or USA, as the cost of food and other daily costs tends to be much higher in countries like Japan. It is important that the tour manager gets a signed receipt or gets a signature on the touring envelope every time pds are paid out. Sometimes pds are paid out every two or three days, whilst other tour managers will pay all the pds in cash at the beginning of the tour. The danger with that approach is that some members of the band or crew may overspend, running out of money halfway through the tour, which will require them to seek a loan.

## Cash Envelope

DATE: _____

VENUE: _____

| FLOAT IN: | From where: | |
|---|---|---|

| FLOAT OUT: | To where: | |
|---|---|---|

| Description | Amount | Signature |
|---|---|---|
| | | |
| | | |
| | | |
| | | |
| | | |
| | | |
| | | |
| | | |
| | | |
| | | |
| | | |
| | | |
| | | |
| | | |
| | | |
| | | |
| | | |
| | | |
| **TOTAL** | | |

## Festivals and Conferences

One of the best routes to international recognition is to play music festivals. Some festivals stick rigidly to one specific musical genre, such as heavy metal (e.g. Sonisphere in France and Italy), reggae (e.g. Reggae Sumfest in Montego Bay, Jamaica), 80s pop (e.g. Rewind in the UK and Retrolicious in Singapore), folk (e.g.

The Newport Folk Festival in the USA) or electronic music (e.g. Ultra in Miami, Fusion in Germany or Electro Beach in Puerta Vallarta, Mexico). Others pride themselves in being as eclectic as possible, booking a wide range of artists and bands from different musical genres. Both types of festival are important for gaining international recognition and profile. One of the most eclectic and successful festivals is the Glastonbury Festival in England, which takes place in June once every two years. The capacity of the festival is 177,000, making it the largest greenfield music and performing arts festival in the world. The festival is best known for its contemporary music, but also features dance, comedy, theatre, circus, cabaret and many other arts. Typically the Glastonbury festival features around 400 different live performances on over 80 stages. The tickets go on sale about nine months prior to the festival happening and such is the demand that they all sell on the first day regardless of who is performing. Glastonbury is a trusted brand and those that are lucky enough to purchase tickets know they will get an amazing three-day musical experience, even if they have no idea who will be appearing when they purchase the tickets. Glastonbury mixes artists as diverse as U2, JayZ, Tony Bennett, Fatboy Slim, Lee Scratch Perry, David Guetta, The Rolling Stones, Nile Rogers, Mumford & Sons, BB King and Paul Simon, and also features a wide range of music from developing countries, thus creating a very successful festival with no musical barriers or limits.

One opportunity for artists from developing countries to perform in other countries is to try to get a booking at one of the WOMAD festivals. The World of Music Arts and Dance (WOMAD) organization was established by Peter Gabriel in 1980. Gabriel, who had a very successful career as lead singer of Genesis and later in his own right as a solo artist, had a particular interest in African music and wanted to set up an organization which would promote music from all over the world. Together with Thomas Brooman and Bob Hooten, Peter presented the first WOMAD festival in England in 1982. Since then, 160 WOMAD festivals have been organized in 27 countries. There are currently about 10 WOMAD festivals each year worldwide. The festivals feature live performances by artists from all over the world, workshops for musical instrument players and singers as well as dancers. Artists wishing to be considered for a booking at one of the WOMAD festivals should send an email with a link to the artist's music (e.g. on SoundCloud or YouTube) to artist.demos@womad.org, including a link to the artist's website or social media page. WOMAD will need to easily find a one-page biography, information about how many band members there are, where the band or artist have played previously and of course the artist or manager's contact details. Go to www.womad.org for more information.

Another very useful organization for artists from all over the world is WOMEX. Berlin-based WOMEX (World Music Expo) organizes showcase and networking events in several international cities each year. WOMEX book most of their showcase artists via SonicBids, so it's important to have a presence there. Their events are frequented by many booking agents, record labels, music journalists and media and technology representatives. WOMEX events are a mixture of a trade fair, a conference, a networking opportunity and a venue for artist showcases. Artists will have to pay their own expenses, but it may be possible to get help with these from the artist's government or national arts organization. WOMEX also publish a top five music chart for world music every month, compiled by world music radio programmers in 25 European countries. Go to http://bit.ly/XJ8xYR for a PDF of the top 150 World Music tracks as compiled by Johannes Theurer on behalf of the World Music Workshop of the European Broadcasting Union (EBU). In 2012, for example, the No. 1 world music album in this chart was 'Bouger Le Monde' by Staff Benda Bilili from the Democratic Republic of the Congo on the Brussels-based Crammed record label (http://www.YouTube.com/watch?v=rt-G_6Ba_rk). Go to www.womex.com for more information on WOMEX and/or to subscribe to their free e-newsletter.

Managers may benefit from attending WOMEX not just for networking, but also to find opportunities for their artists, even if their artists are not performing. They may also consider attending the two big world conferences: Midem in the South of France, which takes place every January, and SXSW (South by SouthWest) which takes place in Austin, Texas every March.

There are some artist showcases at Midem, but it is mainly a music business conference with an emphasis on publishing and recording, where managers, publishers and phonogram producers can meet licensees and potential new licensees. It has excellent and informative conference panels and presentations on every aspect of the music business, particularly digital services and developments. Media futurist Gerd Leonard usually gives a very interesting Midem presentation on the future of music, which he immediately puts up online via his website. Midem themselves also make videos of the panel discussions available on YouTube, so if an

artist or manager doesn't have the money to attend Midem they can at least view these invaluable presentations online at no cost. The cost of attending Midem varies depending on the category of application and when the booking is made, but it can be anything from $350 to $1000. There are a range of 'early bird' rates if a booking is made some months beforehand. Various music trade bodies, such as the various Music Managers Forums around the world, and Independent Record Company organizations who are members of umbrella organization IMPALA can often offer rates far lower than advertised on the conference sites. It may be worth joining one of the trade bodies offering a discount, as the joining fee may be less than the conference discount on offer. If attending, it is best to purchase tickets as early as possible, not only to save money, but also so that the list of participants can be accessed online and appointments can be made well in advance, especially if the aim is to license recordings or to find sub-publishers. Key participants' diaries fill up very quickly, so make sure appointments are booked in November if possible. The author of this book has been known to take over 100 meetings at Midem over a five-day period. One of those meetings resulted in the Japanese synchronization license described on page 112.

SXSW in Austin is far more geared to artist showcases. Again, it is essential to plan any participation as early as possible, particularly if participating in a showcase. If based outside the US, the work visa process for the US can take up to five months to complete. Don't even think about performing without a visa, as if this is discovered by the US immigration authorities it may be that the artist can never perform in the US again. The SXSW website (www.SXSW.com) offers some advice on US work visas. Be very careful to get this right. There have been some horror stories of bands investing thousands of dollars in air fares and accommodation, only to find that their visas have not come through in time and their trip and show had to be cancelled. Managers attending SXSW would not need a work visa but would need to travel under the US Visa Waiver Program. It will be necessary to apply for an ESTA (Electronic System for Travel Authorization) at https://esta.cbp.dhs.gov. An ESTA can be applied for online for a small fee of around $15 but must be obtained in advance of travel. SXSW Music Badges for the conference cost anything from $400 to $1000, depending on the type of pass and how early it is booked. Another conference to consider is the CMJ conference in New York, which takes place every October (www.cmj.com).

If the artist's music is in any of the electronic/dance genres, then the best conference to attend is the Amsterdam Dance Event, which again takes place in October each year. The ADE features over 300 events in 75 venues, including over 500 DJ sets, and attracts up to 200,000 people (http://www.amsterdam-dance-event.nl). The other big dance event is the Winter Music Conference which takes place in Miami every March (http://wintermusicconference.com). Many managers, artists, licensors, licensees and other music industry people attend both SXSW and the Winter Music Conference, as they follow on from each other and are relatively close geographically.

The ILMC (International Live Music Conference), which takes place in London in March, is also worth considering. It attracts the biggest promoters, booking agents, ticketing services and venue owners in the world and often sells out in advance (http://www.ilmc.com).

The United Nations Scientific and Cultural Organization (UNESCO) can also provide a wealth of information on music festivals around the world and other music information (www.unesco.org/music). For information on booking agents, promoters, concert venues and festivals, Pollstar publishes several directories which have comprehensive information (www.pollstar.com/about_pollstar.pl?page=Directories).

# CHAPTER 15
## MERCHANDISING

Merchandising can provide an immensely important income stream for an artist, if handled correctly. An astute manager will spend time researching the kind of merchandise that fans of an artist will want to buy. This can include T-shirts, sweatshirts, hoodies, CDs, DVDs, memory sticks, hats, mouse mats, jewelry, bumper stickers, tour books, mugs, posters, framed signed photographs, canvas prints, drumskins, specially numbered limited editions etc. It is always a good idea to have at least one high-priced piece of premium product for über-fans. If the artist is playing smaller venues, with perhaps up to a 700 capacity, it is important for the artist to sign CDs, DVDs or photographs in advance and these can be sold at a premium. Personally signed CDs and DVDs are always in demand by fans and are highly valued. A developing band should always come out to meet fans by the merchandising stand as soon as they have come off stage, in order to sign merchandising items and even sell merchandising themselves. Fans expect direct contact with the artist much more in the modern era and will buy items if they can get them personally signed. The artist should also engage in conversations with fans and be prepared to have their photograph taken with fans if requested. If a fan has a good direct-to-artist experience, they are likely to become a fan for life. It is essential to have the merchandising stand in a well-lit area so the merchandise can be clearly seen. This will also allow the artist to request that any fan photos be without flash, as there should be adequate light for a photo without flash. It's okay to have a few photos taken with flash but anything more than that will often end up with the artist suffering a severe headache or even migraine, such is the power and intensity of flash on the latest digital cameras. Carrying spot-lamps is a very good idea so that the merchandising stand looks professionally lit. It is also very important to position the merchandising stand where there is the maximum amount of audience traffic. This is usually in the foyer near the entrance, or even in the venue itself near the

entrance point to the main venue space. If the merchandising stand is poorly lit or in a position around a corner where nobody sees it, merchandising sales will be low.

It is a good idea for the manager or tour manager to present and talk about the key pieces of merchandising on stage just prior to the band being announced. This can double merchandising sales. It is important that the merchandise stand or table is set up and fully operational prior to doors opening at the beginning of the evening. It's also very important that the person selling and in charge of the merchandising stand has good knowledge of the artist's career and the merchandise on offer. A trusted fan is ideal, but in any case the person needs to be well briefed prior to engaging with the audience. If this person is supplied by the venue and is therefore different every night, the artist or manager should have a printed two-page description of the band's history and the merchandising on offer that the sales person can read and refer to. It is also a good idea to have information about each piece of merchandise clearly visible for members of the audience to see, together with the price of each item. One of the artists represented by the author played a concert in Perth, Australia to 700 people. Two of the CDs available were pre-signed, there was a good all-round level of stock, a piece-by-piece presentation of key pieces of merchandising on stage prior to the artist performing, and the artist came out to meet the audience after the show. Sales of merchandise were just under A$10,000 which equated to over A$14 per person, which is a very good per-head figure.

If the artist becomes very popular and regularly sells more than 700 tickets for a show, it may be impractical to come out and meet the audience after the show as there simply won't be time to meet all those that would like to meet the artist. If members of the audience have waited for some time after the show and are then unable to meet the artist, it can be counterproductive and they may lose interest in the artist altogether. In this case it may be better for the artist not to come out at all. However, if the artist is a developing artist or a 'heritage' artist who is still able to tour successfully but who had hits years ago, merchandising sales and direct after-show contact with the audience are paramount. An extreme case of this was the US singer/songwriter and guitarist Richie Havens, who was very popular in the late 1960s, particularly as a result of his appearances at the Woodstock and Isle of Wight festivals. He would sit down at a table and talk and sign items for as many members of the audience as possible after a show and was known to do this in some venues

until 3.00 am, if the venue allowed it. (Sadly, Richie Havens passed away in April 2013 but his legacy lives on.) On a personal health note, it is best for an artist to wash their hands thoroughly after a meet-and-greet session. It will be inevitable that some members of the audience will have a cold or even the flu. If the artist contracts a bad cold or flu as a result, and half the tour is subsequently cancelled, that will not be a good outcome.

On a tour, it is important to control the merchandise stock carefully. If the right stock is not at the venue, income will obviously suffer. There is nothing worse than having an audience clamoring to buy merchandise and there being very little to sell. If an artist becomes more popular, selling perhaps over 1000 tickets per show, it is worth considering hiring specialist merchandisers. These are companies who can organize everything including design, manufacture and stock control and who will also transport and sell the merchandise at each venue. For this service they will take a percentage of sales. They may also be prepared to pay an advance to the artist prior to the tour, which can help the tour's cash flow. At some venues, particularly larger ones, the venue itself will also require a percentage on sales which can be anything from two T-shirts, 5% or as much as 30%. This may be negotiable but sometimes it will be a case of 'take it or leave it'. It is important that the manager works closely with the merchandiser, the promoter, the booking agent and the venue to ensure that the pricing structure of the merchandise is such that it is affordable for the consumer yet still allows a reasonable margin for the artist. It is important for the artist manager to instruct the booking agent to negotiate the venue's merchandising percentage at the time of the booking. There are many specialist merchandising companies. These are examples of some of the world's largest: Backstreet International Merchandise (based in New York and London, www.bsimerch.com), Bravado (based in Stockholm, London, New York, Los Angeles and San Francisco, www.bravado.com), Live Nation Merchandising (worldwide, www.lnmlicensing.com), Cinderblock (based in Oakland, California, www.cinderblock.com), TSP Merchandise (based in Australia, www.tsprint.com.au) and Gene Pelc (based in Japan, http://pelc-ent.com). With the major phonogram producers increasingly insisting on 360 degree agreements which often include a percentage of an artist's merchandising income, Sony and Warners have created their own merchandising divisions. Some of these companies, such as Bravado, are more geared to touring merchandise, whereas others such as Backstreet are more geared towards e-commerce online merchandising. Two other pioneering services to consider are Sandbag (www.sandbagheadquarters.com) and Topspin (www.topspinmedia.com), both of which offer complete merchandising, ticketing and fan engagement solutions. Sandbag won a Grammy Award for their pioneering and revolutionary campaign for the Radiohead album 'In Rainbows' wherein fans were asked to pay whatever they thought was reasonable to download the album.

An online merchandiser, such as CD Baby, Backstreet, Sandbag or Topspin, will also distribute CDs and DVDs for an artist via their own online web-store or via a web-store created especially for the artist. A typical arrangement for this service is for the online web-store provider to take 20-30 percent of all sales, depending on the volume shipped. This assumes the artist provides the online merchandiser with manufactured finished product. If the merchandiser manufactures the merchandise and/or CDs at its own cost, the percentage taken can increase to 60 – 70 percent, leaving the artist with a net 30 – 40 percent of sales. The processing of physical merchandising and recorded product sales online, including processing the credit card payments and shipping the product, is sometimes referred to as 'fulfillment'. Credit card, debit card or PayPal charges as well as postage and packing charges are usually added to the price of the merchandise and paid by the purchaser as an extra charge.

Another issue in regard to merchandising is that of 'bootlegging', i.e. rogue sellers of illegal merchandise selling to fans outside the venue. This is particularly common outside large venues for very popular artists. Many countries have laws which allow for the prosecution of such illegal sellers, but it is essential for the artist to have registered trademarks for his/her name and artwork in that country. There was a case in Aylesbury in the UK where the trading standards officers wanted to prosecute sellers of illegal merchandise outside a very large local venue, the Milton Keynes Bowl. The concert was being given by a very successful US band. Unfortunately, the band did not have a valid trademark registration in the UK for their name and the band's artwork, so Trading Standards officers were unable to prosecute the bootleggers. There are specialist trademark lawyers and agents who can assist in securing national and international trademark registration for artists. (See the section on trademarks on page 40.)

# CHAPTER 16
# SPONSORSHIP AND BRANDING

Another income stream that is becoming increasingly important is that of sponsorship and tie-ins with established brands who want to increase sales by associating themselves with music and artists. As we move further into the digital revolution, more and more brands are discovering the importance of associating themselves with music, artists and digital services. Not surprisingly, brands are usually more interested in high-profile established artists and bands rather than artists who are trying to establish themselves, so the more successful an artist or band becomes, the more interested brands will be. Many brands, such as Apple, Coca Cola, Pepsi, Starbucks, Bacardi, Diesel, Budweiser and Red Bull have long been connected with music because they see it as a core marketing opportunity to reach their customers and increase sales. Apple is the most extreme example. Their launch of the iPod, iTunes and the iTunes store were successful business ventures in their own right, but the real value was to vastly increase sales of Apple computers, which in 2011 resulted in Apple becoming the largest corporation in the world. Apple is now bigger and more valuable as a corporation than the entire US retail sector, and this was largely due to the way they innovated their products with music. Telecoms such as O2 in the UK have become involved with music by investing heavily in the sponsorship of live music venues. The most high-profile of these is the O2 Arena in London, which grosses more income in ticket sales than any other venue in the world. This has worked so well for them that they have also sponsored the Academy group venues all over the UK, rebranding them as 'O2 Academy'.

Some brands also provide opportunities for unsigned bands (i.e. bands without a recording agreement with a phonogram producer) or bands who release their own recordings. These often take the form of competitions to take part in a brand-sponsored compilation album or a live event. When an artist is starting out, it is important to take any opportunities which will result in a higher profile, and a sponsored unsigned band competition is certainly one of the ways to do that.

A way for an artist to save money is to approach musical instrument and equipment manufacturers and suppliers to see if they would be interested in sponsorship (sometimes referred to as 'endorsement'). In the early stages, this may only mean that the artist is able to purchase instruments and equipment at wholesale prices rather than retail price. As the artist becomes better known, this may be extended to the loan of equipment free of charge. It may also be that the manufacturers or suppliers of musical equipment wish to publish photographs of the artist playing or using their equipment or instruments in their magazine or in advertisements. They may also expect the artist to provide feedback and reviews of their latest products. Some brands may want the artist to sign a sponsorship agreement for two or three years, whereas it could just be a one-off arrangement for a tour or some specific event.

There are also agencies called brand entertainment consultants who represent brands and provide ideas and connections which will help to sell the brand through music. It is worth trying to contact these agencies to make them aware of the artist's music, and to provide them with news of the progress being made. One of the largest is CAKE (www.cakegroup.com), which represents such brands as American Express, IKEA, Sony, BurgerKing, Honda, Orange and, in the US, Volvo, Sears and Anne Klein, amongst others. Another is Citizensound (www.citizensound.net), which specializes in music strategy for brands and artists. They describe themselves as a sonic branding and music marketing collective and represent brands as diverse as Nissan, Sagres Beer and Ethiopian Tourism.

One way many brands use sponsorship is by sponsoring tours. For example, US band The Maroon 5, who have for a long time been associated with brands, were sponsored on one of their tours by Honda Cars. They also participated in Coca-Cola's 'Coca-Cola Music' initiative by participating in a 24-hour session in which they wrote and recorded a song, 'Is Anybody Out There'. Opening up the session to global fans via Facebook and Twitter, fans could tweet in ideas for the song lyrics, the recording production and musical arrangement live during the 24-hour session. It gave fans a

unique insight into how the writing and recording process works at the top level, in addition to direct participation. Coca-Cola made 100,000 free downloads of the track available from their website and made a donation to The Coca-Cola Africa Foundation's Replenish Africa Initiative (RAIN) to provide access to clean water to communities in Africa for every download. At the end of the day everyone was happy. The band recorded a new track paid for by Coca-Cola, the fans loved the experience and were able to get a free download (if they were quick), African communities benefited and Coca-Cola came out as the 'good guys', with enhanced brand association and recognition.

Established artists have to think carefully before attaching themselves to a brand which may not fit in either with their style or their ethical views. The Maroon 5 were heavily criticized when, unbeknown to them, a promoter for their show in Jakarta, Indonesia received sponsorship for his concert series from tobacco company Gudang Garum and their Surya Professional Mild cigarettes. When the band discovered this, they immediately demanded that the tobacco association with their name be removed from all advertising or they would not be performing. This is a good example of how careful managers have to be with live work. The band had no direct sponsorship with the tobacco company, but the promoter's concert series did, thus giving rise to an unwelcome association on the posters and advertising with the band.

In the early days, brands would associate themselves with music by 'badging' live events, i.e. the brand would have their logo on all advertising for the event and usually a banner at the back or sides of the stage. They would also often provide fans with a free download and/or tickets, or in the very early days a free ringtone. As the music branding space gets more crowded, brands are finding that they have to be far more innovative with their campaigns, often partnering with digital services, phonogram producers and artists to achieve integrated, engaging and wide-reaching market penetration. A good example of this is a campaign put together by Budweiser in the US to increase sales of their Budweiser Light beer. They called the campaign 'Bud Light Music First' and staged 50 concerts, one in each of the US's fifty states, all of which took place on the same day. The campaign was a collaboration between Budweiser, the world's biggest concert promoter, Live Nation, the biggest phonogram producer in the world, Universal Music, and the new MySpace. Budweiser created iOS and

Android apps which allowed fans to scan QR Codes on bottles of Bud Light from which they could win headphones, concert tickets, Universal Music downloads and even cash. MySpace created a special hub from which fans could stream all 50 shows, as well as access band information and interviews. All this provided a highly engaging and viral music experience for the music fan. It also helped developing artists who participated in the concerts to reach a much wider audience. Because the fans had to download a free app on to their smartphone or tablet, they were in effect taking the campaign around with them, which allowed the brand to keep in touch with them and further develop the campaign later. The MySpace streaming allowed not only ticketholders but many millions of fans all over the world to watch the concerts and for the brand to connect with them on a global level.

Energy drink company Red Bull have taken a different approach with their Red Bull Amplifier Accelerator program, which targets innovative start-up services rather than the artists themselves. Their aim is 'to make music experiences better and redefine the idea of accelerating a start-up'. Other brands, such as Coca Cola, have provided free Spotify subscriptions, and Spotify itself has launched brand apps for companies such as Intel and McDonalds. Beer company Tuborg have launched a very innovative campaign which opens up access to different music around the world via tastemaker service Pitchfork and Tuborg's 'Tuborg Music Hunter' website. According to the site, 'This summer Tuborg is seeking filmmakers, videographers and journalists with unique visual styles and a flair for first-person story telling. The Music Hunters will be sent into the field, accompanied by Pitchfork.tv production staff, to film and document their trip as they travel to and from festivals around the globe.' Some other brands such as Bacardi, Toyota and Mountain Dew have actually started their own record label and have signed artists directly.

According to IEG Research, in 2012 in the US alone brands spent in excess of $1.2 billion on music- related campaigns, and according to Neilson, 30% of those who engage with a campaign will try the product.

The golden rules for artists who are prepared to have themselves associated with brands are as follows:

1. Make sure the product in question is compatible with the band's image and beliefs. Don't just go with the brand that is offering the most money.

2. Fans usually dislike their artists engaging with brands, so try to manage this situation and bring the fans onboard by explaining that the money is being used to create better shows and better recordings.

3. Engage with the digital services the brand intends to use.

4. Try to get the brand to share data information (particularly email addresses) so as to expand the artist's fan base.

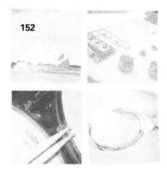

# CHAPTER 17
# THE DIGITAL REVOLUTION

## A Short History

Before the Internet came into popular use, the rules of copyright were developing and working quite well for authors, performers, phonogram producers, publishers, retailers etc. There was still a lot of work to do to fill the gaps in international copyright law, such as introducing a public performance right in sound recordings for performers and phonogram producers worldwide, and the introduction of a treaty that would provide international rights for audiovisual performers, which was finally agreed in Beijing in 2012.

In 1996, in a visionary way, WIPO Member States introduced the so-called WIPO Internet treaties, the WIPO Performances and Phonograms Treaty (WPPT) and the WIPO Copyright Treaty (WCT). At the time they were introduced, however, it was impossible to predict just how fast the new technology was moving, where it was going and how it would develop. When the Internet first started, it was accessible via slow dial-up connections which were fine for emails and other text-based communication and information, but not fast enough for the transfer of music or film. It was possible, but uploading and downloading music took a long time and did not present traditional sound carrier sales such as CDs and DVDs with too much competition. With the introduction of compressed digital MP3 files, download speeds became faster but they still took some time to download.

When high speed broadband came along, everything changed. Suddenly it was possible to upload music and film in a fraction of the time that it would have taken with a dial-up connection. Consumers, instead of being obliged to play by the rules of the music industry and the national copyright legislation of the country in which

they lived, quickly realized that this new technology gave them the power to take the initiative, albeit illegal and unauthorized. Consumers all over the world, particularly students, raced ahead with the new technology, keen to explore all its possibilities. One such US student was 18-year-old Shawn Fanning, who in 1999 developed the Napster software program, which allowed simple online peer-to-peer file-sharing of MP3 music files. It was called Napster because that was Sean's nickname at school. What began as an idea in the head of a teenager proceeded to redefine the Internet, the music industry and the entire way we think about intellectual property. The Napster software program itself was not illegal, in that it could be argued that if the copyrights in the music were owned by the uploader and they wished to share their music with others there was no copyright infringement. Napster was the first system of its kind which allowed one consumer to remotely access another consumer's hard drive and share files. Napster had a central index server which linked users to other users computers so that downloads could take place. The MP3s themselves were not stored on Napster's central server. The Napster program and those that followed, such as Limewire, iMesh, Grokster, Kazaa and Morpheous, were enthusiastically embraced by consumers and advertisers. Many consumers either ignored the rules of copyright or were unaware of them and exchanged copyright-protected music files in their millions, which resulted in no royalties flowing through to performers, authors, phonogram producers or publishers. The quality of MP3 files, although not as good as that found on a CD, was still good enough for most people and was certainly better than that from cassettes or vinyl.

It is perhaps fair to say that phonogram producers in particular were caught napping, and were very slow to embrace the new business opportunities that the online environment offered. In the same way that the US railroad owners tried to stop the building of airports when commercial air travel first became viable, the phonogram producers defended themselves by prosecuting consumers for copyright infringement rather than working to roll out attractive legal alternatives. As, in some countries, phonogram producers were unable to identify the infringers in law until they sued them, they found themselves suing children and grandmothers, which was not well received in the popular media. From a public relations point of view, this litigation almost certainly did more harm than good. The Record Industry Association of America (RIAA), which is the US umbrella trade body for US phonogram producers, not only sued individuals using Napster-type programs but also successfully sued Napster itself, which resulted in Napster filing for bankruptcy in 2002. The Napster name was later re-introduced as a legal download service and later still was acquired by Rhapsody. These legal challenges and the enormous publicity they generated fed even more interest in file-sharing amongst consumers. Other, more sophisticated file-sharing programs such as Kazaa evolved and attracted consumers in their millions. Illegal file sharing became almost a part of the culture, particularly amongst the young who increasingly regarded music as 'free' in the same way as music via the radio is, or at least feels like, 'free'.

It was not until 2003 that a substantial legitimate digital download market started to emerge. Steve Jobs, the CEO of Apple Computers, convinced all of the major phonogram producers to license their recordings to his new iTunes download service. This proved to be very popular, particularly amongst law-abiding music fans, who felt uncomfortable about illegally downloading copyright-protected music even if the chances of being caught were remote. Most people are honest and would prefer not to break the law. iTunes offered the first legitimate service with an extensive catalog of recordings. It also offered marketing possibilities and would email its customers with news of new releases that were of a similar genre to a previous purchase. In the early years, sales of downloads on iTunes increased exponentially and other legal download services such as Amazon MP3, 7digital, Playdigital, Beatport, Rhapsody, eMusic and Deezer were launched. Despite these other services entering the market, Apple's iTunes continued to dominate the legal download market, accounting for between 80-90% of the world's legal download sales. Although these legal services offered the music industry hope and encouragement, illegal downloads continued to dominate, particularly in developing countries where few legal services (if any) were available.

By 2011, global legal download sales were starting to flatten as fans moved away from the download model to streaming services such as YouTube, Pandora and Spotify. For a decade, gross global legal sales of physical and digital recordings in financial terms fell year on year. In 2012, however, they posted their first rise, with a small but significant increase in worldwide sale of recorded music (physical and digital combined) of 0.3%, according to the IFPI.

Prior to the online digital era, music was purchased either as a single disc, an extended play single (EP) or as an album. In the days of vinyl, it was only possible to

record around 45 minutes of music on a long-play vinyl disc, so albums were restricted to that time duration, unless the album was sold as a double or triple album containing two or three 12-inch discs. A vinyl album would typically contain ten tracks averaging around four minutes each. When the CD came along, this extended the amount of music that could be recorded on an album from 45 minutes to a maximum of approximately 74 minutes. Phonogram producers made most of their profits by selling albums rather than singles or EPs. The online environment is changing that too. Rather than having to buy a whole album, which may include tracks that the fan doesn't particularly want, many fans would rather just download the one track they heard on the radio, TV, on a computer game or in an advertisement. It is unlikely that the album will become extinct, but there has been a shift away from albums back to singles. Some artists are considering releasing tracks one by one online as soon as they are recorded, mixed and mastered, thus abandoning the album concept altogether.

## Digital Rights Management and Technical Protection Measures

TPM (Technical Protection Measures) are a subset of DRM (Digital Rights Management). DRM can include copy protection TPM systems and also digital information such as identifying numbers and other information which is used for functionality, accumulating data and for marketing purposes. The copy protection TPM systems can be applied to physical digital sound carriers such as CDs, as well as digital music files, so that access to, and copying of, these products is restricted or prohibited without authorization. Such systems were the cornerstone of the 1996 WIPO Internet treaties which included appropriate enforcement language. The WIPO Internet treaties obliged Member States to introduce national legislation which would make it a criminal offence for individuals to circumvent such copy protection measures, if they were applied by the right owners to recordings made available for sale to the public. It was thought, quite reasonably, that this would be the perfect solution which would protect copyright and related rights through the digital revolution. These DRM copy-protection applications, however, were disliked by consumers who had been used to buying a CD and then doing whatever they liked with it. They might want to copy it on to a cassette for use in their car or make a copy for a friend. When such TPMs were first applied to CDs, they provided an immediate downgrade to the value of a CD. One of the restrictions was that the CD could not be played in a computer's CD drive. With computer CD drives becoming more and more common, consumers became even more annoyed. Things came to a head in 2005, when Sony-BMG introduced their 'rootkit' TPM software. It was discovered that this rootkit software had infected eight million CDs comprising 51 titles with copy-restriction technologies that covertly installed themselves, hid themselves from users and made users vulnerable to hackers and viruses. An estimated 500,000 networks were infected, including many government and military networks. Following this, Sony-BMG destroyed millions of their CDs and removed all copy protection TPMs from their future physical sound carriers, a policy that was quickly followed by the other phonogram producers.

In the world of legal digital downloads, the application of TPM has restricted its development. On the one hand, a consumer could access a recording illegally via one of the file sharing networks with no copy protection, and on the other, the consumer could pay for a legal download which had copy protection applied to it. Given this choice, even some of the most law-abiding consumers elected to take their chances with the free illegal download. In 2007 EMI came to a landmark agreement with iTunes to provide EMI downloads to consumers using Apple's AAC format with no copy protection, but at a slightly higher price than for a download with copy protection. This was a major breakthrough for consumers and the music industry. TPM copy protection quickly became a thing of the past and now nearly all purchasable legal downloads are TPM-free. DRM is still incorporated into sound carriers and audio music files, but the copy-protection technology has been removed. The exception is 'tethering' which is attached to downloads from such subscription services as TDC (in Denmark), Spotify Premium and Deezer. With these services, provided monthly subscriptions are paid, the subscriber is entitled to download tracks to a registered computer or mobile device. However, if the subscription payments cease, the downloads become unplayable.

One of the historic problems with digital music files was that Apple's AAC files were only playable on Apple devices and would not play on MP3 players. In 2006 Apple made it possible to convert their AAC files to MP3 files in the iTunes 'Advanced' drop-down menu which provided the interoperability that fans and the industry had demanded for so long.

## Digital Marketing and Distribution

### Building a Website

The most important tool for the modern artist is to have a well-designed and fully functioning website which acts as a hub for all the artist's activities. Once that has been created, it needs to be regularly updated and managed.

The most empowering element of the Internet is that it provides rapid access to information. With the evolution of fast search engines, information on almost anything is just a click away. The other remarkable aspect of the Internet and the World Wide Web is that it is geographically neutral. It doesn't matter if an artist is based in the Sudan, Mongolia, Vietnam or Barbados: once the website exists, the whole world can access it instantly. In the online environment, if an artist or artist manager has access to a computer with a broadband connection, most processes and digital tools cost very little or nothing at all, at least at entry level. For example, sending an email to an artist's fan base costs very little or nothing, depending on the size of the fan base, and is instant. Compare this with the cost of mailing information in physical form via the post office, and the length of time such information would take to reach the recipient, and it can easily be seen that the savings in terms of time and cost are substantial.

It is essential to create an artist website as soon as possible in an artist's career and to find a webmaster. If one of an artist's core fans is tech-savvy, they might be the ideal person to be the webmaster, or it could be a member of the band or the band or artist's manager. An enthusiastic fan will usually be happy to be the webmaster for free, at least in the early stages.

So how does an artist or an artist's webmaster build their first website, and is it necessary to engage a professional website designer? The answer is that anyone with the most basic computer skills can build and design their own website. As an artist becomes more popular, it might be a good idea to engage the services of a professional website designer, but there's no reason at all why an artist cannot do it themselves at least in the beginning, and at very little cost. Daniel Piechnick has set up a very useful website which has easy instructions on building a website or blog: http://www.websitesetupguide.com.

The first thing to do is to choose a domain name which should be as descriptive, simple and short as possible. Domain names have to be unique, so it is mandatory to choose one that nobody else in the world is using. There may be an annual charge for a domain name, although some web-hosting services such as fatcow.com, justhost.com or ipage.com will provide the domain name for free, provided that their commercial web hosting service is used. If an artist's first choice is already taken, it might be worth considering adding the word 'music', 'live' or 'beats' to make the name unique. Another good idea is to add the musical genre, e.g. if the artist is a reggae artist named Martin Black it might be an idea to choose www.martinblackreggae.com if the domain name www.martinblack.com has already been taken (which it has). The top-level international domain name endings are .com, .net and .org. These are the ones recommended. However, an artist might want to consider using one of the national domain name endings such as .co.uk if the artist is based in the UK or .it if an artist is based in Italy. If our fictitious reggae artist Martin Black lived in Jamaica, he might want to consider the domain name endings .com.jm, .net.jm or .org.jm. This would immediately tell visitors to the site that this reggae artist is the real thing and comes from Jamaica, the home of reggae. Generally for an artist with international ambition .com would be the most prestigious and easy to remember domain name ending.

There are several free social media tools available, such as 'smartURL' and 'PO.ST', which will digitally shorten a domain name so that it effectively shortens links. These services also feature several other very useful marketing tools around real-time information and analytics.

The next step after choosing a domain name is to engage a web hosting service provider. The web hosting service will host an artist's website on a computer wherever the hosting service is based. It doesn't matter where the service is geographically based or where the artist is based, so an artist has the whole world's website hosting services to choose from. There will be a monthly charge for web hosting, but this can be as little as US$3 – 4 per month for a basic service. Check out www.top10bestwebsitehosting.com for the latest reviews and prices.

The next stage is to design and manage the website. The easiest way to do this is to download one of the many website templates that are available. One of the most

widely used for artists is Wordpress (www.wordpress.com), which provides website templates at no cost. Another would be Wix (www.wix.com), who also supply templates for free, or an artist could consider website template services such as Template Monster (www.templatemonster.com/category/music/) who charge license fees for more sophisticated templates. Another way of creating a website is to use Tumblr, which integrates directly with Facebook and Twitter.

The first page on a website is the home page or landing page, which introduces the artist and the artist's music to the world. This is the artist's shop window and it's essential that it is well-designed, interesting to view and lets the viewer understand immediately the genre of music, where the artist comes from and the image of the artist, so that the viewer will want to go further into the site. It is best to avoid animated or moving image 'flash' applications on the homepage, as this slows up the loading process and could result in the viewer immediately moving on to another site. Most fans will not wait for pages to load for more than a few seconds.

It is generally a bad idea to feature automatic music when the home page is opened. Fans who return regularly to the site may get tired of this. It is preferable for music to be accessible by a click rather than for it to be automatic, unless the automatic music is changed regularly. The home page needs to be designed so as to lead the viewer easily and quickly to other parts of the site and also to facilitate the all-important data-capture. (See the section below on 'Building a Fan base'.) It is also important that the design style of the landing page should have references to the artist's musical genre.

It is imperative to keep the website up to date by removing out-of-date information quickly and constantly posting new, interesting information to encourage fans to regularly return to the site. It is better to have no website than one that is dormant or out of date.

Contact details should also be easy to access using a tab on the website's landing page. Some artists prefer not to provide telephone numbers, but it is strongly advisable to have some telephone number and email contact on the contact tab. In the early days in particular, an artist needs as much contact and support from the fans as possible.

As was stated in the 'Signing to a Phonogram Producer' chapter, it is important that the artist own their own website if possible, as they will then have complete control over it. It is very important to have a presence on all the social media networks' artist pages in addition to the artist's website, but if an artist only depends on artist pages on one of the social media networks, the rules governing those sites are in the hands of the social media network itself and can be changed, or the social media network could even disappear, at any time. In some recording agreements, particularly 360 degree agreements, it may say that the phonogram producer owns the artist website and the fan database. It is very important to try and negotiate this out, particularly regarding ownership or access to the fan database. If the artist is dropped by the phonogram producer, it's quite easy to build a new website, but without the fan database the artist will be back to starting from scratch. The fan database is the most valuable asset the artist has. The best situation is that the artist owns the website and the fan database, or at least that both are co-owned by the artist and the phonogram producer, with clear wording as to how the database can be used in the event that the phonogram producer and the artist go their separate ways.

**Adapting the Website for Mobile**

Initially the website will usually be designed for viewing on a laptop or a desktop computer. It is important that when viewed on a smartphone or tablet it resizes and operates smoothly on those other formats. In the past, most professional businesses have created completely separate mobile websites for each device, each of which runs parallel with the main website. The latest approach in website design is 'responsive design' which automatically resizes and adapts the main website for mobile devices. As the user switches from their laptop to their tablet or to their smartphone, the website needs to automatically switch to accommodate for resolution, image size and scripting abilities, i.e. the website should have the technology to automatically respond to the user's preferences. If the website was designed on a Wordpress template, there is an excellent Wordpress plugin called WP Touch which will do this, automatically transforming the website for mobile devices such as the iPhone and iPad as well as Android, Windows and Blackberry smartphones. There are other services that can be considered to achieve this mobile transformation, one of which is Songpier, which claims to be 'the artist's Swiss Army knife in promotion'. By adding all the artist information in Songpier's backend, it allows the artist to build mobile apps, websites, widgets and the artist's Facebook page simultaneously, which will automatically adapt

to all screen sizes and formats. It's like a one-stop shop where one update will instantly go to all the artist's fan-connection channels.

**Search Engine Optimization**

When an artist creates a website, it is important to consider maximizing the site's Search Engine Optimization (SEO). SEO is the process of maximizing the visibility of an artist's website or web page in a search engine's search results. The goal is to appear as near to the top of the first page of search results as possible and ideally to be the very first listing on the first page. Search engines work by software rules known as algorithms.

Search engines such as Google, Yahoo, Baidu, Yandex, Ask Jeeves or Bing work by sending 'crawlers', sometimes referred to as 'spiders' or 'bots' (short for 'robots'), across the Internet, which scan for web pages being entered in a 'search' by using natural algorithmic search results. Google offers Google Webmaster Tools for which a free XML Sitemap feed can be created and submitted to ensure that an artist's website and other webpages can be found. Google is by far the world's most used search engine. According to comScore, in 2012 Google had a worldwide market share of over 65%, with Chinese search engine Baidu coming in second with 8% and Yahoo third with 5%. In Europe, Google has a market share in excess of 80%. Research has shown that around 70% of all traffic to a website is via search engines, so efficient and effective SEO is very important. Many music fans go directly to YouTube for searching music. Whilst YouTube isn't a conventional search engine, as it deals only with audio-visual content, it is very important in worldwide music search. In the UK and the US for example, YouTube is the second most widely used search engine after Google (see the section on YouTube on page 182).

**Here are some useful tips to ensure good SEO:**

1.  As has been stated previously, it is advisable to choose an unusual and preferably unique name for the artist or band. This will ensure that the artist is not competing with other websites that contain the same or a similar name when a search is made. For example, there is a band from France called The Forks, which is a great name, but because it is a common name it will compete with all kinds of other businesses and web pages with the same name, e.g. there is an historic site called The Forks in Winnipeg, Canada, and in Washington state in the USA there is a small city named 'The Forks'.

Businesses selling cutlery will also appear in the search results. If, however, the band had spelt their name 'The Forcs' or 'The Forcks', the name would almost certainly be unique, which would immediately give them excellent SEO.

2.  Make sure there is plain text on the website, or if there is designed text that the image file is correctly tagged in normal text, particularly on the landing page. Crawlers cannot read graphically designed lettering unless the image file is tagged with the same lettering in regular text. It is important to include keywords such as the name of the artist or band, the genre of music (e.g. 'metal', 'gothic', 'folk', 'soca' or 'rap') and possibly the country where the artist is based. The word 'music' also helps. Download Google's free Keyword Tool to find out more about effective keywords. Other free keyword information services are Wordstream and Soovle, which will give instant information showing the most effective keywords.

3.  The most important aspect of increasing SEO is to update the website as often as possible. The crawlers will detect this and prioritize those sites. The crawlers will also monitor how many visitors a site has. The greater the number of visitors, the better the SEO.

4.  If the artist has some history, make sure that there is a Wikipedia entry containing as much information about the artist as possible. This can be done using the Wikipedia Article Wizzard. Make sure that this is updated every six months or so. Wikipedia always ranks high in search results and will help to lead fans to the official website.

5.  Links on the website to trusted quality third party sites such as CNN, BBC, New York Times, The Guardian, Huffington Post etc. raise the search profile. It is also important to make sure that any links on the website are correct and functioning. If there are dead links on the site, the crawlers will detect this and lower the SEO.

6. If an artist's site is built on a Wordpress template, try the Wordpress SEO by Yoast free plugin. This will rate an article or post on an artist's website and provide advice on how to improve the SEO.

7. There are many agencies who will for a fee increase a site's SEO, but at the beginning, when finance is usually in short supply, there are many things an artist and the webmaster can do to increase the website's SEO without resorting to these services.

**Selling Music Directly from the Website**

Another important part of the website (if the artist is not signed to a third-party phonogram producer) is to make the artist's physical music product such as CDs and DVDs as well as other merchandise available for purchase directly from the website. Here are some of the ways of doing that:

1. Build a web store and open a merchant account with a bank which can process credit card transactions via a secure encryption service such as Protx or Verisign and sell directly from the artist's website. Fulfillment (processing and dispatching orders) will usually be in-house.

2. Build a web store and use a transaction company such as PayPal. Using this structure, customers can sign up to PayPal before they purchase anything from the store, paying through PayPal or by credit card via PayPal. Organizations such as PayPal take a higher commission from the seller than is the case with a merchant account but are very convenient and easy to use.

3. Outsource all the physical web sales to a merchandising company such as CD Baby (www.cdbaby.com), Backstreet (www.bsimerch.com), Sandbag (www.sandbagheadquarters.uk.com) or Topspin (www.topspin.com). With this method, all that is required is a link from the artist's website to the third party merchandiser who will, for a percentage, look after all the financial transactions and fulfillment.

4. Apply for an online e-commerce account with services such as Amazon. These services will facilitate the sale and the financial transactions for physical product, but the artist or manager will be expected to expedite and dispatch the physical product promptly. If fulfillment does not take place promptly, Amazon or a similar service may close the account. The

service will take a percentage, but many artists find that it is worthwhile having an Amazon or similar account in addition to any in-house or other third party web store structures, as it seems to generate additional sales.

One method of maximizing purchases of physical product is to create a limited edition wherein the first 500 or 1000 CDs or DVDs are numbered and/or signed by the artist. This makes them collectable and the personalization of the signature(s) is something fans tend to value highly.

In developing countries, it may be difficult to set up a structure for selling music directly from the website due to a lack of financial infrastructure, such as difficulties in being able to open a bank account. One answer may be to form a co-operative artists' group which can collectively open a bank account from which several artists can access income. Such a group may also be able to facilitate a broadband Internet connection in a central location or via a satellite dish if such connections are not easily available or affordable to individual artists. It may be that national or local governments can help set up or provide such a facility in various locations as part of their arts, music and culture program. The important element of online music purchasing transactions is that the consumer must feel secure about parting with credit card information, which should be the case with any good e-retail payment processing system. The credit card or PayPal information is encrypted so that it cannot be read by anyone except the purchaser and the financial organization that receives the money. Credit card details cannot be seen by the artist, the webmaster, the ISP or anyone else in the processing chain.

Whichever purchasing structure is chosen when designing the website, it is important to provide a clear means of purchasing physical product and downloads with one click, preferably from the home page. Some artists feel uncomfortable about 'pushing' the sale of their work, but it is essential to at least make purchasing as easy to do as possible if they are to succeed. It should not be too blatant but can be simply done by having a 'purchase music' or 'shopping cart' tab on the home page. Clicking this tab should take the viewer straight to the store page of the website or provide a link to a third-party store website.

**Aggregators – Digital download and streaming sales**

For digital downloads and streaming, the artist and manager of an artist who is not signed to a third- party phonogram producer will need to engage an aggregator, who is effectively a digital distributor. An aggregator will place an artist's music on up to 150 download and streaming sites around the world, the most important of which is iTunes. The aggregator will usually take a commission of perhaps 10-30% and then forward the balance to the artist's bank account or PayPal account at regular intervals. Some aggregators also charge an additional one-off fee for placing an album on all the digital stores they distribute to. Other aggregators work on the basis of charging the artist a fixed amount per month for a range of services in which digital distribution is included. In this case, 100% of sales income is forwarded to the artist, provided the artist only releases a limited number of tracks per year and pays the monthly subscription. Examples of aggregators are Believe (http://www.believedigital.com), AWAL (www.awal.com), CD Baby (www.cdbaby.com), IODA (www.iodalliance.com), Tunecore (www.tunecore.com), The Orchard (http://www.theorchard.com) and Reverbnation (www.reverbnation.com). For a territorial list of aggregators as officially recommended by iTunes, go to:

https://itunesconnect.apple.com/WebObjects/iTunesConnect.woa/wa/displayAggregat ors?ccTypeId=3

Some, such as Reverbnation, operate as a one-stop shop for independent artists' digital marketing and distribution, all included in a monthly subscription. As with many digital services, Reverbnation offer a free basic package which includes a free artist Android app but no digital distribution. Sales commissions, cost per track for placement on stores and/or subscription rates across aggregators vary considerably, so it's worth looking at each site and reading the sign-up agreement carefully before deciding who to use. Try to use a service which does not lock an artist in to an exclusive agreement for a period of more than one year. In addition to digital download stores, make sure the aggregator distributes to the on-demand streaming services, such as Deezer, Spotify and Google Play Music All Access. They should also be able to set up and collect any YouTube partnership income on behalf of an artist, if required. Alternatively, the artist could become a YouTube partner directly (see section on YouTube on page 182).

There are also download and streaming services which specialize in certain musical genres. For example, if the artist is in the electronic/dance music field, it is essential to sign up to such services as Beatport (www.beatport.com), which will distribute directly to DJs all over the world. This can be done independently or via an aggregator. These specialist digital music services can arrange downloads of CD quality, which is the format most DJs need if they are to play the music in clubs and on the radio etc.

**Building a Fan Base**

The importance of developing and building an artist fan database has been mentioned several times throughout this book, so let's now look at creative ways of achieving that in more detail. As has been stated above, the artist's fan database is the most valuable asset the artist will ever own or have access to.

The most important thing for a new artist or band is to perfect their skills as musicians and singers, write great songs and learn the art of giving great live performances. The internet hasn't affected this first law of art at all. The only way an artist is going to attract fans is to be great at what they do and provide fans with the music and live performances they like.

Once an artist or band has embarked on this journey, it is essential to build a fan base and a mailing list in order to keep the fans informed about upcoming releases, events and shows. As ex-*Wired* magazine executive editor Kevin Kelly famously wrote, if an artist can create a database of over a 1000 serious fans and the artist treats them with respect and care, it may be possible to live from those fans for the rest of the artist's life. That's why it's important to manage the fan experience and to constantly be seeking to expand and develop that fan base. This need not cost much money, but it will require time, effort, some original thinking and regular attention.

Every artist should have the ambition to play live as much as possible, particularly in the early stages. At every show give out postcards or forms with info and an image of the band/artist and invite the recipient to comment on the performance and sign up to the artist's fan base by providing their email address. Make sure the postcard or form has at least one question on it. Questions are very effective tools in

achieving fan engagement. Most people stick with one email address for years or even life, and that email address identifies and is controlled by that person. Who knows if Facebook or Twitter will still be around in the future? Whilst Facebook and Twitter are very valuable tools in the whole process of building a fan base, a personal email address of a genuine fan is the most valuable piece of data of all.

Another approach at live shows is to have a friendly and enthusiastic fan go around the venue with a clipboard, collecting email addresses. It is also useful to get the fan's zipcode (postcode) or nearest large city to where they live so that they can be kept informed of shows in their area. There's not much point giving a fan in Paris info about a show in Tokyo. It's important early on to find out who the hardcore fans are. These fans are referred to as 'über-fans' or 'sneezers' and it's extremely important to look after them and give them extra benefits, such as access to the artist or backstage passes. With any luck, these über-fans will make it their life's mission to spread the word on the artist's music. They are invaluable.

It is usual to offer a potential new fan something in return for providing their email address at live shows or on the artist's website. This could be one or two free track downloads or maybe free tickets for some future event. A free download could be a track from the artist's album, a live recording or a rare unreleased track. Even the most successful artists often give away one or two tracks from an upcoming album as a taster. Free music, interviews with the artist, audiovisual footage of the artist in the recording studio or elsewhere (usually via a link to YouTube) and downloadable podcasts should be a feature of any artist's website. By doing this, the fan who feels that he/she is getting something back from the artist feels part of the artist's community. Data capture (i.e. email address capture) should ideally be right on the artist's website's landing page, so that one of the first things a potential new fan sees is the possibility to get a free download. In order to get this, all they have to do is enter their email address.

An artist can use analytics to track where their fans are. The most classic case of this was social media queen Imogen Heap, who noticed that the analytics on Facebook and Twitter were showing a big spike in Jakarta in Indonesia. Very few phonogram producers operate there, as unauthorized file sharing is the norm. Imogen had never been to Indonesia and had never done any promotion there. Imogen's manager spoke to Imogen's international booking agent in London and asked him if he knew any promoters in Jakarta. He did indeed know promoters in Jakarta and contacted them to see if they would be interested in booking Imogen for a concert. After doing some local research, one of the promoters came back and said that he would be interested in booking Imogen and suggested a 4500 capacity venue and a very large fee plus all expenses. When tickets went on sale, it sold out and turned into one of the most financially and artistically successful concerts of Imogen's career. The spike was almost certainly caused by a few Indonesian über-fans sharing their enthusiasm which then went viral.

Fans want to feel they are a part of the artist's community rather than just consumers. It's therefore essential to involve them as much as possible in the artist development process. For example, it could be a good idea to set up a link to three new tracks via the artist's website that can be streamed and to ask fans to rate them and to make comments. An artist should send their music to genre-specific blogs for their consideration and run public remix competitions and/or other competitions or lotteries. Prizes could be sitting at the side of the stage at a live show, attending the sound-check, attending an after-show party or some other privilege which involves direct contact with the artist. The artist could also consult fans about artwork, favorite tracks, where they should play live etc. Some artists run competitions wherein fans submit artwork for the next EP or album cover. This can provide the artist with great artwork and keeps the fans engaged, in addition to providing a prize for the winning entry. If this process is being followed, it is important to consider the copyright in the artwork. The usual way of dealing with this is to have a simple licensing agreement with the designer so that the artist can use the design for certain uses such as record covers and merchandising, but the copyright ownership is retained by the designer. Alternatively, the artist might come to an agreement with the designer wherein they offer the designer a financial sum for a complete buy-out of all rights in the artwork, i.e. copyright ownership in the artwork would be transferred to the artist. In either case, it is important to uphold the designer's moral right of attribution by naming them as the designer wherever possible.

As soon as email addresses start to come in, it is important to create a mailing list with a single title so that information can be sent to fans. Services such as YMLP (Your Mailing List Provider), Mailchimp and Fanbridge can help manage mailing lists and allow mailing lists to be larger than would be possible with the artist's ISP. It is

important to issue regular newsletters featuring news about new upcoming shows, events and record releases, but these should not be sent out too often. Once per month or every two weeks is perhaps as regular as they should be unless there is some very important news which requires an immediate press release. If fans receive emails too often, they may just hit the spam button, which means any future emails will end up unread in the fan's junk folder. These news releases are usually sent out by the artist's webmaster but can be accompanied by responses from the artist themselves, either as a mass email mail-out, as posts on Facebook and Twitter, or preferably all of these together. Whilst fans appreciate contact with the webmaster and the manager's office, there is nothing that means more to a fan than receiving an email or a response on Twitter or Facebook directly from the artist. It is important that the webmaster or others don't issue posts and messages making out that such posts and messages are actually from the artist when they are not. Transparency, honesty and trust should be the cornerstones of any artist's website and fan communication. It should always be clear from whom the email, post or tweet has come from. Whoever responds to an email from a fan, it is important to respond promptly. Likewise, if a free download is on offer in exchange for an email address, it is important to make this automatic and instant using such services as Fanbridge, Mailchimp or SoundCloud's Email Unlock, which is a free app. It's also important for an artist to have their music available via SoundCloud, as it's fast becoming far more than an audio-sharing platform. Recent developments have seen it emerging as a social network in its own right.

Another good idea is to have a 'guest book' where anyone visiting the site can leave comments about the artist's performance at a recent show or their opinion of the artist's latest release etc. Similarly, many sites have chat rooms and forums. Chat rooms are areas where fans can chat with each other live in real time. Forums are like chat rooms, but the text stays permanently in the forum area so that fans can add comments as and when they feel like it and look back at previous comments. The webmaster should monitor these chat rooms, forums and mailing lists to some extent, making sure that they do not get abusive or do not drift too far 'off-topic'. It is essential that someone is managing the artist's website, social networking and fan communication on a daily basis in a way that is compatible with the artist. This is why webmasters are becoming more and more important as key members of a successful team.

## Podcasts

Podcasts which can be downloaded from the website are another important promotional tool. A podcast by definition is an audio or video file that is attached to an RSS feed as an enclosure so that any user who wants to receive it can 'subscribe' via a piece of software known as a podcatcher. RSS stands for Really Simple Syndication. There are many different podcatchers available both for Apple's iOS system and Google's Android. Anyone can create a show using freely-available software (e.g. Audacity – http://audacity.sourceforge.net/download/) and create an RSS feed to submit to any number of hundreds of podcast directories. A free online RSS feed creator can be found at http://www.podcastblaster.com/podcast-feed/. A podcast is a file that can only be downloaded to a computer, or mobile device at the request of the recipient. In other words, it is not possible to send out podcasts as spam to people who did not ask for them. The podcast can contain an interview with the artist, with or without music, and any other content of interest to fans. It can be audio only or audiovisual. If done well, podcasts can enhance the fan experience and lead the fan to explore other parts of the artist's website, as well as possibly purchasing merchandise and music. If the podcast contains music, it is important that the rights in that music are either owned by the artist or cleared for use by the relevant third party rights holders.

## Social Networking

There is an ancient Chinese proverb that says "Tell me and I'll forget, show me and I may remember, involve me and I'll understand." This is the basic philosophy of social networking, which is all about fan involvement and engagement. It is essential to engage with fans via the social networks to further expand and build an artist fan base. At the time of writing, the most widely used services are Facebook, Twitter and YouTube, so the following section looks at these three services in more detail. There are other social network services such as the new MySpace, Instagram, Pinterest and Google+ which should also be used, but the three mentioned are the biggest. As time goes by, these social networks may become less important and new ones may emerge, so an artist and an artist manager must always keep up-to-date with the latest developments in digital services.

## Facebook

At the time of writing, Facebook was the most widely used social networking site globally, so it is worth having a look at how it can be used and how it works in more detail. The following will hopefully provide a basic guide in the short to medium-term, but there will be constant developments and new features, so the reader is advised to keep up to date with such developments via digital music information providers such as Musically (www.musically.com).

Facebook as a social networking service was launched in 2004 by Mark Zuckerberg and his college friends. It is one of the greatest success stories of the modern era. In September 2012, it had over 1 billion monthly active users (MAUs) and over 580 million daily active users (DAUs). It is without doubt a very important tool for any musician or artist to embrace and needs to be fully understood. Most basic features can be used for free.

Many people have personal Facebook pages, but it is also important for an aspiring artist or musician to set up their own Facebook Fan Page. A Fan Page (sometimes referred to as a Facebook Artist Page) is a single page separate from a personal Facebook account. Think of the Fan Page as something quite similar to a traditional band website, but where the fans can interact more easily with the artist. The Facebook Fan Page should be a one-stop shop where people can find all kinds of current information as well as getting to know the band and feel a connection with the artist.

A fan's personal Facebook page will have the following basic features: the 'Newsfeed' or 'Home Page', which will show what some of the fan's personal friends are up to. It will also show some of the posts from the Facebook pages that the fan likes. The newsfeed is private to the fan. Only when they share, comment or like something do others get to see what they see. The fan's 'Timeline' (or 'Wall') is what is happening in the fan's life according to Facebook. If the fan scrolls down right to the bottom of their Timeline, they will see the date they were born and above that everything they have ever posted on Facebook in chronological order. The fan's Timeline is also where their friends can write them a public post. The fan's friends can see the fan's Timeline. The artist's Facebook Fan Page will also have its own Timeline.

## Likes

The way fans interact with the artist's Fan Page is by 'liking' it. Once someone has liked an artist's page, they will receive some of the artist's status updates and will be able to view all parts of the artist's Fan Page, in a similar way to when an individual becomes friends with people on a personal Facebook page. It should be high on any aspiring musician's list to get as many genuine 'likes' as possible. Not only is it a great way of communicating and building a fan base, but it is also looked at by many key industry people in the recording, publishing, media and live sectors as an indicator of the popularity of a band and whether they should invest money or airtime in them. Large numbers of Facebook 'likes', and hence the implication that a band has a huge fan base, have become very important. This has led to some labels and individual artists paying for likes by using agencies who have huge teams who they pay or reward for liking an artist. This practice is looked down upon and is not recommended. It can be quite obvious to someone at radio or in other parts of the music industry when a band has purchased many ten of thousands of likes. If, for example, there are a very large number of likes but very few posted comments, that immediately sounds alarm bells. Once a 'tastemaker' feels that a band is basically cheating, they are very unlikely to support that band going forward.

In addition to the total number of 'likes', there are other important statistics that are viewable on Facebook Insights (Facebook analytics) to consider, particularly:

'People Talking About This'. This is the number of people who have commented or created a story about an artist's page in the previous seven days. Many people in digital marketing regard this as the most important Facebook statistic of all, as it reflects genuine fan engagement.

'Friends of Fans'. The number of people who are friends of the artist's fans. When a fan of the artist's page likes, comments or shares an artist page post, the post will then appear in their friends' newsfeeds as well. This provides double or triple the exposure than would otherwise be the case.

'Total Reach'. The number of Facebook users who have seen any content associated with the artist's fan page in the previous seven days.

There are several excellent videos on YouTube explaining how to use Facebook Insights.

**Building a Facebook Fan Page**

Here are some basic guidelines for building a Fan Page:

1) Give it the correct name

   An artist should set up a Fan Page the moment they decide they want to make a career in the music industry. The first thing they will be presented with is naming the page. It is vitally important that the artist page is named correctly, as it is very difficult to change the name once the page is active. Make sure people are going to be able to find it easily and be sure to check Facebook for artists with the same name and consider if this will cause confusion.

2) Get the information up

   All the information fans would expect to see on a traditional band website should also be on the Facebook Fan Page. Be sure to include band members' details, biographies, upcoming live dates, contact information and make all this information as clear as possible. Amy Sciarretto from Road Runner records states, 'One thing I find frustrating and think bands can improve on, is posting their biographies and their names on Facebook. It is helpful for journalists needing or wanting to fact check'.

3) Get the page looking great

   Spend time thinking about the banner which can be inserted at the top of the page . The page should be easy to navigate and should not look cluttered.

4) Differentiate between personal page and the Fan Page

   An artist should make their personal page only for true friends, family and fellow musicians. The fan page should be the main conduit with fans. If the artist name is the same as the artist's real name, they should consider using a pseudonym on the personal page. It is important fans have one conduit so that all the likes appear on one page.

5)   Allow fans to be able to post directly

The Facebook page should be set up to allow fans to post directly onto the page, thus creating a forum and giving them the freedom to make their own comments, rather than only reacting to those of the artist.

## Posting On Facebook

The key when authoring a post is 'engagement'. The writer should make the post as engaging as possible to their audience, with the aim of interacting with the fans. Before discussing the best ways of authoring engaging posts, it is important to understand how Facebook posts work within Facebook.

## Edgerank

Edgerank is an internal system ( Facebook calls it a proprietary ranking algorithm) within Facebook which determines the success of a Facebook post. Not everyone who follows an artist or individual will see every post they write, as there are simply too many people on Facebook. Edgerank is the system which decides what appears in individuals' or artists' newsfeeds. It is very important to understand the system, as it determines how many fans will see an individual post.

In a given week posts will only reach an average of 16% of an artist's fans. This is a frustrating statistic when one considers how hard it can be to get Facebook likes. By improving the Edgeranking it will be possible to increase this percentage. Edgerank is determined by three factors:

1.   Affinity Score – this represents how connected the fan is with the artist. If the fan frequently interacts with the artist's Facebook page, then they have a higher affinity score than someone who rarely or never interacts with the page. If a fan has previously engaged with the artist's Facebook page, then that increases the chances of fresh content appearing in their newsfeed.

2.   Edge weight – this measures the type of post and its performance, photo and video posts typically having the highest score. The performance of a post is determined by the interaction a post gets. The kinds of interactions are rated, so a comment is considered more valuable than a like, for example.

3.  Time Decay – How current a post is. Fans will see newer posts first. The older the post, the more it drops down in a fan's newsfeed. Facebook also looks at how often a user will login and will update their newsfeeds accordingly. Therefore someone who logs in once a month will see posts with high affinity and edge weights above more recent posts with low scores in the other two categories. The average lifetime of a post is around three hours.

Facebook will not reveal the 'Edgerank' of a particular post. Instead, the best way to judge the success of a post is to look at the Facebook Insights on 'How many people saw this post'. The best posts on Facebook are engaging by their nature and hence attract a high Edgerank, and will therefore be seen by more fans. There is a social media tool called 'Edgerank Checker' which will provide information about how engaging a post is and the best time to place a post to get maximum impact. It has a free trial period followed by a subscription of around US$15 per month.

## Ensuring Content Gets Seen

### Add a photo or video

When posting on Facebook, it is important to make a visual impact by attaching an image or video. It is well researched that posts with images are much more engaging. The image itself needs to be good, of course. Commentator Fred Parotta states, 'not all images are equal on Facebook. The best images are funny, evoke an emotional response, are shocking, or make the person sharing it look good, funny, smart, or in-the-know'. Doug Barash, Director of New Media at Verve / Universal Music, states, 'Any time an artist does any kind of status update, include a photo, because a photo speaks volumes'.

### Post a question

Another very good idea is to post a question, e.g. "What is your favorite track on the new EP?" or "Who is coming to the gig in Kingston on Friday?" If a question is posted, a fan is much more likely to comment, which improves a post's Edgerank. Another example might be to post three possible artwork ideas for an album and ask fans for their preferences and input. There are internal Facebook systems such as Facebook Questions which can be considered, which reach a far wider and more targeted range of friends as they reach friends of friends.

### Be a Role Model

Fans will want to know more than just about the music the artist or band makes . If an artist posts what they are passionate about, it is likely the artist's fans who relate to the music may well also relate or aspire to the artist's fashion, politics and loves in life. Artists should share things they find interesting on their Facebook page.

### Don't oversell

Fans will only tolerate a small amount of 'buy now' from Facebook posts, and artists should be very subtle on how they market themselves using Facebook. A 'Buy It Now' post could be made on the day of release, but even then it would be far better to say that the new record is 'available' or 'released today' and then provide a link to the artist's webstore, iTunes, Amazon etc. It is much more effective to let the artist's fans do the marketing on an artist's behalf by posting positive comments. Constantly provide information such as which is the artist's favorite track, who played on it and where it was recorded etc. In addition, let fans know of any success the record is having, such as radio-play or how it's 27 in the local hip-hop chart etc. Be a friend and a trusted source of information, rather than a salesperson.

### Comment on fans' comments

If an artist posts something and it receives lots of comments, then they should engage with these comments by commenting on their own post. Form a sense of companionship and access amongst the fans. This will also increase the post's Edgerank, and hence the number of fans who will see it.

### Post regularly and intelligently

An artist should only make posts that will interest the fan base and should post reasonably frequently to maintain engagement, build loyalty and form an affinity with fans. Remember that only an average of 16% of fans will be sent a post and even then most of them won't see it. There is no accepted rule as to how frequently to post. Some artists put the effort into making interesting and quality posts every two or three days, whereas others feel that daily or even hourly posts have the maximum effect in maintaining engagement.

### Über-fans

Hard core über-fans should be treated with the greatest respect and encouraged to become ambassadors for the artist on Facebook. An artist should encourage and engage personally with them and look after them by occasionally putting them on the guest list or allowing them backstage for shows etc. Fifty loyal über-fans are worth more than five thousand casual fans.

### Paying Facebook to promote a post

Facebook allows users to promote or 'boost' their posts. In basic terms, this means a payment is made to Facebook to increase the number of fans who will see the post. It could be regarded as improving a post's Edgerank. There is also an option with promoted posts for friends of fans to see a post. As a rule, a post will only be worth promoting if it is already proving to be a highly engaging post with fans.

### Engage with other artists' fan pages

In the same way that by supporting other artists at a show can increase an artist's fan following, the same applies to Facebook. An artist should befriend other artists and encourage them to post about them. Studies show that the best way to promote anything is by recommendation. This is totally true in the world of music. Fans look up to bands as tastemakers, and will follow their musical tastes and recommendations. If an artist comments on numerous other artists they like or who have influenced their music, they may well return the favor.

### Offer exclusives and giveaways

Offer special deals to fans on Facebook. These could be priority tickets or a free audio track. Various free apps allow fans to get access to a free download or similar in exchange for liking the page. It is also a good idea for an artist or the singer in a band to ask the audience to engage with the artist's Facebook page at live shows, saying that if they like it they can receive a free track.

### Include the Facebook fan page link on everything

If the artist is printing flyers, designing their website, creating cover art for recordings, even artist T shirts etc. It is important to always include the 'f' Facebook symbol and name of the artist's Facebook page on all artwork. This prompts fans or would-be fans to discover and engage with the artist's Facebook page.

### Take photos with fans

Posting photographs with fans is very popular with fans on Facebook and can be very effective. Also post on Instagram (which is owned by Facebook), Pinterest, Flickr and other photo sharing sites.

### Advertise

It can be quite expensive to advertise on Facebook, but it's an excellent way to reach a very specific music fan demographic. For example, if an artist feels that their music will greatly appeal to fans of another artist in the same genre, it is possible to advertise as simply as 'Like This Artist? Then check this artist out'. An advert can be created which specifically targets people who like a particular artist, e.g. all fans of heavy metal over 35 years old within a 40-mile radius of a specific city or town.

### Facebook Events

For special shows, it is a good idea for an artist to set up a dedicated Facebook event page via their fan page. It is not a good idea to do this for every show, but for special ones where an artist might want to try to impress music industry people to sign them, launch a new EP/album or celebrate the band being together for a year or five years (for example), it is well worth it. The first thing to do is to give the event a name. It is usually more appealing to fans to call it a 'party' rather than a 'music event'. Another good idea is to create a package admission price which includes a free CD, i.e. rather than charge $8 for a ticket, charge $13 which includes the ticket and a free CD or tracks on a memory stick. The artist should tell their fans why this event is so important and how much fun it will be. Try to make the description of the event as compelling as possible and include good photos, video and artwork. Stories about what happened at the last show in the same venue (if there was one) always appeal to fans, and stories about what unusual clothes the band intend to wear etc. are also appealing. Once the event page is set up and fully functional, an artist will need to invite all their friends, which should also include the other band members and other people associated with the band. Make it clear that they need to click the RSVP button and point out exactly where it is. The artist should then write personal invitations to the artist's über-fans explaining why this show is so important and asking them if they would invite all of their friends. Don't bombard fans with too many reminders. After the initial invite, one more invite, maybe two days before the event, could be okay, but no more.

## Facebook Apps

As a band gets bigger, it may be worth considering building a dedicated Facebook app. Facebook is basically a large privately owned friendly internet in its own right, and Facebook apps are walled gardens within that structure which need to be downloaded by fans. In 2011 Facebook launched its new 'Open Graph' app structure which has been successfully integrated by services such as Spotify and Bandpage etc. More general artist apps are available from services such as 'Mobile Roadie' and 'Shout Em'.

## Facebook coverage

As has been explained above, on average only 16% of an artist's Facebook fan page friends will actually receive a post unless it is a promoted post, which costs money. As a result, many artists are focusing on getting information out via their own website mailing list first, which will get to 100% of the fans that they have email addresses for. It is therefore advisable to prioritize the mailing list and supplement it with Facebook and Twitter activity.

Here is an example (from the author's Friars Aylesbury club in the UK) of how all artwork and advertising produced should always alert viewers that the artist (or in this case club) can be found on Facebook and Twitter:

## Twitter

Many artists use Twitter as their main communication channel with fans. Twitter is a micro-blogging tool that can be used conversationally or to follow trending topics. A trending topic is one that is most tweeted about by city, by country or globally. At the time of writing, Twitter had approximately half the number of users as Facebook and has an open API (Application Platform Interface). It is essential to understand how to navigate and use Twitter, so it's a good idea to sign up personally and use it for a while to fully understand how it works. The difference between Twitter and

Facebook is that whereas a Facebook post can be quite long and detailed, with lots of information, a tweet is limited to a maximum of 140 characters (including spaces). It takes some practice to get used to this limitation and to get the most from each tweet. Whereas Facebook friends have to be approved using a Facebook friend request, there is no such process with Twitter. Anybody can 'follow' anybody they choose to follow. It is therefore important for an artist to get as many genuine Twitter followers as possible and to tweet regularly.

Many of the points in the section on Facebook above also apply to Twitter, but here are some specific Twitter guidelines:

### Create an artist Twitter account

Choose the name carefully so that potential followers can easily find the artist. The artist account could be from the whole band using the 'We' approach or could be from individual band members from time to time. In the latter case, it would be good to start with something like 'Chris here'. Tweets can also be posted by managers or webmasters on behalf of the artist (with their permission), but it should always be clear who is tweeting. It should never appear to be a tweet from the artist when it isn't. For example, Lady Gaga's manager occasionally tweets on her behalf but he always makes it clear that it is he who is tweeting. When creating a Twitter profile, an artist should match the artwork with other artwork being used on the artist's website and Facebook page etc.

### Try to get as many genuine followers as possible.

This can be done by an artist making it clear on the artist's website and other places that the artist is active on Twitter. Start to follow other artists and people connected with the same musical genre to pick up followers from them. Most people choose to be notified when a new person is following them. When they see that an artist is following them, they may in turn want to follow the same artist and receive the artist's updates. As with Facebook, the Twitter logo with the name of the Twitter feed should be clearly shown on all artwork.

### Tweet regularly

Each artist is different. Some artists tweet once per day, others several times a day. As with Facebook, an artist should try to make the tweets as interesting as possible.

It should be remembered that each tweet will only be read by a small fraction of the artist's fans, so an artist should not be shy about tweeting often. Several artists are on record as saying 'Write each tweet as if it were your last'. That's a bit extreme, but there is some truth in that statement.

### Tweet at the right time

For maximum effect, an artist should tweet at peak Twitter hours. This tends to be in the afternoon and evening. Engagement also increases dramatically towards the end of the working week, so Thursdays and Fridays are the best days to tweet.

### Using @ and #

If someone has commented on a tweet, users can type the '@' symbol to directly message other users. It is useful to create and continue conversations between users and to pass on links.

The '#' or hash symbol is used to follow trending topics. e.g. '#Sofia' would be a hashtag and could be used in a tweet to talk about shows going on in Sofia in Bulgaria. Users can click on the hashtag to find all the tweets that discuss this topic. It's a good idea for an artist to create a special hashtag to promote a new record or a live event, e.g. #phonatlive for live shows by the artist 'Phonat'. Some artists are even including the hashtag as part of the track or album title in order to get trending activity, e.g. Jennifer Lopez titled her 2013 single '#liveitup'. Use of the '#liveitup' hashtag on Twitter caused the number of uses to rise from 500 to 22,000 per day. It is good to keep the hashtag as short as possible. Use the hashtag everywhere, including daily tweets, press releases, the artist's website and on all marketing materials. If done consistently, a hashtag promotion can effectively encourage other people to promote an artist's work. Their followers will see the hashtag and may choose to follow the artist or the promotion as it unfolds.

### Encourage re-tweeting

An artist should write tweets that encourage re-tweeting and replying to help spread the word. There is nothing wrong with openly saying 'Please re-tweet' within the tweet if an artist is trying to reach the maximum number of people, concerning a record release or a special live performance etc. However, this should only be done for important tweets and shouldn't be done too regularly, as it may come over as a bit desperate.

### Don't oversell

As with Facebook, avoid 'buy now' tweets. By all means provide information about new releases and add a link to where they can be purchased, but keep the tweets informative and engaging rather than direct advertising.

### Including links (URLs)

When including links on a tweet, be aware that Twitter automatically shortens a URL to 20 characters using its t.co service. So if an artist includes a link, there will be 120 characters left in which to write the message. Research has shown that links are more effective if placed near the beginning of the tweet rather than at the end. A tweet has also been shown to be more effective if nearly all the 140 characters are used, i.e. longer tweets are more effective than short ones.

### Promoted tweets

In the same way that it is possible to pay for a promoted Facebook post to give information a higher profile, it is also possible to pay for a promoted tweet on Twitter. Promoted tweets (sometimes called 'sponsored tweets') are ordinary tweets which can be used to reach a wider group of users and also ignite more engagement from existing followers. Sponsored tweets are clearly labeled 'promoted', but other than that they behave exactly the same as a normal tweet. They can be re-tweeted, replied to, favorited etc.

### Twitter apps

There are many Twitter apps which can assist an artist in their social networking marketing. One very useful app is SoundCloud's 'Social Unlock', which allows an artist to give access to a download to a fan in exchange for a tweet, a social interaction or an email address. Another useful app is 'Tweetdeck', which is owned by Twitter. Tweetdeck is a social media dashboard app for management of Twitter and Facebook accounts. Like other Twitter apps it interfaces with the Twitter API to allow users to send and receive tweets and view profiles.

### YouTube

Created in 2005, YouTube is a video-sharing website which allows users to upload, view and share videos. It uses Adobe Flash Video and HTML5 technology to display

a wide variety of audio-visual content, including music videos, movie clips and TV clips, as well as amateur audio-visual content such as video blogging and educational videos. In November 2006 YouTube was bought by Google. YouTube makes money by placing video ads at the beginning of a video or by placing static and banner ads around the video viewing area.

YouTube is the biggest music discovery service on the planet, so it's essential for an artist to have a good presence there. Even if no video exists for a track, it is still worthwhile posting audio tracks with static artwork. It's very important to try to get decent quality video of live performances on YouTube as soon as possible, as well as promotional videos if money allows. A promotional video is a specially directed video based on a storyboard and usually features the artist acting or performing in situations that complement the song and the lyrics. Fans also love entertaining and funny audiovisual dressing room conversations and antics. Video interviews with fans are also easy to create at live performances and work really well on YouTube. Any of this non-musical video can go viral, particularly if it's funny/entertaining. In places like the UK, comedy is the new rock'n'roll, with many home-grown comedians selling out multiple nights at 10,000 capacity arenas. Never underestimate the appeal of humor, even if the music is serious, e.g. PSY's 'Gangnam Style', which is the most viewed video in YouTube history.

Here are some guidelines for maximizing the promotional value and income from YouTube.

**Buy or borrow a video camera**

An artist should never underestimate the power of YouTube. The industry is moving from an audio-only industry to being an audio-visual industry. It is therefore becoming very important for an artist or the artist's manager to carry a video camera around with them at all times if possible. Video the artist in all situations, including traveling, recording, in dressing rooms, talking to fans etc. As technology progresses, good video cameras are becoming less and less expensive. Even video from a smartphone can be acceptable if the content is interesting.

**Download and read the YouTube Creator Playbook Guide for Music**

This comprehensive free guide published by YouTube explains how an artist can set up their own YouTube channel and maximize promotional value and income from

YouTube. It explains how to become a YouTube partner so that an artist can receive income every time their video is viewed. Go to:

http://services.google.com/fh/files/misc/music_playbook_guide.pdf

## Create an artist YouTube channel

If an artist is signed to a phonogram producer, it will be the phonogram producer's job to create a channel for the artist or a label channel for all the artists signed to that phonogram producer. If the artist is not signed to a third-party phonogram producer and has their own label, it will be down to the artist and manager to create a channel and upload videos.

## Become a YouTube Partner

If an artist is signed to a phonogram producer, the phonogram producer will need to become a YouTube Partner and pay through royalties to the artist according to the artist's recording agreement. If the artist/manager have their own label, it will be necessary for them to become YouTube partners. By doing this, the label will receive income every time a music fan views the video by receiving a share of the advertising revenue. It used to be the case that payment was made for every time the video was clicked, but YouTube changed the system so that it is now based on 'watch time' or 'engagement time', i.e. the metric is for how long a viewer views a video, which gives a better measure of video engagement. If a video goes viral (i.e. its number of views rises exponentially based on YouTube viewers recommendations to each other), a very large amount of income can be achieved.

One such non-music video was a 56-second home movie called 'Charlie Bit my Finger', which was videoed and posted on YouTube by the British parents of two young boys so that their godfather, who lived in the US, could view it. The video went viral with over half a billion YouTube views, which gave rise to income exceeding $150,000 for the parents after they became YouTube partners, according to Britain's *The Times* newspaper. In order for an artist or label to receive payment from YouTube, it will be necessary to create and associate an 'Adsense' account with an artist's/label's YouTube account.

**Make sure the metadata is correct**

As YouTube is the biggest music discovery platform, it is essential to optimize videos to maximize the chances of music discovery by potential fans. Most music fans discover YouTube channels by search results, so getting the metadata right is very important. The information that follows uses a fictitious band called The Mombasa Lions. They have made a video for a track called 'Concrete Jungle' and it is from a fictitious album called 'Movin Kenya'. Here are some of the main points to get right:

(a) **Titles:** Put heavily searched names first, such as track title, artist name and album or EP Title, e.g. 'Concrete Jungle', 'The Mombasa Lions', 'Movin Kenya'

(b) **Tags:** Use generic and specific keywords, e.g. music, Kenya, reggae, soca, Mombasa Lions

(c) **Description:** Place the call to action at the top, e.g. 'Watch the new Mombasa Lions video for 'Concrete Jungle' here (add link). Follow this with links to stores, live dates, biography, band members names, lyrics, links to website and Facebook page etc.

(d) **Create a 'thumbnail image' for the video.** Use close-ups and bright images for maximum impact. In the same way as the cover of a book is very important for sales, the thumbnail is equally important for YouTube views.

**Releasing an EP or album**

An artist should create lots of good video for the artist channel, including a video trailer for the new release, an official promo video for the first single, interviews with band members, audio-visual content taken in the recording studio, live performance videos etc. This should be introduced one at a time throughout the launch period and flagged on Facebook and Twitter with video links.

186

## Case study – The Young Tigers

So let's look at how to set about building a fan base using the example of a fictitious band, The Young Tigers. Some of the digital services mentioned will inevitably fall by the wayside and new services will emerge, so, as has been said earlier, it's important to keep up-to-date with the latest developments.

The Young Tigers meet at college and form a band making electronic indie crossover music. After a long period of practicing, rehearsing, writing and recording a debut EP, they are ready to do as many live shows as possible. They meet a well-connected and capable manager who is genuinely enthusiastic about their music. They realize that there is nothing more important than getting on the road and performing to people. The band and the manager create their own band website using a free Wordpress template and a mobile version of the site using the free WP Touch Wordpress plug-in which resizes the website for iPhone, iPad, Android, Windows and Blackberry platforms. They sign-up to a website hosting service such as iPage.com, fatcow.com or justhost.com who will provide a free domain name. They choose a .com domain name as this is the most widely used in the commercial world. The band's website will be the hub for everything they do.

At each show, they ask friends and family to collect as many email addresses and postcodes from the audience as they possibly can, using pens and clipboards and approaching audience members individually. They also have postcards printed with a good photo of the band and some basic information such as the band's website address. The postcard asks the recipients to e-mail in what they thought of the show and ideas for improvement. In return for signing up to their email list they send the new fan two free downloads of the band's music, via a link to SoundCloud, as soon as possible after the show. They collect these email addresses and use a mailing list program such as YMLP, Mailchimp or Fanbridge. The basic SoundCloud account, and the entry level accounts for YMLP Fanbridge and Mailchimp cost nothing, so all they need to invest at this stage is their time. They carefully organize their data so the e-mail addresses and geographical location can be used to alert fans in each area the next time they play a show in their region. At each show, the band sells their debut EP and T-shirts and try to meet and talk with as many fans as possible, as well as

actually selling merchandise after the show. Because the band have very little money and can't afford hotels, they invest in $15 inflatable beds and request to be able to sleep on fans' floors. This creates a bonding with fans wherein the fans/hosts become life-long friends and supporters. They make sure their EP is streamable on Spotify and YouTube and is available to purchase online, particularly from iTunes and Google Play, as well as specialist online stores such as Beatport. They sign up to one of the indie aggregators/digital distributors such as AWAL (Artists Without a Label), The Orchard, Believe, CD Baby, Tunecore or Reverbnation, who will place their music for sale on up to 150 digital stores worldwide. They open a band bank account and a PayPal account so that the aggregator can pay them regularly on any sales income.

They create a Facebook artist page, Twitter account, SongKick account and become a YouTube Partner. They encourage as many people as possible to 'Like' their Facebook page, using a simple download for a like app such as BIA, Inboundnow or SoundCloud's Social Unlock, which gives fans a free track in exchange for a Facebook 'like' or a Tweet. Using Facebook, they post interesting updates, anecdotes and funny stories and observations about being on the road. They don't 'hard sell' and over-message their fans with 'buy our EP', keeping a careful balance. They notice that if they embed a photograph or a video with their Facebook posts they get far more likes and comments, so they do that as often as possible. The band do the same with Twitter. The singer encourages the audience every night to follow the band on Twitter. They use social media tools such as SmartURL or PO.ST which shorten the band's domain name, which shortens links. They make banners and T-shirts which just show a graphic with the name of the band and a QR Code. Members of the audience can then take a picture of the QR Code with their smart phones which will link them directly to The Young Tigers website. The manager signs them up to Sonicbids, which helps them to get more live bookings.

They set up their website to act as a hub for Facebook and Twitter feeds. They use SongKick to list their live gigs and embed this in their site. They embed their SoundCloud player on the website and on their Facebook page. The band also use SoundCloud to build their fan base sharing their tunes with other users and developing respect amongst their peers. SoundCloud is the world's leading social sound platform where anyone can create sounds and share them privately with their

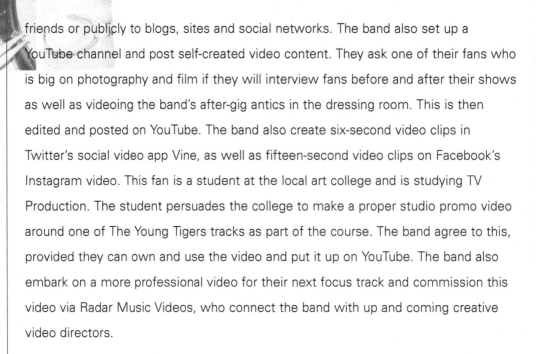

friends or publicly to blogs, sites and social networks. The band also set up a YouTube channel and post self-created video content. They ask one of their fans who is big on photography and film if they will interview fans before and after their shows as well as videoing the band's after-gig antics in the dressing room. This is then edited and posted on YouTube. The band also create six-second video clips in Twitter's social video app Vine, as well as fifteen-second video clips on Facebook's Instagram video. This fan is a student at the local art college and is studying TV Production. The student persuades the college to make a proper studio promo video around one of The Young Tigers tracks as part of the course. The band agree to this, provided they can own and use the video and put it up on YouTube. The band also embark on a more professional video for their next focus track and commission this video via Radar Music Videos, who connect the band with up and coming creative video directors.

The band also make sure that they send their music to music identification giants Gracenote and Shazam. These services can only provide audio identification services to the public if they have The Young Tigers' music. The band's manager takes out a subscription with 'MusicAlly' so that she can keep up to date with the latest digital music services and trends. She and the band use 'Musicmetric', an artist analytics dashboard which not only tracks legitimate sales but also illegal BitTorrent downloads, which she finds useful information, particularly when planning where to play live.

Having done all these things, the band is now reaching out to blogs and sharing links. More fans are discovering them on these blogs, so the band then presents music to specialist radio stations. They have used the BBC introducing service and also send links and info to their favorite specialist DJs who 'break' new artists. They find that some of the most influential specialist radio stations in the world for their music are KCRW in Los Angeles, BBC 6 Music, BBC Radio One, BBC Radio One Extra and XFM in the UK. The band's manager ensures that these stations and other tastemaker stations have The Young Tigers EP.

Being an electronic crossover band, The Young Tigers offer to remix other artists tracks on a reciprocal basis, i.e. they will create a remix for another band if the other band creates a remix of one of The Young Tigers tracks. No money changes hands,

but this cross-pollination process spreads awareness and can create many new fans for both artists. They also develop their skills as DJs as well as playing live and record DJ mixes which they share with their fans and send to small online radio stations and specialist radio programs. They post charts on Beatport every month. They record monthly podcasts which they make available on their website, and record a weekly show with Ideal Clubworld DJs.

All the time, the band are creating as much interesting content as possible to support their music and engage and create loyalty with their fans. They are recording videos, posting cool comments on Facebook and Twitter, giving away free tracks to blogs and setting up competitions. They involve and interact with their fan base as much as possible. They write a song where their fans help contribute to the lyrics. They mobilize their fans in each town when they visit to help advertise the show in that area. The Young Tigers understand that in order to create a loyal fan base they must create a fan community. They never do a hard sell on their fans, as they know that this will dampen enthusiasm for the band. The band also engage via image social networks Instagram, Pinterest, Flickr and Snapchat.

As CD, T-shirt and other merchandise sales increase, the band engage a company such as Topspin, Backstreet, or Sandbag to market their physical items on a larger scale. Some of these services can also sell live performance tickets on behalf of the band.

Creating a fan base is still fundamentally the same as it was 40 years ago. In order to be successful, The Young Tigers have used old-fashioned techniques, such as getting on the road, gigging hard and collecting fans contact details at each show, but they have also fully embraced the modern online technology available to them. Combining all of this, and provided The Young Tigers continue to make great music, they will build a loyal and enduring fan base. Once they have achieved many tens of thousands of genuine likes on Facebook, thousands of followers on Twitter, hundreds of thousands of YouTube views and drawn good attendances at small indie gigs, the band and the band's manager soon find publishers, booking agents and record labels knocking on their door, ready to propel them to the next level. Knowing the band has a genuine and enthusiastic fan base will mean radio and the media will regard them as serious contenders. They are on their way.

## The Future

We are moving into the era of the screen. We are seeing newspapers, books, CDs and DVDs being replaced by their digital on-screen equivalents. This is good news for the environment as less trees are being cut down to create newspapers, books and audio and audio-visual packaging, and less chemical processes are taking place as the demand for CDs and DVDs diminishes. Many music fans are digitizing their physical record collection and are carrying their whole library around with them on their mobile phone so that they can listen to their favorite music anytime and anywhere, whether this be via actual downloads on to their phone or via cloud services. Physical sound carriers will always exist but they will be dwarfed by the unstoppable tide moving to digital ubiquity and convenience.

The future will be social, local, mobile and fluid. Social, via Facebook, Twitter, Instagram and the many other social networks that exist or are yet to be invented. Local, via such services as Four Square, SongKick, Tripadvisor and other services that give fast local information. Mobile, as the networked information society moves ever-faster towards more and more sophisticated smartphones and tablets. Fluid, as the number of click-throughs in each process diminishes and pay-walls become automatic, allowing fans to get to the music or information they need faster. A good example of this is Amazon where they keep customers credit card details and postal billing and delivery addresses on file, making purchasing very fast and simple with just a few clicks.

When radio first started to broadcast music, the music industry at the time vigorously opposed it, saying that if music was played on the radio it would effectively kill the music industry. What actually happened was that radio was the medium that gave the biggest boost to the music industry that it has ever known. Fans would hear music on the radio and if they liked it would often go out and buy the record from their local record store. The internet will almost certainly repeat that evolutionary process. The challenge will be how to monetize the online consumption of music so that authors and performers can make a living from music, but which at the same time, is set at a reasonable price to the music fan. The early years of the music digital revolution have seen conflict and mistrust between the music rights owners, on the one hand, and the technology industries on the other. The reality is that the

technology giants need music content and the music content copyright owners need the technology companies for 21st century distribution. In the future, there will have to be more and more symbiotic co-operation and partnership between the two. This is already happening as we see Google, who have long campaigned for more flexible copyright laws and an open Internet, launching services such as Google Play and Google Play Access All Music, which are built on the laws of copyright.

In many of the poorer areas of the world, even basic radio and television is still not available, particularly in areas away from the big cities. People in these areas are skipping these services and are leap-frogging straight into the online connected world. When the remaining three billion in the world come online and have instant access to all the information and music the world wide web offers, the world's music will inevitably experience a massive boost. For artists, they will find that the income per download or per stream continues to be low, but if that micropayment can be scaled up sufficiently, income from recorded music will once more become significant. Rather than receiving a royalty of perhaps $2 for every album sold, artists may find they receive maybe something of the order of $0.005 per track streamed, which for a ten-track album would amount to $0.05. If the artist sold 50,000 albums and received $2 per album that would equate to $100,000. To generate the same money from streaming, the artist would need to receive payment of the order of four million album streams, but how much better it would be to reach 4 million fans rather than 50,000. The implications for an artist's live work in this scenario are massive.

It will be almost like returning to the days before Emile Berliner's invention of the gramophone, when performers were in complete control of their rights. They either performed live or they didn't. In the future, an artist's fan base will have the potential to be far larger than it is today, which will open up far more opportunities to earn more money from playing live to ever-larger audiences. Cities and private corporations will need to invest in new high quality venues with state-of-the-art facilities so that this increasing demand for live music can be satisfied. Small 100-200 capacity venues, medium sized venues with capacities of 200-1000 and large venues and arenas with capacities of 1000- 20,000 will be needed in every major city. This is why artists will need to work harder than ever on their live performances, as they will be in a highly competitive market where audiences demand great live shows. Audio systems, lighting and stage production will continue to evolve and play an increasingly important role in the success of live performances. Mirroring the success of YouTube, bespoke projected images during the performance are already becoming an essential part of the show for many artists and will continue to become more important in the future. Increasingly, live performances will become multimedia events with fans sharing their experiences in real time.

Income from branding will continue to become increasingly significant, with brands creating ever more innovative campaigns using the 'brand + live + digital' structure on multiple platforms. With phonogram producers providing less funding for new artists, crowd funding and finance from brands will increasingly provide the resources needed to launch an artist's career.

As always, governments will need to continue to adapt, monitor and harmonize laws and appropriate enforcement provisions for the new digital ecosystem. The future will depend on cooperation between artists, phonogram producers, publishers, CMOs, technology/media companies, governments, users and consumers to ensure that new innovative digital services are able to operate and thrive. In the digital world, consumers are an essential and interactive part of any business model. Successful digital businesses will focus on social engagement with consumers, so as to constantly receive feedback and ideas for improvement and development. The social networks are providing a powerful voice for consumers and music fans that never existed before.

A nation's music is one of its most valuable assets and should be regarded in the same way as oil or minerals or any other national asset. Regulatory systems and structures need to be put in place where artists receive fair compensation for their creative work so that a nation's culture and identity can be exported and enriched.

The concept of copyright will survive, but new mechanisms and regulations may have to be devised for consumers to pay for the music they wish to enjoy. One vision of the future is that consumers would be obliged to pay a monthly fee for music in the same way as they pay for electricity or gas. The payment for this blanket license could be made via the consumer's Internet service provider or their mobile service provider which would entitle them to download or stream any music

they liked. It would operate in the same way as the BBC broadcasting license in the UK. Every household in the UK has to pay around $200 per year for the BBC's television, radio and website services (including the very popular interactive BBC iPlayer) which are delivered with no advertising. With this music blanket licensing model, Internet music traffic could then be monitored using digital identifiers and the appropriate payments could be made to authors, performers, publishers and phonogram producers via a CMO. Whilst this is a very logical model in theory, it is difficult to see how it will come about in practice, with all the different interests of the various stakeholders. The Spotify Premium model, wherein music fans can pay a monthly subscription of $10-$15 for all the music on the service, is very close to this model and at the time of writing was growing and working well, although the amount of money trickling down to authors and performers seems disproportionally low, particularly if they are signed to a phonogram producer. One of the biggest independent phonogram producers, Beggars Banquet, has introduced a very fair 50/50 income share for its artists for streaming income, which if sustainable will hopefully become the new norm across the whole recording industry. The key to the success of streaming services is that ALL music has to be available on the service. Some bands are holding out as they do not think services such as Spotify would pay them adequately, but at the time of writing bands such as Pink Floyd and The Eagles, after abstaining for years, are finally coming on-board. In the future, the concept of ownership will be increasingly replaced by access, but this will depend on ubiquitous broadband network coverage, not only in the cities, but in rural areas as well.

The creation of a global repertoire database will need to be a priority, as it will assist significantly in making collective management more efficient and effective in the future. In addition to the WIPO International Music Registry initiative, the Global Repertoire Database for authors' works will hopefully become a reality and will significantly improve accurate international payments for authors and publishers in the future. The ideal scenario for some time in the future would be for a combined authors, performers and phonogram producers global database to be created, with compatible and harmonized software which would result in efficient and accurate cross-border payments.

Education on copyright, music and technology will be increasingly important, as the younger generation find it even more natural to multi-task by monitoring several screens at the same time. Children who are growing up in the era of the digital screen think nothing of viewing TV, a smartphone, a tablet and perhaps a game console all at the same time and switching priority from one to the other on a second-by-second basis, according to what is happening. As this generation grows older, those engaged with the digital world will find this to be a natural and normal process. Smartphones will increasingly be regarded as a second brain that travels with a person constantly. Leaving a smartphone at home by mistake will be akin to leaving the house with no clothes on.

The Apps market will continue to grow exponentially as consumers make it clear that they are prepared to pay for convenience and collation. Whilst an artist's audio and audio-visual content can be found at various places on the Internet, fans will pay for the convenience of it all being brought together in one easily accessible place via an app. More and more accessing and paying for music will be by social recommendation. It can also be expected that higher CD quality downloads will be available to music fans in the future at a premium price.

Advertising will increasingly be targeted only at those that might be interested in the product or service being advertised. New generation smart TVs will have an option to view the viewer, sense what mood they're in and whether they are male or female. Advertising will then be specifically tailored to ads that might be of interest to that particular viewer. In return for allowing this interactive advertising, the viewer would be given perhaps free access to sport or films.

Despite all this exponential change, one thing remains the same: those artists wishing to make a living from music need to work hard at their craft. Musicians still need to put in their 10,000 hours of practice and focus on original songwriting and performances, just as they have for centuries gone by. Those that succeed will be those who are not put off by failure and who keep believing in themselves and the music they create. Some things never change.

# ANNEX A
## DEFINITIONS AND INDEX

**AAC file:** An Advanced Audio Coding file used by Apple for its iTunes and iPod technologies. AAC is an audio compression technology that is part of the MPEG-2 and MPEG-4 standards. AAC, especially MPEG-4 AAC, provides greater compression and better sound quality than MP3, which also came out of the MPEG standard.

**Advance:** An amount of money paid to an author or a performer before royalties are earned and which is usually recoupable against future royalties.

**Advertising agency:** A business which provides ideas and which manages an advertisement or an advertising campaign on behalf of a product, brand or service.

**Aggregator:** A Digital Music Aggregator (DMA) is a person or business licensing and receiving income from a number of digital music retailers on behalf of an artist or a phonogram producer.

**Album:** A collection of recorded tracks together on one recording medium such as a CD. An album typically comprises 10-14 tracks.

**Alpha Testing:** The initial testing of a newly developed software product, wherein employees and friends of the developing company test the product for bugs, glitches and functionality. (See Beta Testing.)

**A&R:** Artist and Repertoire. An A&R person in a phonogram producer's business is the one with responsibility for finding new artists and offering them recording agreements and who supervises the recordings of artists on behalf of the phonogram producer.

**API:** Abbreviation of 'Application Platform Interface'. API is a set of tools, protocols and routines for building software applications. An API makes it easier to develop programs by providing the building blocks for a programmer/developer. (See Open API below.)

**App:** Abbreviation of 'Application'. An application is computer software designed to help the user perform specific tasks.

**Arbitration:** The hearing and determination of a dispute by an impartial referee selected or agreed upon by the parties concerned. Unlike 'Mediation' (see below), an arbitrator will issue a binding judgment on the parties in the same way as a court.

**Artist:** A performer who may or may not also be an author.

**ASCAP:** The American Society of Composers, Authors and Publishers. One of three US public performance right CMOs collecting license fees on behalf of its author and publisher members. ASCAP analyses and distributes license fee income as royalties to those of its members whose works have been performed in public.

**At source basis:** Payments made as a percentage of the gross income (rather than the net income) received, less any sales or value added taxes (VAT).

**Audit rights:** The right to examine a contracting party's financial accounting records, to ensure that correct accounting has been implemented.

**Author:** The person or entity who creates a work. This can be the creator of the musical composition, the musical arrangement or the lyrics, or a combination of any of them. In some countries, interpreters of lyrics may also qualify as an author.

**Back-end income:** Income based on results rather than from an initial advance. The opposite of front-loaded.

**Beta Testing:** The final stage of testing for a newly developed software product, before it is available to be sold to the public. Beta testing involves allowing a limited number of public users the chance to test the software and provide feedback on any problems or ideas for improvement.

**BIEM:** The international umbrella organization representing mechanical rights CMOs on behalf of publishers and authors.

**Blog:** A website on which an individual or group of users record opinions, information etc. on a regular basis. A blog is an open Internet-based diary: a contraction of the word 'weblog'.

**BMI:** Broadcast Music Incorporated. One of three US public performance right CMOs, collecting license fees on behalf of its author and publisher members. BMI distributes license fee income as royalties to those of its members whose works have been performed in public.

**Boiler plate:** The legal detail and standard provisions to be found in an agreement.

**Booking agent:** Someone who interfaces with promoters and venues on behalf of an artist in order to secure live performance bookings.

**Bootlegger:** Someone who illegally manufactures and/or sells copyright and related right-protected recordings and works, or copyright-protected merchandise without a license and who makes no payment to the legitimate copyright or related rights holders.

**BRIC:** Short for the combined territories of Brazil, Russia, India and China, which together account for over 40% of the world's population.

**Brief:** A concise statement or summary.

**Broadband:** A high-speed Internet connection capable of supporting a wide range of electromagnetic frequencies, typically from audio up to video frequencies. It can carry multiple signals by dividing the total capacity of the medium into multiple, independent bandwidth channels, where each channel operates only on a specific range of frequencies.

**Busking:** Playing music in public places in the hope that members of the public who pass by will voluntarily pay money into a hat or instrument case placed near the performer(s).

**Carnet:** A temporary customs document allowing the holder to temporarily import equipment and/or merchandising to a foreign country for the purposes of a live performance or tour without having to pay duties or posting bonds.

**CD:** An optical digital audio compact disc capable of storing up to 700 Mb of information or 74 minutes of high fidelity stereo music. A CD is 120mm in diameter, recorded on one side, with individual tracks playable in any sequence.

**Choreographer:** The person responsible for creating and arranging the movements of a dance routine.

**CISAC:** International Confederation of Societies of Authors and Composers. The international umbrella organization representing authors and publishers public performance CMOs, who in turn represent their author and publisher members.

**Cleared:** When the rights in a work or a performance have been authorized for use by the legitimate rights holders.

**Cloud computing:** The practice of using a network of remote servers hosted on the Internet to store, manage and process data, rather than a local server. Cloud computing allows businesses to reduce the cost of information management, as they do not need to own their own servers, but can use capacity leased from third parties via the internet.

**Cloud storage:** Networked online storage where data is stored on remote servers, generally hosted by third parties. Businesses and individuals who require data to be hosted can buy or lease storage capacity from them. (See Cyberlockers).

**CMO:** Collective Management Organization

**Compilation album:** An album comprising a collection of recorded tracks by different artists.

**Contract period:** Each option period in an agreement.

**Copyright:** The right to authorize or prohibit the making of copies of a work. (also used in reference to the copying of recordings in some common law countries).

**Cover:** A performance by a performer who is not the author of the musical work.

**Cover record:** A recording by a performer who is not the author of the musical work contained in the recording.

**Cure Period:** A provision in a contract which allows a defaulting party to correct the default within a defined time period after being notified by the other party.

**Cyberlocker:** A cyberlocker is a third-party online service that provides file-storing and file-sharing services for media files and other data. Cyberlockers can be accessed globally over the Internet and are online data hosting services that provide secure remote storage.

**Dial-up:** A low-speed Internet connection accessed by a telephone connection via a modem operating on Internet connection speeds below 100 Kbps. A 56 Kbps modem and basic rate ISDN are examples.

**Distributor:** A business that distributes sound recordings and/or audiovisual recordings on behalf of owners or licensees of sound recordings and audiovisual recordings.

**Domain name:** A string of letters, numbers and hyphens that are used to define the location of a website. Domain names are used as pointers to IP addresses, e.g. www.wipo.int or www.bobmarley.com.

**Download:** Any digital file such as an mP3 file or an app which can be transferred from an online server to a local computer and stored on the local computer.

**DRM:** Digital Rights Management. Any digital technology used to protect the interests of copyright owners and service providers. DRM includes TPM and identification technologies that can be used for marketing and operating purposes.

**ECSA:** The European Composer and Songwriter Alliance. The umbrella European organization representing professional music authors in 22 European countries.

**Embed:** The process of the incorporation of a media player or video into a website or blog.

**Encryption:** The conversion of data into cipher text that cannot be understood by unauthorized people. Decryption is the process of converting encrypted data back into its original form, so that it can be understood.

**Encryption service:** A business that provides encryption, usually in the context of financial transactions in order to avoid fraud.

**EPK:** An electronic press kit. This usually includes a biography, still photographs and a video interview with the artist. Sometimes called a DPK (Digital Press Kit).

**Escrow Account:** An account created in which funds deposited are safeguarded and put in the custody of a third person. Money can only be accessed and paid out under certain specified conditions.

**Equitable remuneration:** Fair (usually equal but not necessarily) remuneration between two rights holders who are entitled to share a single payment.

**Exclusive:** Not divided or shared with others.

**Exclusive right:** The holder of an exclusive right has the power to authorize or prohibit certain actions or use.

**Extended play single:** A single with extra tracks so that it falls between a single and an album in length. Sometimes called an EP.

**Facebook:** A free social networking website available in 37 languages that allows registered users to create profiles, upload photos and video, send messages and keep in touch with friends, family and colleagues. In the case of music, it is a key tool for digital marketing and communication with fans.

**FIA:** The International Federation of Actors.

**FIM:** The International Federation of Musicians (Fédération Internationale des Musiciens). The international umbrella organization representing national musicians' unions.

**Fixation:** When a performance is recorded or fixed on to a magnetic tape or digital disc or any recording medium. (The definition in the WPPT is 'the embodiment of sounds or of the representations thereof, from which they can be perceived, reproduced or communicated through a device'.) Also known as a fixed performance.

**Front-loaded agreement:** An agreement where there is a substantial initial advance rather than one where most of the income is based on results (back-ended).

**Front-of-house engineer:** The engineer responsible for mixing the sound that the audience will hear through the PA system.

**Fulfillment:** The process of managing financial transactions, handling and shipping customers' orders.

**GAS:** Short for the combined territories of Germany, Austria and Switzerland.

**Geolocation:** The detection of the physical location of an internet connected computing device.

**Genre:** A type or style of music, e.g. chillout, soul, heavy metal, folk, reggae, electronic dance etc.

**GESAC:** The European umbrella organization representing the largest European authors and publishers CMOs.

**Gig:** Slang for a show, concert, event or performance.

**Google Play:** A digital application distribution platform for Android developed and maintained by Google. (Formerly known as the Android Market.)

**Gracenote:** A commercial internet-accessible database containing information about audio recordings. It provides software and metadata to businesses such as iTunes that enables their customers to manage and search digital media.

**Harry Fox Agency:** The US CMO responsible for mechanical licensing, collection and distribution for music publishers.

**Hashtag:** The # symbol is used to mark keywords or topics in a Tweet or Facebook post. It was created organically by Twitter users as a way to categorize messages.

**Heads of agreement:** A brief summary of the main points of an agreement without the legal detail (boiler plate).

**Home Copying Levies:** a levy or tax that is placed by national governments on recordable media (such as recordable CDRs, DVDs and tape) and/or recordable hardware (such as computer hard drives/analogue and digital recording devices) to compensate rights holders for music copied by consumers within the domestic environment. The income is usually distributed to the rights holders (authors, performers, publishers and phonogram producers) via CMOs.

**ICMP:** International Confederation of Music Publishers. The umbrella trade organization representing music publishers worldwide.

**ICT:** Information & Communications Technology.

**IFPI:** The International Federation of the Phonographic Industry. The international umbrella trade body representing phonogram producers and affiliated industry organizations.

**IMMF:** The International Music Managers Forum. The international umbrella trade body representing Music Managers' Forums (MMFs) worldwide.

**IMPALA:** The Independent Music Companies Association. The international umbrella trade body representing independent phonogram producers worldwide.

**Intellectual property (IP):** A non-tangible product of the intellect that has commercial value, including copyrighted property such as literary, musical or artistic works, and ideational property, such as patents, business methods, and industrial processes.

**In perpetuity:** Something that lasts for life or forever. In copyright terms, it refers to the full length of copyright protection permitted by law, i.e. life of copyright.

**Instagram:** An online photo-sharing and social networking service owned by Facebook that enables users to apply digital filters to their pictures and share them on social networking sites such as Facebook and Twitter. A distinctive feature is that it confines photos to a square shape similar to how Kodak Instamatic and Polaroid used to, rather than the 16:9 ratio used by most mobile device cameras. Initially a purely photo-sharing service, Instagram incorporated video sharing in June 2013, allowing its users to record and share videos lasting for up to 15 seconds.

**Interactive streaming:** Streaming wherein a member of the public can access a specific recording/work at a time and a place of their own choosing, sometimes referred to as

'non-linear streaming'. (See also 'webcasting', 'simulcasting', 'linear streaming' and 'making available'.)

**Internet:** An interconnected system of networks that connects computers worldwide via the TCP/IP protocol.

**ISP:** Internet service provider. An ISP is a business that provides individuals and businesses with access to the Internet and other related services such as website building. An ISP has the equipment and the telecommunication line access required to have a point-of-presence on the Internet for the geographic area served. The larger ISPs have their own high-speed leased lines so that they are less dependent on the telecommunication providers and can provide better service to their customers.

**iTunes:** A digital music service owned, operated and developed by Apple that incorporates a media player and a media library application. It is used to play, download, and organize digital audio and video on personal computers running the OS X and Microsoft Windows operating systems.

**JASRAC:** Japanese Society for Rights of Authors, Composers and Publishers. The sole CMO in Japan responsible for authors' and publishers' public performance right income and mechanical income.

**Karaoke:** A musical sound system providing pre-recorded accompaniment to popular songs that a performer (usually a member of the public in a bar or club) sings live by following the words on a video screen.

**License/licensing:** When rights owners authorize the use of their rights to third parties under certain conditions, whilst retaining ownership of the right.

**Licensee:** A person or business that licenses a right from a right owner (the licensor) under certain conditions.

**Licensor:** A right owner who licenses the use of the right under certain conditions to another person or business (a licensee).

**Linear streaming:** Streaming wherein a member of the public has no control as to which recording/work is being streamed. (See 'interactive streaming', 'webcasting' and 'simulcasting'.)

**Lyrics:** The words of a work.

**Making available:** The exclusive right for authors, performers and phonogram producers to authorize or prohibit the interactive use of their works or recordings by wire or wireless means via the Internet, such that members of the public may access a work or recording from a place and at a time individually chosen by them.

**Mailing list:** A list of e-mail addresses with one title that is used to send out information to multiple recipients. With one click all the recipients on the list will receive the information.

**Manager:** An artist manager is a person who manages an artist's business affairs and an artist's career.

**Manufacturer:** A business that creates the physical copies of recordings for sale and/or distribution to the public.

**Master recording:** The finished mixed and mastered version of a recording.

**Master re-use license:** A license issued by a phonogram producer or a performer or by whoever holds the related rights in a particular sound recording for the right to use the sound recording in conjunction with visual images in a film, a television production, a video game or an advertisement.

**Mastering:** The final stage of the recording process, in which a mixed recording is processed by a mastering engineer using equalization and dynamic enhancement so as to make the recording sound as good as possible prior to manufacture, downloading, streaming and broadcasting.

**MCPS:** The Mechanical Copyright Protection Society. The sole UK CMO that issues mechanical licenses and collects mechanical royalties and other income on behalf of authors and publishers.

**Mechanical license:** The license issued by the copyright owner of a musical work (or a CMO representing the copyright owner for mechanical rights) to a phonogram producer, which permits the phonogram producer to exploit recordings containing the work.

**Mechanical rate:** The rate set or recommended in a country as a percentage of PPD, or as a rate per track, payable by phonogram producers to copyright holders of works (or a CMO representing the copyright owner for mechanical rights) for each record sold.

**Mechanical royalties:** Royalties paid by owners or licensees of sound recordings to the copyright owners of musical works (or a CMO representing the copyright owner for mechanical rights) for the right to record, copy and distribute works in such recordings.

**Mediation:** A dispute settlement process wherein both parties mutually agree to appoint a mediator who facilitates a settlement between the parties that they both agree to. (See Arbitration above.)

**Merchandiser:** A person or business who sells an artist's merchandising products to the public on behalf of the artist.

**Merchandising:** The sale of T-shirts, books, CDs and other artifacts relating to an artist at the venue where an artist is playing live or through a website or retail outlet.

**Metadata:** Data about data. The title, format and other information embedded into a digital music file such as an MP3.

**Minimum commitment:** The minimum number of works or recordings required to be submitted or released during each contract period.

**Mixing engineer:** The engineer responsible for mixing the separate tracks of a recording in a studio, resulting in a master recording.

**Modem:** Abbreviation of modulator/demodulator. A communications device that converts digital signals to analogue and then from analogue to digital for transmission of data via telephone or cable lines.

**Monitor engineer:** An engineer who ensures that performing artists can adequately hear their stage performance and the stage performances of others playing with them, by way of on-stage monitor speakers or in-ear radio monitoring systems.

**Most favored nations (MFN):** In a situation where there is more than one licensor (such as with an audiovisual synchronization license where there are usually two separate copyright holders – the publisher and the phonogram producer), the licensee agrees to give all parties the most favorable terms negotiated by any one of the licensors.

**MP3 file:** A computer file created with compression technology commonly used to make digital audio computer files relatively small while maintaining high audio quality. MP3 means MPEG-1, Audio Layer 3 and is an audio-specific format. The compression takes off certain sounds that cannot be heard by the listener, i.e. outside the normal human hearing range. It provides a representation of pulse-code modulation-encoded audio in much less space, by using psychoacoustic models to discard components less audible to human hearing, and recording the remaining information in an efficient manner.

**MPEG:** Moving Picture Experts Group. An ISO/ITU standard for compressing digital video. Pronounced 'em-peg', it is the universal standard for digital terrestrial, cable and satellite TV, DVDs and digital video recorders (DVRs).

**musicFIRST Coalition:** A pressure group which includes the AFofM, Sound Exchange, the US Music Managers Forum, the Grammy Foundation and the RIAA etc. who campaign for the introduction of a public performance right in sound recordings for free-to-air radio in the US.

**Music supervisor:** A person who has the responsibility to find and clear suitable music and manage the music for a film, television production, video game or an advertisement.

**MySpace:** A social networking service with a strong emphasis on music. In June 2006 it was the most visited website in the US but then fell into decline. Purchased in June 2011 by Specific Media and Justin Timberlake for relaunch in 2013.

**NDA:** Non-disclosure agreement. A clause in a contract wherein one or all of the contracting parties is/are prohibited from disclosing the conditions of the agreement to third parties.

**National treatment:** A principle in international law wherein a member state grants equal treatment and rights to foreigners as it does to its own citizens, provided that the two countries are both parties to the same relevant international agreement or treaty.

**Net income:** Gross income less any sales or value added taxes and less all or certain specified expenses and costs.

**Non-Linear streaming:** Interactive streaming wherein a member of the public can access a specific recording/work at a time and a place of their own choosing. (see 'linear streaming')

**Online:** Via the Internet.

**Open API:** An open application platform interface is one where a service provider makes their API openly available to third-party developers so that new apps can be created using their service.

**Option:** The right of a phonogram producer or of a publisher to future recordings or works at their discretion (usually accompanied by a further advance to the performer or author).

**Overage:** Any additional sums payable over and above the guaranteed sum in an agreement.

**PA system:** A public address sound system, consisting of amplifiers and speakers used to amplify an artist's performance so that an audience can hear it clearly.

**PD:** *per diem*: A daily financial allowance for each member of a band and touring crew to cover food and other incidental costs whilst working away from home.

**Peer-to-peer (P2P):** A network computing system in which all computers are treated as equals on the network and have the capability to share files with each other. Napster was the first mainstream P2P software that enabled large-scale file sharing.

**Performer:** An entertainer who plays musical instruments and/or sings and/or dances or performs a dramatic work.

**Phonogram:** An audio-only fixation of a performance or other sounds.

**Phonogram producer:** An entity that holds the related rights in a recording and exploits that recording by way of advertising, promotion and distribution for sale to the public, sometimes referred to as a record company or record label.

**Pinterest:** A pinboard-style photo-sharing website that allows users to create and manage theme-based image collections such as events, interests and hobbies. Users can browse other users' pinboards for images, re-pin images to their own pinboards, or 'like' photos.

**Piracy:** When related right protected recordings, possibly containing copyright protected works, are manufactured and sold or made available for download and sold illegally with

no license and no payment being made to the legitimate copyright or related right holders. The term 'piracy' is also sometimes used when illegal copyright protected merchandise is sold.

**Plug-in (or Plugin):** An add-on software component that adds a specific feature to an existing software application which allows customization. Examples are the Adobe Flash Player, QuickTime Player, the Java plug-in and Wordpress's WPtouch plug-in.

**Plugger:** Someone who is paid to try and persuade a radio or TV station to play a record.

**Podcast:** An audio or video file that is attached to an RSS feed as an enclosure so that any user that wants to receive it can 'subscribe' via software known as a podcatcher.

**Podcatcher:** A software computer program used to download various media via an RSS or XML feed.

**Point:** A percentage point. 3 percent of PPD is sometimes referred to as '3 points'.

**PPD:** The published price to dealers of a recording as published by a phonogram producer or distributor. (Sometimes referred to as the wholesale price)

**PPL:** Public Performance Limited. The sole UK CMO that collects public performance income on behalf of performers and phonogram producers.

**Production company:** A business that offers a recording agreement to an artist, makes and pays for recordings, and then licenses them to other phonogram producers or distributors.

**Production manager:** A person who supervises the provision of all the stage equipment, sound equipment and lighting and special effects equipment associated with a concert or tour.

**Promoter:** Someone who engages an artist to appear live at a venue and is responsible for organizing, advertising and selling tickets for the event as well as paying the artist for such a performance.

**Promotion:** Anything that assists an artist to become better known to the public including press and website interviews, radio and television appearances etc.

**PRS:** Performing Right Society. The sole UK CMO that collects public performance income on behalf of authors and publishers, latterly rebranded as 'PRSforMusic'.

**Public domain:** The period of time after copyright or related rights protection in a work or a recording has expired. For a work or a recording to be 'in the public domain', it is no longer protected by copyright or related rights and any member of the public can use it or sell it without needing permission or authorization.

**Publisher:** A person or business that commercially exploits the works created by authors.

**Publishing agreement:** An agreement whereby an author licenses or assigns the works they create to a music publisher for commercial exploitation of those works.

**QR Code:** A two-dimensional barcode readable my mobile phones with cameras, smartphones or QR scanners to access information such as contact details or website addresses.

**Real tones:** Actual sound clips of recorded music and sounds which can be downloaded to a mobile phone and which will play when the mobile phone receives an incoming call.

**Receipts basis:** Payments made on the net rather than the gross income.

**Reciprocal agreements:** When one organization in a country has an agreement with another organization in another country to pay through royalties to authors or performers resident in either country, from one to the other.

**Recoupable cost:** A cost that can be offset against royalties earned by a performer or author, by a phonogram producer or publisher.

**Recoupment:** The point at which the royalties earned under an agreement equal the advances and other recoupable costs.

**Related rights:** Intellectual property rights granted to performers, broadcasters and phonogram producers.

**Remuneration right:** The right to receive a payment every time a work or a recording is used without the ability to authorize or prohibit such use.

**Restraint of trade:** A common law doctrine relating to the enforceability of contractual restrictions on the freedom to conduct business.

**Retainer:** A minimum monthly sum of money which is guaranteed whether or not work is required in that month in order to retain first call on a person's services.

**Retention period:** The period after the term of a publishing agreement has expired whereby the works covered in the agreement continue to be exercised by the publisher.

**RIAA:** The Recording Industry Association of America. The trade association that represents most US phonogram producers.

**Ring tones:** The sound (usually polyphonic) made by a mobile phone to indicate an incoming call.

**Ringback tones:** Music offered by a mobile network operator that becomes the audible sound heard on a telephone by the caller while the phone they are ringing is being rung.

**Roadie:** Someone who sets up and takes down an artist or band's equipment on stage and supervises the stage equipment during the performance.

**Royalties:** Compensation payments made to an author, performer or other entity for each use or sale of a work, recording or merchandise item by a publisher, phonogram producer, computer game manufacturer or merchandiser etc. A royalty is expressed as a percentage of receipts or as a payment for each unit sold.

**Royalty rate:** The percentage at which royalties are paid.

**RSS feed:** Short for 'really simple syndication' or 'rich site summary', an RSS feed is a digital delivery vehicle for news or other web content such as is contained in a podcast or a blog.

**SACEM:** (Société des Auteurs, Compositeurs et Editeurs de Musique) The sole CMO representing authors and publishers in France.

**Sample:** The use of a portion or part of an existing recording or work (or both) and the integration of this into a new recording or work (or both).

**SCAPR:** The Societies' Council for the collective management of performers' rights. The international umbrella body for CMOs responsible for collecting income from public performance licenses on behalf of performers.

**Score:** A musical composition in printed or written form, also used to describe the soundtrack to a film.

**Search engine:** Software code designed to search for information on the internet using web-crawlers (sometimes known as 'spiders' or 'bots').

**SEO or search engine optimization:** The process of increasing the visibility of a website or web page in a search engine's search results.

**Serial number:** A number in a series that is marked on a piece of equipment by the manufacturer to give that piece of equipment a unique identifying number.

**SESAC:** One of three US public performance right collection societies, collecting license fees on behalf of its author and publisher members. SESAC distributes them as royalties to those SESAC members whose works have been performed.

**Shazam:** One of the largest music identification services that allows mobile users to identify commercially released tracks from any device which is playing music via a loudspeaker (TV, radio, PA system etc.). By holding the phone to the music for several seconds, the audio sample is sent to the Shazam datacenter which compares it to a database of millions of song fingerprints and identifies it.

**Sheet music:** Musical notation of a work printed or written down, which usually shows the notes, chords, lyrics and other musical information for the performance of the work using voice, piano, guitar and/or other musical instruments.

**Simulcast:** A simultaneous webcast of a radio or television broadcast or cable broadcast (see 'interactive streaming', 'linear streaming' and 'webcast').

**Smartphone:** A cellular mobile phone with built-in applications and which has the capability for internet access.

**Smart TV:** Televisions that have built-in applications and which can be connected to the internet to provide a more interactive experience for users.

**Snapchat:** A photo messaging application ("app") wherein users can take photos, record videos, add text and drawings, and send them to a controlled list of recipients. These sent photographs and videos are known as "Snaps". Users set a time limit for how long recipients can view their Snaps (1 to 10 seconds), after which they will be hidden from the recipient's device and deleted from Snapchat's servers.

**Sound carrier:** Any physical medium including CDs, tapes, vinyl discs and memory sticks which contain recorded music or sounds.

**Sound-check:** The process of performers testing and balancing the front of house sound mix and the on-stage monitor mix in a venue prior to a live public performance.

**SoundCloud:** SoundCloud is an online audio distribution platform based in Berlin, Germany that enables its users to upload, record, promote and share their originally-created sounds.

**Sound Exchange:** The sole US related rights CMO responsible for licensing and collecting digital income (where such rights exist) on behalf of performers and phonogram producers from the public performance of sound recordings in the US.

**Spotify:** A commercial music streaming service, based in Sweden, providing streamed content from phonogram producers and artists, either on a free limited ad-supported subscription basis or on a premium ad-free subscription.

**STIM:** (Svenska Tonsättares Internationella Musikbyrå) The sole CMO for authors and publishers in Sweden.

**Studio producer:** The person who is responsible for supervising the creation of a sound recording in a recording studio, also sometimes referred to as a record producer.

**Soundtrack album:** A collection of songs put together to comprise an album which are taken from or associated with a film.

**Spam:** Indiscriminate and unsolicited bulk email (UBE). Spam is usually associated with unsolicited commercial advertising and is sometimes referred to as 'junk mail'.

**Splitter bus:** A vehicle that provides seating in the front of the vehicle and a separate compartment at the back for equipment.

**Sponsorship:** Financial payment or payment in kind by a third party to the artist or other entity in return for promotion of the third party's products or brand.

**Streaming:** Data that can be accessed via a local computer from an on-line server, but which cannot be downloaded or stored on the local computer. (See 'linear streaming' and 'interactive streaming')

**Sub-publisher:** A publisher in a foreign territory which represents the interests and collects income on behalf of the domestic publisher and pays through that income to the domestic publisher after taking an agreed commission.

**Synchronization license:** The license issued by a publisher or an author when the author's work is synchronized with visual images, usually moving images.

**Telecoms:** Businesses in the field of telecommunications such as mobile phone companies.

**Term:** The period of time for which an agreement is effective.

**Tethered downloads:** A digital music file downloaded from a music subscription service that has embedded TPM technology which only allows the file to be played on a computer registered to the account.

**Tour bus:** A bus used for touring which usually has sleeping facilities, a kitchen, a lounge and bathroom facilities on board. The bus will often travel to the next city on the tour overnight while the artist and crew are sleeping.

**Tour manager:** Someone who manages an artist's live performance work on behalf of the artist's manager and/or the artist.

**Tour support:** A payment made to an artist, usually by the artist's phonogram producer to cover the financial shortfall of a tour. This payment is usually recoupable from artist's royalties.

**TPM:** Technical protection measures. A sub-set of DRM, TPM are digital technology applications designed to prevent or limit unauthorized copying.

**Track:** A single recording of a performance of a work. There are typically 10 to 14 tracks on an album. Each track often comprises many sub-tracks which are recorded individually and which are then mixed to create the finished track.

**Trademark:** The registered name or symbol identifiable with goods or services to ensure exclusivity and protection from others using the same name or symbol for commercial benefit.

**Twitter:** A free social networking micro-blogging service that allows registered users to broadcast short posts known as 'tweets'. Users can create tweets of no more than 140 characters and 'follow' other users tweets by using multiple platforms and devices. A key tool for digital music marketing.

**Über-fan:** A hard core fan who is a very loyal and passionate supporter of an artist.

**UGC:** User-generated content. Content created by members of the public such as home-made videos which are then posted on sites such as YouTube for non-commercial social sharing.

**Underscore:** Background music in a film.

**UNESCO:** The United Nations Educational Scientific and Cultural Organization, which encourages international peace and universal respect by promoting collaboration among nations.

**Venue:** The place or building where a live performance takes place.

**Vine:** A social video app owned by Twitter. Videos can only be created within the app and are limited to six seconds which are then looped. Captions and hashtags can be included to make the videos easily searchable and shareable on Twitter and Facebook.

**Viral:** The process whereby a track or a video becomes popular by fan-to-fan recommendation rather than marketing. There is no such thing as viral marketing.

**Visa (work visa):** The appropriate immigration document, usually stamped in or attached to an artist or crew member's passport, which permits that person to work in a foreign country for a limited period of time.

**Webcast:** The online equivalent of broadcasting, but only by streaming via the Internet.

**Webmaster:** Someone who builds and/or supervises an artist's website.

**Website:** A collection of web pages, which are documents coded in HTML that are linked to each other and very often to pages on other websites. For musical artists it is usually their primary presence on the internet.

**Widget:** Short for 'window gadget', a widget is a standardized on-screen representation of a control that may be manipulated by the user. Scroll bars, buttons and text boxes are all examples of widgets.

**WIPO:** The World Intellectual Property Organization, an agency of the United Nations, based in Geneva, dedicated to developing a balanced and accessible international intellectual property (IP) system which rewards creativity, stimulates innovation and contributes to economic development while safeguarding the public interest.

**WOMAD:** The World of Music Arts and Dance. An international organization that promotes festivals featuring artists from all over the world.

**WOMEX:** World Music Expo. An organization promoting artist showcases and networking opportunity events for artists from all over the world.

**Work:** Any author's musical creation, including the musical composition and/or lyrics, and/or the musical arrangement. In some countries, those that translate the lyrics may also have rights in a work.

**YouTube:** A social networking video sharing service that allows users to watch videos posted by other users and upload videos of their own. Owned by Google, it is the world's number one music discovery website and is a key tool in digital music marketing.

## INDEX

## H

## I

## J

## K

## L

## M

# ANNEX B
## EXAMPLE OF A SHORT-TERM LETTER OF ENGAGEMENT

To: (Artist(s) Name(s) and Address(es)), hereinafter referred to as 'Artist' or 'You'

Date.............................................

Dear ...........................................

Further to our recent meetings and discussions, please accept this letter as confirmation that.......................(hereinafter referred to as 'Manager', 'Us' or 'We') will act as your exclusive manager throughout the world for a trial period of (.........) months from the above date, after which either You or Us must give 30 days' notice to the other to effect termination.

During this trial period you agree to pay Us commission of (......) % on any income received by You in the entertainment industry, except for any income specifically intended as recording costs, video production costs or as tour support. You further agree to reimburse reasonable expenses incurred by Us on your behalf as per the attached schedule. In regard to live performances the commission payable to Us will be reduced to (......) % of the gross income received.

At the end of the trial period You or Us may decide to terminate the management relationship or move forward with negotiations for a long-form artist management agreement. In either case payment of commission and expenses must be paid to Us within 60 days of receipt of the invoice which We shall submit.

In signing this letter You are entering into a legally-binding agreement.

If the above is a correct reflection of the agreement we have reached, please confirm this by your signature(s) below:

Yours sincerely

...........................(Manager)

Date...........................................

Confirmation of agreement by (name and address of Artist(s))

Signature.......................................

Date...........................................

Expenses as per the example that follows should be attached to this temporary letter of engagement. The Manager's Expenses are paid by the manager from his/her own resources, whereas the Artist's Expenses are repayable to the manager from the artist's gross income in addition to any commission payable.

### Example of an Expenses Schedule

1.  *Manager's Expenses – Manager's general office and business costs, including:*

    *Office rent*

    *Local property tax on office*

    *Management staff salaries and wages*

    *Management staff social security payments*

    *Manager's office equipment, including:*

    *Computers*

    *Fax machines*

    *Photocopiers*

    *Mobile phones*

    *Office telephone systems*

    *Audio and audiovisual equipment*

    *Manager's car and associated costs*

    *Manager's legal fees*

    *Local telephone, fax and email costs*

    *Miscellaneous office expenses*

2.  *Artist's Expenses – Any expenses reasonably incurred in connection with the Artist's career, whether incurred by the Manager or the Artist, other than the Manager's Expenses, including but not limited to the following:*

    *Commission payable to a booking agent or other agents*

    *Costs/wages payable to a tour manager*

    *Mail shots on behalf of the Artist*

    *Advertising on behalf of the Artist*

    *Artwork on behalf of the Artist*

    *Management long-distance phone and fax charges If specifically on behalf of the Artist*

    *Accommodation costs*

*Air, rail and sea fares*

*Courier charges on behalf of the Artist*

*Manager's reasonable subsistence (food etc.) when on tour or away on business on the Artist's behalf*

*(___) per mile for the Manager's car journeys (to be reviewed annually)*

*Car hire, taxis and other travel costs when business being carried out on behalf of the Artist by the Manager or the Manager's personal assistant*

*Legal costs incurred when the Artist contracts with third parties*

*Expenses incurred by the Manager prior to the commencement of this agreement in the sum of (_____)*

*The above to be pro rata if work for other artists is also being carried out.*

The mileage rate charged for the manager's car journeys will vary according to the car's engine capacity. The local tax authority or automobile association should be able to supply the acceptable current mileage rates. This mileage rate not only covers fuel but also road tax, maintenance and servicing as well as depreciation etc.

# ANNEX C
## EXAMPLE OF A LONG-FORM ARTIST MANAGEMENT AGREEMENT

(with explanatory notes)

Every situation is different and will present its own unique set of circumstances. Some countries follow different industry practices which may not be the same as the following example. It is therefore intended to be a guide to understanding long-form artist management contracts, hopefully assisting in arriving at a fair agreement for both parties.

This example is in two parts: the contract and the schedule. Example clauses are shown in italics with notes on the clauses in normal type.

### THE CONTRACT

1.  *The Artist hereby appoints the Manager who agrees to carry out the Manager's duties in relation to the Artist's career throughout the Territory during the Term.*

2.  *The Artist shall pay commission to the Manager at the Commission Rate during the Commission Term on all commissionable income earned by the Artist from the Artist's career.*

3.  *The Manager shall pay the Manager's Expenses as defined in the Schedule.*

4.  *The Artist shall pay the Artist's Expenses as defined in the Schedule.*

5.  *The Artist and the Manager shall each have the right to audit the other's accounts, although not more than once in any (_____) month period. Such audit shall require 30 days written notice and must take place within normal office hours. If no objection is raised to an accounting statement rendered by either party within (_____) years of its date, such statement will be deemed correct and binding.*

With audit rights, it is common to agree that if the party being audited is shown to have underpaid by more than 10 percent, then in addition to reimbursing the shortfall (plus interest) that party is also obliged to pay the cost of the audit. The right to audit is usually limited to no more than once in any six or twelve-month period. The period when an objection may be raised is typically two – three years.

Then either:

> 6. *The Manager shall, during the Term, collect all income on behalf of the Artist and shall pay it into a bank account exclusively dedicated to the Artist. The Manager shall only use funds deposited in such account for purposes directly connected to the Artist's career.*

or:

> 6. *The Artist shall be responsible for all accounting concerning the Artist's career including all book-keeping, tax returns, invoicing, receipts and payments etc. From time to time the Manager will invoice the Artist for Commission which shall be paid within (___) days of receipt.*

If adopting the second approach, ignore sections 8, 9.4 and 9.5 of the Schedule.

It is important that the manager keeps a separate bank account for each artist. The period by which the invoice should be paid could be anything from ten-thirty days.

> 7. *After the expiry of the Term, the Artist shall every (_____) months produce statements to the Manager showing all income and Commission due, and shall on receipt of an invoice from the Manager pay the Commission due within (_____) days of receipt of the invoice.*

It is normal for the artist to be obliged to produce statements every three months. The period by which the invoice should be paid could be anything from 10 – 30 days.

> 8.1 *The Artist and the Manager shall each have the right to terminate the Term by written notice if the other:*
>
> 8.1.1 *is declared bankrupt, or enters into a composition or agreement with his or her creditors; or*
>
> 8.1.2 *is convicted of an offence involving dishonesty; or*
>
> 8.1.3 *is in material breach of this agreement and shall not have remedied that breach within thirty days of written notice requiring him/her to do so; or*
>
> 8.1.4 *is incapacitated due to illness or accident for a period exceeding (_____) days.*

The normal period of incapacity is three – four months but it could be anything from six weeks to twelve months. A contract might also provide for a temporary replacement manager in such circumstances. Anyone can have an accident or fall ill and it seems unreasonable that managers, having suffered one misfortune, then have to suffer another by losing their artists. A period of at least three months would therefore seem reasonable. The thirty-day period to correct a breach of contract is often referred to as a 'cure period'.

> *8.2. If either party terminates the Term, this shall not affect either party's rights or obligations that are intended to continue in force beyond the Term.*
>
> *9. No variation of this agreement shall be binding unless made in writing and signed by both parties.*
>
> *10. Any notice or consent to be given under this agreement shall be effective if sent by registered post or recorded delivery to the other party at the address given in the Schedule. Service shall be deemed to take place on the day after the postmark.*
>
> *11. Nothing herein shall constitute a partnership between the Artist and the Manager.*
>
> *12. The Artist and the Manager hereby acknowledge that they are advised to seek independent specialist legal advice from a qualified music business lawyer before signing this agreement.*
>
> *13. The Manager has the right and authority to negotiate with third parties on the Artist's behalf.*
>
> *14. This agreement shall be governed by (________) law and both parties agree to submit to the jurisdiction of the courts in (________).*

A manager dealing with an artist who is based in another country and who insists on dealing according to the law of that country must be very careful to research the laws concerning contracts. For example, in California in the USA contracts for personal services are restricted to seven years.

> *15. Terms used in this Agreement shall have the meanings described in the Schedule which is incorporated into this Agreement.*

## THE SCHEDULE

*1.   The Artist: (_____)*

The artist could be an individual, a partnership or a corporation/limited company. The artist's real name should appear here together with his/her stage name (if any) and current address. If the artist is a band, each member's real name together with their stage name (if any) and their current addresses and the current name of the band should be shown. If the artist is a band, there could to be provision here for changes in the band's personnel with an obligation for new members to be party to this agreement, or this provision could be included in a separate band agreement. If the artist is contracted as a limited company, it will be necessary to prepare an inducement letter in which the artist is held personally responsible for the provisions of the agreement.

*2.   The Manager: (_____)*

The manager could be an individual, a partnership or a corporation/limited company. If contracted as a partnership or a corporation, the artist may wish to have a 'key man' clause inserted in the agreement obliging the manager's personal services to be available, failure of which would be a breach.

*3.   Territory: (_____)*

If a manager is not managing the artist worldwide, he/she would need to ensure that it is clear who the other managers in other territories are and their roles in the international context. If the manager is the principal manager, then he/she should have the right to appoint third-party managers in foreign territories. In this case it is important for the manager to ensure that the commission arrangements are clear and that the artists are not paying double commission. Sometimes the principal manager will take half the commission rate in those territories where there is a separate manager, e.g. if the commission rate were twenty percent, the principal manager would take 10 percent and the foreign manager would take 10 percent.

*4. Term (_____) years/months commencing (_____). Thereafter the*
*Term continues until either party gives (_____) months' notice of*
*termination.*

The term could be anything from six months to seven years. Some managers prefer
to opt for a comparatively short term, perhaps 12 months, and to have a three-month
notice of termination from either side after that period so that, for example, the term
continues indefinitely after 12 months until one party gives notice to the other that it
will end three months after the notice is served. The advantage of this is that the
manager is in a stronger negotiating position in regard to the other terms of the
contract. Artists are also reassured that, if things don't work out, they are not tied to
the manager for a long period of time.

On the other hand, some managers feel they will need to invest a great deal of hard
work (and sometimes money) in an artist's career in the early stages, probably with
very little commission, and that they therefore need a longer term in order to feel
secure about making an investment of their time, effort and possibly money.

Another common arrangement is to have a term of perhaps two or three years with
options for a further one or two years. The options can only be taken up by the
manager if certain income levels for the artist have been achieved.

Yet another approach is to define the term in albums rather than in years. In the
1970s an artist would typically release one or more albums per year. For example,
David Bowie released three of his best albums, *'The Man Who Sold The World'*,
*'Hunky Dory'* and *'The Rise and Fall of Ziggy Stardust and the Spiders from Mars'*
within a 12-month period from July 1971 to June 1972. These days, however, an
artist may be lucky to get two albums released in four years. For example, Peter
Gabriel releases only one album every eight years or so. It may therefore be a much
better approach to define the term as two or three albums in the same way that it is
defined in recording and publishing contracts. If this approach is adopted, it is
essential that a long-stop term be included as a contract cannot be open-ended. For
example, two years from a certain date or until six months after the release of the
third album, whichever is the longer, provided that in no circumstances will the basic term
exceed five years.

In some cases the manager may reach an arrangement with the artist whereby, if the manager is unsuccessful in obtaining a recording or publishing agreement within, say, 12-18 months, then the artist has the right to terminate the agreement.

> 5. *Commission Rate: (_____) %*
>
> *Notwithstanding anything to the contrary in this Agreement, the Commission payable to the Manager by the Artist in respect of touring and live performance income shall be (_____) % of the gross fees in respect of touring and live performances or (_____) % of the net profit from touring and live performances, whichever is the greater.*

The generally accepted commission rate for managers in the music industry is 15 – 20 percent. In practice, however, this can range from 10 percent to 50 percent. Let us take the example of a manager investing a lot of money in a new band and expending a tremendous amount of time and energy. In such a situation, it might be reasonable for the manager to take 25 percent or more. It may also be appropriate for a manager to take 25 percent if he or she agrees to manage the artist exclusively. In such a situation it is common to agree that the commission rate reduces to 20 percent if the manager manages more than one or two other artists.

When a very well-established artist seeks a new manager, the latter will know that there is very little or no risk involved and that the artist already enjoys a high level of income. In such a case the manager might be willing to agree a commission of 10 – 15 percent or even operate on a flat fee basis.

At the other extreme, there has been a new phenomenon in recent years whereby a high-level manager has created a band by holding auditions or by taking a band on via a TV talent competition such as 'Pop Idol' or 'The X Factor'. With the manager virtually guaranteeing massive TV exposure or, in the case of the manager creating the band and investing very large sums of money, commissions as high as 50 percent have been known. Whether a court would find this level of commission acceptable in such circumstances remains to be tested, but in such a case it may be better to enter into some kind of joint venture with the band or artist, as will be briefly discussed later in this section.

## TOURING INCOME

In practice there are many different arrangements in place for touring income, varying from a straight 20 percent of the gross to 20 percent of the net profits only. Many tours lose money or break even, and often need record company tour support. If the manager only receives 20 percent of the net profits, this means he or she cannot take any commission on the tour. Furthermore, the manager has had to pay all of the management staff and office costs etc. connected with the tour. In such a case, the manager has done a tremendous amount of work (usually much more than the booking agent) and ends up with a considerable financial loss. Also if there is tour support from a record company, this represents a further loss to the manager as it is usually fully recoupable from royalties which would otherwise have been commissionable. It is therefore clear that 20 percent of the net profits only is unreasonable from the manager's perspective unless the tour is making a substantial profit. A good compromise would be for the manager to take 10-15 percent of the gross touring income (less VAT/other taxes) or 20-30 percent of the net profits, whichever is the greater.

Another approach is for the manager to take a fixed fee for managing the tour or for an arrangement to be worked out on a tour-by-tour basis by reference to the budgeted costs and income. Yet another basis is that the manager is paid at least the same as the highest-paid person on the tour. The level of an appropriate touring commission rate can be influenced by several other factors: is the manager also the tour manager or the booking agent or both? Is the artist a solo performer or a band? Who is in charge of touring costs? For example, if the manager also provides and pays for the services of a tour manager, it would be quite reasonable to fix an all-in touring commission rate of perhaps 17.5 – 20 percent of the gross.

If an agreement is reached for a percentage of the gross and the artist is unable to pay the manager due to cash flow difficulties, then the amount should be put aside, with interest, and paid when the artist is in a position to do so. This process also applies to commission generally.

Merchandising and sponsorship income associated with a tour or a retail merchandising agreement should be treated separately and should be commissioned at the normal Commission Rate rather than included in the calculation of touring losses and profits. However, some phonogram producers may insist that merchandising income forms a part of the overall tour budget and will only pay tour support after such income is included.

When negotiating tour support with a phonogram producer, the manager should insist that management commission is an acceptable tour cost. It is also important to clarify that merchandising income should not be included as tour income in the tour accounts. Some phonogram producers accept booking agency commission as a bona fide expense but refuse to accept management commission. Apart from being illogical, this is also unfair to managers and artists. It is important to raise these issues with the phonogram producer as early as possible and preferably when the recording agreement is first negotiated. That is the only point at which the manager may have leverage over the phonogram producer. It may also be possible to negotiate with the phonogram producer that they pay the manager a fixed weekly fee when on tour, plus international airfares in the early stages of the artist's career when touring will need support.

A 'tour' might be defined as a series of more than six dates in any four-week period. If several 'one-off' dates occur in a month, then these can be grouped and the commission calculated on a monthly basis.

As record sales have decreased due to unauthorized file-sharing, an artist's income is in many cases shifting from recording and publishing income towards touring income. For artists who have ceased to produce hit albums and hit singles, touring income represents their main income stream, so it is very important to consider the above carefully and arrive at fair and workable percentages for both parties.

*6. Commission Term: (_____)*

An accepted principle of artist management agreements is that the manager should continue to receive commission after the term has expired for achievements during the term. In many countries this is known as 'post-term commission'. In the US it is known as the 'sunset clause'.

Many managers believe strongly that commission should be payable in perpetuity on income resulting from work carried out during the term. If an album is successful, it is generally so because of the combined efforts of the artist, the manager and the phonogram producer. Many recording contracts are for the life of the related rights protection, which for sound recordings is currently 50 – 70 years from first release in most countries, although in some countries it is longer. In the US for example it is 95 years (or more if it is not deemed to be a Work Made for Hire) and in Mexico it is 100 years. Therefore the artist and the phonogram producer will receive income in perpetuity (or the life of the related rights protection), so why shouldn't the manager? The manager is usually a key component in the success of an album, and that expertise and hard work deserve to be rewarded if quality managers are to be attracted to the industry. Similarly, the life of copyright for authors currently often lasts for 70 years after the death of the last person who participated in the work, which in practice could be 150 years if the song was written when the author was 15 and he/she died at the age of 95. Post-term commission in perpetuity is something that is likely to be challenged by artists' lawyers, but if it applies to the phonogram producer why should it not apply to managers?

It may be the case that a compromise is reached by which the manager's commission is payable at full rate for a period after the term, which is then followed by one or two periods in which the commission reduces, the last of these being in perpetuity. For example, full rate for the first two or three years following the end of the term of the management agreement and half rate in perpetuity (or until copyright or the related right expires by law) thereafter.

If commission does reduce, a second manager may be able to negotiate with the artist for the difference between the commission being paid to the first manager and the commission rate. If the previous works and/or recordings were commissionable at the full rate in perpetuity by the first manager, it may be a good idea to approach the original manager (with the approval of the artist) to negotiate a commission split on previous works and/or recordings. If a new manager invests a tremendous amount of effort on current and future works, and the work is successful, this could well stimulate back catalogue sales, which would benefit the original manager. It may therefore be in the original manager's interest to encourage the new manager to try very hard in this respect by agreeing to a split commission which would provide a further incentive.

In any case, except in unusual circumstances, the aggregate of the commissions of the old manager and the new would not normally exceed the commission rate. It is also important to define which works will be commissionable on a post-term basis. It could be any of the following:

(a) Anything created during the term (writing or recording)

(b) Anything recorded during the term (either demos or masters)

(c) Anything released during the term.

7. *Artist's Career: All activities in the (_____) industry including, without Limitation, the creation of Works or Recordings as defined in 11 below.*

Either 'music' or 'entertainment' should be inserted here. 'Entertainment' has broader scope and would include such things as literary and dramatic works if appropriate.

8. *Artist's Bank     Account: Bank Address: (_____)*
   *Bank Account No: (_____)*
   *Signatories: (_____)(_____)*

Interest if either party owes money to the other: (_____) % over the (_____) base rate. This clause allows either the manager or the artist to charge interest if the other party owes them money beyond the normal trading term arrangements. An invoice is usually payable within 30 days. If a payment of income or corporation tax is late, the tax authority will normally automatically charge interest and the situation should be exactly the same in the music industry.

9. *Manager's Duties:*

9.1 *To use the Manager's reasonable endeavors to advance and promote the Artist's career.*

9.2 *To advise and consult with the Artist regarding collection of income and the incurring of expenditure and to use the Manager's reasonable endeavors to ensure that the Artist receives payment.*

It is important that the manager and the artist regularly consult and discuss the development of the artist's career both in terms of assessing its past and present success and its future direction.

> *9.3 To consult regularly with the Artist and keep the Artist informed of all substantial activity undertaken by the Manager on the Artist's behalf, and to discuss the Artist's career development generally and to periodically offer constructive criticism.*
>
> *9.4 To maintain records of all transactions affecting the Artist's career and to send the Artist a statement within (_____) days of the end of each calendar quarter disclosing all income, the source of income, expenses, commission and other debts and liabilities arising during the preceding three months.*

The period between the end of the quarter and the statement can be anything from 30 to 120 days. It can often take a considerable time to document and account the financial activity of a particular quarter, especially if the artist is on a world tour. If the accounts are late for any reason, an artist may feel he/she has a reasonable claim for breach of contract. Supplying the accounts 120 days after the quarter end is not unreasonable, and for those cases where a tour straddles two accounting periods it may be necessary to have a one-off agreement signed to the effect that the accounting will be deferred to the end of the period following the end of the tour. In such a case it is important to have a clear written agreement signed to this effect before the start of the tour.

> *9.5 To obtain the Artist's approval for any expenditure over (_____) for a single check or (_____) over a period of one calendar month.*

This is sometimes seen in artist management agreements, and provides the artist with some protection against the manager misusing his or her money. In practice, it is vital that there is trust between the artist and the manager. This limitation can also be a practical problem if, for example, the manager is in South Africa and the artist is in Australia and funds are needed quickly.

*9.6 To advise the Artist on appointing booking agents, accountants, lawyers, sponsors, merchandisers and other agents, with due consideration to the Artist's moral views.*

It is important that both the artist and the manager feel comfortable and are able to work with third-party professionals. It is also important that the manager is aware of the artist's political and moral views and does not commit the artist to anything inappropriate.

| | |
|---|---|
| *10.* | *Artist's Duties:* |
| *10.1* | *To carry out to the best of his/her ability and in punctual and sober fashion all reasonable agreements, engagements, performances and promotional activities obtained or approved by the Manager.* |
| *10.2* | *To attend punctually all appointments and to keep the Manager reasonablyinformed of the Artist's whereabouts and availability at all times.* |
| *10.3* | *To reveal to the Manager all income, including but not limited to public performance income, touring overages and radio and television appearance monies paid directly to the Artist.* |
| *10.4* | *To refer promptly all approaches and offers from third parties concerning the Artist's career to the Manager.* |
| *10.5* | *Not to engage any other person to act as the Artist's manager or representative in connection with any aspect of the Artist's career during the Term.* |
| *10.6* | *To consult regularly with the Manager concerning the development of the Artist's career and to accept that it is part of the Manager's job to offer constructive criticism from time to time.* |
| *10.7* | *To keep the Manager fully informed and to consult regularly concerning all anticipated expenditure to be incurred by the Artist, and to obtain the Manager's approval in regard to recording costs, video costs, equipment costs and touring costs.* |
| *11.* | *Works and Recordings shall include:* |

11.1     Sound recordings (including demos).

11.2     Visual and Audio-visual recordings, including film and video.

11.3     Literary, dramatic and musical works.

11.4     Merchandising, branding and sponsorship of any name, logo, artwork or trademark owned by or associated with the Artist.

11.5 Performances and appearances by the Artist in concert, on radio, television or film.

11.6 Recordings of other artists produced, engineered, programmed or arranged by the Artist.

In each case (11.1 – 11.6) created or substantially created during the Term.

12.   Income shall mean both 12.1 and 12.2:

12.1 Commissionable Income:

All gross fees and sums of money payable and accruing to the Artist in respect of exploitation of the works and recordings or otherwise arising from activities in the artist's career excluding non-commissionable income.

12.2 Non-Commissionable Income:

12.2.1   Sums paid by or on behalf of the Artist as budgeted, recoupable recording costs or budgeted recoupable video costs.

12.2.2   Royalties, advances or fees paid or credited by or on behalf of the Artist to any third party producers, mixers, programmers or engineers to an agreed budget.

12.2.3   Monies paid or credited to the Artist as tour support to an agreed budget.

12.2.4   In the event that the Artist enters into a separate production and/or publishing agreement with the Manager, income from such agreements shall be non-commissionable income.

The word 'budgeted' has been included in the above to allow for the commissionable income to be calculated in a fair and reasonable way. The responsibility for budgeting should rest jointly between the artist and the manager, but if, for example, the recording costs for an album go heavily over budget, it may be necessary for them to come to an agreement as to how much commission should be taken.

The modern tendency is for recording contract advances (sometimes called 'recording funds') to be inclusive of recording costs, and if this is the case, the manager and the artist are faced with the problem of deciding how much of the advance should be set aside for recording (which is non-commissionable income) and how much should be regarded as commissionable income. It is a good idea to come to a separate written agreement with the artist every time a new album recording advance is received so that an agreed level of the advance is deemed to be commissionable income. For instance, it could be the case that the entire advance is spent on recording costs, in which case the manager would earn nothing.

It may also be possible to insert a re-assessment clause whereby both parties agree on an adjusted level of commissionable income when the recording of the album has been finished. Also, if the artist buys recording or other equipment with the advance this should be regarded as commissionable income, as the artist is acquiring an asset. Alternatively, an agreement could be reached for the cost of this equipment to be regarded as non-commissionable income at the time of purchase, but that if and when it is sold the manager is entitled to the commission rate applied on the sale price. If the management term expires and the artist wishes to retain the equipment, the artist should pay the manager the commission rate on the value of the equipment on the date of expiry of the management term.

*13. Manager's Expenses:*

See the previous example in Annex B of a typical list of manager's expenses.

*14. Artist's Expenses:*

See the previous example in Annex B of a typical list of artist's expenses.

End of Schedule and example of a long-form contract.

## ACKNOWLEDGEMENTS

I would like to thank all those who have given me help and support whilst writing this book. I would particularly like to thank my son and business partner Joseph Stopps for his invaluable help and guidance, particularly on the sections on audio-visual use of music and digital marketing which he co-wrote. I also give special thanks to family members Nikki, Hazel, Isis, Crispin, Jonathan, and Sue for their constant support and patience. I also wish to sincerely thank the wonderful artists I represent, particularly Howard Jones, Hal Ritson, Tom Bailey, Phonat and Miriam Stockley. For their kind help and advice I would like to thank Francis Gurry, Trevor Clarke, David Uwemedimo, Dimiter Gantchev, Victor Vazquez Lopez, Simon Ouedraogo and Geidy Lung at WIPO, Martin Goebbels (Robertson Taylor Insurance), Andy Allen (Backstreet), Gill Baxter (Baxter McKay Schoenfeld), James Collins (Collins Long), Richard Taylor (Michael Simkins), Jan Uwe Leisse (Grehler Rechtsanwaite), Robert Horsfall (Sound Advice), Dennis Muirhead (Commercial Mediator), Katsu Ogawa (Spectrum Management), Steve Levine, Dr Mihaly Ficsor, Gerd Leonard (The Futures Agency), Mark Livermore (MGM), Tim Gardner (Gale Gardner & Co), Peter Leathem, Laurence Oxenbury and Keith Harris at PPL, Mike Smith (Sony), Martin Mills (Beggars Group), Christine Payne (Equity), John Smith (FIM), Roberto, Francesca, Andrea and Alejandra Quatieri, Erik Berti, Liu Palmieri and Marco Pellati in Bologna, Gary McClarnan (Sparkle Street), Steve Schnur (EA), Rob MacAllister, Claire Mas (MusicAlly), David King (Entertainment Visa Consultants), Alan Durrant (Rock-It Cargo), Geoff Taylor and Kiaron Whitehead (BPI), Mark Kelly (Marillion/FAC), Crispin Hunt (FAC), Roger Armstrong (Ace Records), Stuart Worthington, the members of the UK Music Managers Forum Copyright Committee – Jon Webster, Joe Taylor, Tony Crean, Peter Jenner, James Barton, Tim Clark, David Enthoven and MMF UK Chairman Brian Message. Special thanks too to Nigel Parker, Jazz Summers, Jef Hanlon and Phil Nelson, for their invaluable contributions to the example of a long form artist management agreement. I would also like to thank

**238**

Sara Ronaghy for her endless support during the writing of this book. Special thanks too to my fellow touring road warriors Tony Creaney, Robbie Bronnimann, Jonathan Atkinson, Robin Boult, Simon Bettison, Sean Vincent and Tom Wagstaff, as well as endless personal support throughout from Mike O'Connor, Robin Pike, Pete Frame, Kris Needs, John Braley, Stuart Robb and Rick and Judy Pearce. Also I wish to thank the staff at the Aylesbury Study Centre in the UK, the Sala Borsa in Bologna, Italy and the State Library of Western Australia in Perth, Australia, where this book was written.

Whilst I thank the above wholeheartedly for their advice, help and support, this does not mean that they agree with or endorse anything contained in this book.

# FURTHER READING

## Books

1. *Likeonomics –The Unexpected Truth Behind Earning Trust, Influencing Behavior, and Inspiring Action*
   Rohit Bhargava (ISBN-10: 1118137531; ISBN-13: 978-1118137536)

2. *Working in The Music Industry*
   Anna Britten (ISBN-10: 1845283570; ISBN-13: 978-1845283575)

3. *Collective Management of Copyright and Related Rights*
   Mihaly Ficsor (ISBN 92-805-1103-6)

4. *Collective Management of Copyright and Related Rights*
   Edited by Daniel Gervais (ISBN 978-90-411-2724-2)

5. *The Music Manager's Bible (2012 Edition)*
   Various Authors (ISBN 9781780382371)

6. *Guerrilla Music Marketing Handbook – 201 Self-Promotion Ideas for Songwriters, Musicians and Bands on a Budget*
   Bob Baker (ISBN-10: 0971483892; ISBN-13: 978-0971483897)

7. *The Art of Music Publishing – An Entrepreneurial Guide to Publishing and Copyright for the Music, Film, and Media Industries*
   Helen Gammons (ISBN-10: 1240522354; ISBN-13: 978-0240522357)

8.  *Music, Money and Success – The Insider's Guide to Making Money in the Music Industry*
    Jeffrey Brabec & Todd Brabec (ISBN 10: 0825673461; ISBN-13: 978-0825673467)

9.  *Friction is Fiction: The Future of Content, Media and Business*
    Gerd Leonard (ISBN 9780557224500)

10. *Free Ride – How the Internet Is Destroying the Culture Business and How the Culture Business Can Fight Back*
    Robert Levine (ISBN-10: 1847921485; ISBN-13: 978-1847921482)

11. *Steve Jobs*
    Walter Isaacson (ISBN 978-1-4087-0374-8)

12. *Wikinomics – How Mass Collaboration Changes Everything*
    Don Tapscott & Anthony D Williams (ISBN 10: 1591841380 or ISBN 13: 978-1591841388).

13. *The Longer Long Tail: How Endless Choice is Creating Unlimited Demand*
    Chris Anderson (ISBN-10: 1847940366; ISBN-13: 978-1847940360).

14. *Appetite for Self Destruction – The Spectacular Crash of the Record Industry in the Digital Age*
    Steve Knopper (ISBN-10: 1423375203; ISBN-13:978-1423375203

15. *Perfecting Sound Forever – The Story of Recorded Music*
    Milner (ISBN-10: 1847081401; ISBN-13: 978-1847081407)

16. *Free: How Today's Smartest Businesses Profit by Giving Something for Nothing*
    Chris Anderson (ISBN-10: 190521149X; ISBN-13: 978-1905211494)

17. *Digital Wars – Apple, Google, Microsoft and the Battle for the Internet*
    Charles Arthur (ISBN-10: 0749464135; ISBN-13: 978-0749464134)

18. *The Music Instinct – How Music Works and Why We Can't Do Without It*
    Philip Ball (ISBN-10: 0199896429; ISBN-13: 978-0199896424)

19. *How Soon is Now – The Madmen and Mavericks who made Independent Music 1975-2005*
    Richard King (ISBN-10: 0571243908; ISBN-13: 978-0571243907)

20. *The New Digital Age – Reshaping the Future of People, Nations and Business*
    Eric Schmidt & Jared Cohen (ISBN-10: 1480542288; ISBN-13: 978-1480542280)

21. *The New Business As Usual – Rewire the Way You Work to Succeed in the Consumer Revolution*
    Brian Solis (ISBN-10: 1118077555 | ISBN-13: 978- 1118077559)

## Information and Networking

1. *MusicAlly:* A daily and monthly international digital music marketing information service. Available on subscription. www.musically.com

2. *LinkedIn Free Groups:* Music Industry Network Group
   Music Industry Forum Group
   MusicBiz Group
   Music Promoters Network Group
   Music & Marketing Group
   Music Industry: Worldwide
   World Music Network
   Music Publishing and Licensing Group
   Synch Music Professionals
   The Music Branding Network

3. *Wired* magazine – available on subscription – some articles free to view www.wired.co.uk

4. *Audience magazine:* For the International Contemporary Live Music Industry. Available on subscription www.audience.uk.com

5. *Bob Lefsetz's free email letter blog:*
http://www.lefsetz.com/lists/?p=subscribe&id=1

6. *TEDTalks* – Free presentations from the Ted Conferences viewable on YouTube.

## Conferences

| | |
|---|---|
| Midem | – International Event held in Cannes, France, every January www.midem.com |
| ILMC | – International Live Music Conference held in London every March www.ilmc.com |
| SXSW | – South By South West Music Conference and Festival held in Austin, Texas, every March. www.sxsw.com |
| Eurosonic- Noorderslag | – European Music Conference and Showcase Festival held in Groningen, in The Netherlands, every January www.eurosonic-noorderslag.nl |
| Miami Winter Music Conference | – International festival for electronic/dance music held in Miami every March www.wintermusicconference.com |
| WOMEX | – International networking platform, Trade Fair, Showcase Festival, Conference, and Film programme for the world-music industry. A five-day event held in various locations around the world. |

# ABOUT THE AUTHOR

David Stopps started his career as promoter of the famous Friars Club in Aylesbury, England. From 1969 to 1984 he presented pretty much everybody, but notably David Bowie, U2, Genesis, The Kinks, Blondie, The Police, Peter Gabriel, Queen, Fleetwood Mac, Tom Petty, The Jam, Dennis Brown, Gregory Isaacs, The Ramones and The Clash amongst many others. In 2009 he successfully re-opened the Friars Club after a break of 25 years (www.aylesburyfriars.co.uk). With over 90,000 members, it is the largest music club in Europe.

In 1982 he went into management, originally managing Marillion and then Howard Jones, and later still The Fat Lady Sings. These days he still manages Howard Jones, who continues to make albums and tour and who has now sold in excess of 8 million albums worldwide. He is also management consultant for Miriam Stockley who, as the featured singer with Adiemus, has sold in excess of 3 million albums. With his business partner Joseph Stopps, he manages dance mash-up mavericks The Young Punx and Italian multi-genre dance genius Phonat. Stopps is often on tour as manager and tour manager in USA, Canada, Europe, Japan and Australia.

David Stopps is Director of Copyright and Related Rights for the Music Managers Forum UK. He was also a member of the British Copyright Council and from 2002 to 2010 was the United Nations representative for The International Music Managers Forum who had NGO status at WIPO. At WIPO he represented all featured artists worldwide concerning new international treaty negotiation in the field of copyright and related rights at the SCCR (Standing Committee on Copyright and Related Rights). He is also a member of the Performer Board and the Main Board of UK related rights collective management organization PPL. PPL (Phonographic Performance Ltd.) is the second largest related rights collective management organization in the world.

In May 2008 he received the MMF Roll of Honour award in London.

From 2010 to 2012 he was a Director of 3DiCD Media Ltd., which was an innovative digital start-up which aimed to revolutionize the way digital music is packaged and purchased.

David Stopps is also a Consultant and Educator and has presented a series of international workshops mainly for musical authors, performers, managers, governments and collective management organizations, but also for telecoms, brands and any organization interested in expanding their business using music. He has presented workshops in Jamaica, Barbados, Bulgaria, Canada, Belgium, UK, New Zealand, South Africa, The Netherlands, Kenya, Brazil, Thailand, Antigua, Mozambique, Namibia, The Philippines, Côte D'Ivoire and Indonesia.

In 2011 he became the Senior Advisor on Copyright and Related Rights for the Featured Artists Coalition (FAC) and in March 2013 gave a speech at the European Parliament in Brussels on behalf of the FAC concerning the EU's Collective Rights Management Directive. In July 2013 he made a speech at the WTO's Global Review of Aid for Trade in Geneva.

CPSIA information can be obtained
at www.ICGtesting.com
Printed in the USA
BVHW010128070721
611203BV00014B/217